'Breathtaking, beguiling and brutal. I wanted to reach in and steal that beautiful boy away from all the honesty. I wanted to run with him. I wanted to read, laugh, scrap, cry and draw with him. Keep drawing, kid. Just keep drawing! At last we have the answer to how Vincent Fantauzzo is able to capture all those human portraits with such perfection: the man has lived every sorrow, every fear, every pain, every wild joy to be found in the human experience. It is all here in these pages, too. Wonder, most of all. Read it. Please, please read it.'

Trent Dalton

unveiled

Vincent Fantauzzo

PENGUIN BOOKS

UK | USA | Canada | Ireland | Australia
India | New Zealand | South Africa | China

Penguin Books is part of the Penguin Random House group of companies whose addresses can be found at global.penguinrandomhouse.com.

First published by Penguin Books, 2025

Copyright © Vincent Fantauzzo, 2025

The moral right of the author has been asserted.

All rights reserved. No part of this publication may be reproduced, published, performed in public or communicated to the public in any form or by any means without prior written permission from Penguin Random House Australia Pty Ltd or its authorised licensees.

This book is a memoir. It reflects the author's present recollections of experiences over time. In some instances, events have been compressed and dialogue has been recreated. The names and identifying characteristics of some persons described in this book have been changed.

Every effort has been made to trace creators and copyright holders of images included in this book. The publisher welcomes hearing from anyone not correctly acknowledged.

Cover design by Adam Laszczuk © Penguin Random House Australia Pty Ltd
Front cover image © Nic Walker
Illustrations by Vincent Fantauzzo
All internal photos from Vincent Fantauzzo collection, unless stated otherwise
Typeset in Century Gothic by Midland Typesetters, Australia

Printed and bound in Australia by Griffin Press, an accredited ISO AS/NZ 14001 Environmental Management Systems printer.

 A catalogue record for this book is available from the National Library of Australia

ISBN 978 1 76134 834 1

penguin.com.au

We at Penguin Random House Australia acknowledge that Aboriginal and Torres Strait Islander peoples are the first storytellers and Traditional Custodians of the land on which we live and work. We honour Aboriginal and Torres Strait Islander peoples' continuous connection to Country, waters, skies and communities. We celebrate Aboriginal and Torres Strait Islander stories, traditions and living cultures; and we pay our respects to Elders past and present.

For everyone who dreams

preface

In 2019 I was invited to appear on ABC TV's *Australian Story* to talk about my life. My first instinct was to turn it down. I concocted excuses and cited privacy concerns, but the real reason I hesitated was that the prospect of publicly telling the truth about who I am and what goes on in my head terrified me. I asked my wise friend Michael Gudinski what I should do. 'There are a lot of reasons you should say yes,' he said. 'The big one is because I think it will help you, and I guarantee it will help other people as well.'

I appeared on the show and discovered that revealing some of the dark and complex parts of my psyche *did* make me feel a little more comfortable in my own skin. Afterwards I received a lot of messages and positive feedback from other neurodivergent people in all corners of the country who said hearing my story had helped them make sense of their own. Michael was usually right about those things. Although I felt somewhat unburdened by the *Australian Story* experience, I'd kept most of the real me hidden – a lifelong habit of mine.

It's six years since the program aired and I still have trouble fitting in, knowing who I am and where I belong. The older I've grown, however, the more I've come to realise I'm not alone when it comes to sometimes feeling lost and adrift. I think we all do to a degree, and some more than others. People like me, whose brains happen to be wired differently, tend to be experts in the field. For the longest time I didn't know what I could do about my innate sense of dislocation. I had never heard anyone give advice on how an outsider could fit in.

Although I didn't start with the intention, writing this book turned out to be an exercise in confronting myself wholly and looking for answers within. I don't claim to have found them all but I feel I have a far better understanding of who I am and, in some ways, of the wider human condition. Just as Michael had suggested years ago, today I hope that sharing myself completely and honestly in these pages will allow others living with some kind of diversity in their life – and who never quite knew where they fit in – to see that there is a meaningful and special place for them.

I believe there is great beauty and incredible opportunity to be found in our flaws and imperfections, just as there is in the daily struggle of modern life – no matter which side of the tracks you happen to be born on.

**Vincent Fantauzzo,
St Kilda, September 2024**

I wrote my first suicide note when I was nine years old and I found it really hard. Not the Goodbye World part, not the sad sentiments of a broken-hearted boy – I was very clear about why I wanted to die. My struggle lay in getting the words down on paper. I'd been failing miserably at school since kindergarten. If I wasn't in detention or hived off from the other children in a room by myself, I was fighting in the playground. As my classmates cheerfully sailed through their ABCs and 123s, I was stalled on the start line. It didn't matter how hard I tried or how much I concentrated, I could not come to grips with reading or writing. Simple maths was a problem, too. Not that anyone appeared to care – I was the archetype of schoolyard trouble and my teachers had given up on me. In lonely moments I'd stare blankly at the books in front of me and think, *So this is what it feels like to be stupid.*

I finished the note, though. I contemplated its contents, weighed the words and wrote them down as best I could. It all made perfect sense to me. I left it on the kitchen counter but it was quickly swept away by the winds of chaos that swirled through our cramped and cluttered home. I can only imagine what Mum and Dad or my brothers and sisters would have made of it. To them, my last words would have been gibberish: a jumble of malformed letters, squiggles and shapes. It didn't really matter – I'd put so much effort into announcing my departure from this life that I hadn't considered how I was going to kill myself. It would be a few years yet before I gave serious thought to method.

I soldiered on with life in Shitsville, aka Broadmeadows – a bleak, dormitory suburb that had been dropped onto the flatlands in Melbourne's north and then seemingly forgotten. Mum and Dad had first moved there before we were born. They'd emigrated from Europe in the 1960s as teenagers. My father, Claudio, was from a Sicilian family but he'd grown up in Rome, while my Irish-Catholic mother, Rosaleen, was born in Birmingham.

They first locked eyes in an immigration camp hall in Broadmeadows where Mum was living. Dad had already gone through the process a year or so earlier at the Migrant Reception and Training Centre at Bonegilla in northern Victoria. Then he found work as a printer and got a side-hustle playing the congas in a South American ensemble that entertained new

CHAPTER ONE

Australians in other immigration centres. Mum was only sixteen when Claudio Fantauzzo bossa nova'd his way into her heart one night. I'm not saying it was a mistake for Mum to fall for the guy – I wouldn't be here if she hadn't – but how can you know what you're getting yourself into at sixteen?

Not much was ever said about why Mum's family left England, but I overheard enough half-conversations to conclude her father, Tony Mitchell, had fled his native Ireland after he apparently beat two guys to death. Tony was a bare-knuckle fighter and an angry drunk whose troubles chased the family to Blighty. Finally they had to traverse hemispheres to get a fresh start. In Melbourne, Tony found work as a concreter, building the new airport at Tullamarine alongside teams of Greeks and Italians. While he was at it he constructed a nasty reputation for violence. According to family folklore, Tony had worrying connections to the standover wing of the Painters and Dockers Union.

He's long gone now and I can't verify any of my granddad's fabled criminality. My mum, who has always seen the best in people, emphasised how much he mellowed after he quit drinking in his forties. The old Irishman I remember was indeed gentle and funny: a fountain of limericks, folk songs and poems. Although kind in his ripening age, I had no doubt that the stories starring a younger Tony as a vicious bastard were true. During a game of hide-and-seek I found the two shotguns he kept stashed under his bed and, as I grew older, it was easy to read the trauma he'd imprinted on Mum and Grandma.

So it's not surprising that Mum married Claudio Fantauzzo when she was nineteen. He was a lifeline – her winning ticket out of an abusive household. It wasn't too many years until she realised she'd traded one bad situation for another.

After settling in Broadmeadows, Claudio and Rosaleen welcomed a son, Otis, in 1972. New motherhood concentrated her feelings of disconnection to Australia. She disliked Broadmeadows and reckoned Melbourne was nothing more than a big country town. Most of all, Mum missed friends and family back in Birmingham. She convinced Dad that a return to the other side of the world was necessary.

In England, a daughter, Rachel, joined the fold, followed by me in September 1977. We settled in a strongly Jamaican-Pakistani part of town where young families lived shoulder-to-shoulder in rows of terraced houses. Mum's sisters lived nearby so she had a lot of support looking after us kids while Dad worked at the markets. Apparently, people thought he was Pakistani thanks to his dark olive skin.

For me it was a gloomy time. I fell ill with a severe case of whooping cough at age two, which led to respiratory infections that dogged me for nearly three years. I was in and out of hospital, and at one point doctors worried I might die. I developed an odd way of pronouncing words that sounded like a deaf person speaking, supposedly because my ears were always blocked. As a result, I missed out on a large chunk of normal development between the ages of two and four, and for a time it was thought I was hearing impaired and possibly a bit 'special'.

Although Mum had yearned for the UK, Margaret Thatcher's England fell into painful recession in the early 1980s. Suddenly the big country town didn't look so bad after all, but I don't know if my parents realised Australia was in recession as well. The Broadmeadows-Glenroy community was ready to receive another poor family, but by now the place was cursed by high unemployment, high levels of crime and very low expectations. The downtrodden district became the poorly lit, graffiti-sprayed stage on which my spectacularly misspent youth would play out.

Our street was a long corridor of soulless Housing Commission flats. The Fantauzzos eventually wound up in public housing, too, but to begin with we enjoyed the relative luxury of renting a free-standing house. Two more children completed the clan after our return to Australia – Marianne, and Michael, the baby of the bunch. It was crowded enough with seven of us squeezed into a tiny three-bedroom house, but there were always extra bodies around to fill up spaces where you might have otherwise stretched out. At one point my English grandparents, an aunty and her three children slept on bunk beds in our garage. I often thought of our family as gypsies: everyone in transit to destinations indistinct and fates unconfirmed.

Dad would escape the horde as quickly as he could each day to work in a printing factory on the other side of Melbourne while Mum stayed home to raise five kids as best she could. It's changed a lot over the years, but back then Broadmeadows was populated mostly by Italians, Yugoslavians and good old-fashioned Aussie bogans. My first impression of the Anglo-Saxon locals came from the family who lived across the road. They were definitely bogans – you could tell by their names. In our neighbourhood every second Anglo lad was either Brad, Brett or Wayne.

A lot of them scared me. A Telecom phone booth planted on the footpath outside our house was a punching bag for whatever emotions the local youths needed to release. It was either smashed to bits or set on fire every few weeks in pointless rampages that really put me on edge. It wasn't uncommon for cars to go up in flames in our street, either, blanketing the neighbourhood in acrid smoke and summoning sirens to pierce my dreams.

In our suburban melting pot I learned that violence was the common language. The dog-piss-and-shit-littered grass outside the Commission flats was a low-rent Coliseum where gangs gathered to brawl or assemble on the weekends to scream encouragement as their warring pit bulls tried to tear each other apart.

By the time I was seven or eight years old I needed to have my eyes wide open and my wits about me, otherwise I'd become a victim. If I wanted to go to the milk bar, I wouldn't go alone. If I rode my bike there, someone had to stand guard outside or it'd be gone when I came out. If I wanted to get fish 'n' chips, I had to hide my money or risk being robbed by other kids. I was scared stiff most of the time.

While a lot of the odious things that happened in 1980s Broadmeadows were filed under standard daily life, some events were so grim they made the news. The family of one of my little mates ran a fish 'n' chip shop and they all lived in an apartment upstairs. Bad blood developed between his family and the proprietors of another takeaway joint a couple of doors down the street. One night the fish shop was fire-bombed. Most of the family escaped through a window but my poor friend was trapped and burned to death.

As horrific and devastating as that had been, it was a reminder that things could escalate quickly and I had to be ready to protect myself because no-one else would. Another time, one of our neighbours shot a dog in the street. I don't know why; maybe he was fed up with it barking. Maybe he was mentally ill. Maybe he was evil. When the dog's owner got home and discovered his pooch with a bullet hole in its skull, he found out who was responsible, marched up to the perpetrator's door and shot the guy point-blank. I remember the local kids milling around the crime scene on BMX bikes and being interviewed by Channel Nine after that one.

The Commission flats oozed danger but, having one of the few free-standing houses in the street, our experience was just a bit different. We had a backyard for a start but instead of a dog, we kept a Shetland pony out there. God knows why. We were perhaps a little eccentric but by most measures we were just like everyone else. We faced the same poverty, the same sense of dislocation and the same socio-economic stagnation. The carcasses of dead cars blighted our yard, crap was strewn everywhere and our windows were broken and boarded up like almost every other place in the street.

One upside to being crammed into a small house with four other kids was the abundance of playmates. Since Otis was five years my senior, we didn't hang out together much. My sister Rachel, only eighteen months older than me, was more my speed and we spent a lot of time together. She was a bit of a tomboy who was always up for adventure and any chance to escape to somewhere a little safer. We'd climb on our bikes and hightail it to the nearby Salvation Army outlet where good-hearted and patient volunteers did their best to put on activities for the local riffraff.

Staying out of trouble in Broadmeadows wasn't easy, though. In fact it wasn't really an option if you didn't want your bike stolen, your house broken into or your head smacked in. You had to take a stand – and that meant strife. When Otis was around thirteen he became tangled up in plenty of it. Gangs would turn up outside our place spoiling for a fight. If the phone box happened to be intact, they'd destroy it. They kicked our fence and shouted threats. Sometimes Wayne, the good-hearted but frightening bogan from across the road, would come charging over to scare them off.

Otis became good at scaring people, too. He curated a reputation as crazy-violent – a strategy that also worked in my favour. I noticed people didn't mess with me as much when they thought my big brother had a screw loose. What they didn't know was that I was also frightened of Otis. Still, I could see he was onto something, so I followed his lead. I wasn't tall or muscular or particularly strong – just your average wiry kid. To compensate, when occasion called for it, I also acted crazy. On the inside I was petrified, but the big, unhinged outward show seemed to work most of the time and I was left alone more often than not.

As a young boy I learned to let the violent impulses triggered by fear flow through my synapses unchecked. At the earliest hint of a threat I'd launch a barrage of punches, kicks and headbutts. If I hit first, fast and hard, I survived. To an observer these looked like wild, spontaneous attacks when in reality they were thoughtfully implemented defence manoeuvres.

It didn't matter that I won all my fights, though. I never stopped being afraid.

*

I really don't know why my father bothered having children. When he wasn't at work he did everything he could to avoid us. He had a nasty temper, too. Although he didn't beat me up every day, if he was angry – especially if I started crying – he gave me a proper belting. Dad specialised in painful, full-blooded slaps that left lurid impressions of his big right hand on my legs or back – signature welts that could last a couple of days.

I'd love to know why, but a crying child seemed to stir Dad's fury like nothing else. Whenever I had tears in my eyes, I copped it: 'I'll give you something to cry about!'

Whack!

So I learned to hold my emotions in.

At least Dad didn't drink – a saving grace that may have spared me from worse violence – but he burned through two packets of Winfield Red cigarettes every day by using the tip of the last one to ignite the next. He might have saved on matches, but it wasn't great for his health. Dad smoked everywhere: in bed, at the dinner table – I reckon he could have kept one going in the shower if he had to. On the rare occasions he drove us to school he'd chain-smoke two or three on the way. When we arrived at the front gate it was like a magic trick – the doors would pop open, a great puff of smoke would appear and five kids would tumble out of the car.

Road rage was another of Dad's bad habits. He could be pure evil behind the wheel: he'd scream and bare his teeth, smash the horn, headbutt the driver's side window and glare daggers at people. It didn't just happen now and then, this was his daily demeanour. I even saw my father pull a screwdriver on another motorist once.

I was with him one day when he rolled up next to a guy at a set of lights and launched into his screaming and headbutting routine. The man calmly lowered his window and held up a police badge. The off-duty cop told Dad to pull over and gave him a lecture: 'Mate, you've got a kid in the car and you're acting like that? Grow up!'

It was strangely satisfying to see Dad go from tough guy to Mr Meek in a heartbeat. We drove home in silence.

On top of the ciggies he drank a *lot* of coffee. I sometimes wondered if the nicotine-caffeine mix fuelled his anger, and the addition of young tear-drops caused a chemical reaction that pushed him over the edge. Dad's eyes would bulge out of their sockets, he'd tremble, and veins would appear on his forehead like fat worms. For us kids it was almost a good thing he was hardly ever home. In Mum's case, though, Dad's absence brought no relief at all because he subjected her to a suffocating regime of supervision.

Dad gave Mum a fixed weekly allowance – literally not one cent more – and he knew exactly what she spent it on, where she went, who she was with and everything she did. If he could have read her thoughts he would have. I don't remember Mum going out with her friends once while they were married. I don't remember her *having* any friends.

Mum was a very good-looking, fit and vibrant woman who attracted a lot of attention without trying. I saw it all the time, such as at a petrol station one day when she filled up, went inside to pay and a guy appeared next to me at the passenger window.

'Oooh, is that your mum?' the stranger practically drooled. 'Mate, tell her she's hot.'

Who speaks to a little kid about his mother like that? I told him to fuck off.

She took us to tennis lessons for a while. My brothers and sisters were very good players but I hated the sport, mostly because the coach was a wanker who seemed more intent on flirting with my mum. She played into it to a degree: she stayed to watch the lessons, and she giggled and smiled at him. I'd never seen that side of her before and it confused my ten-year-old brain. I felt embarrassed at the time but now I can see my poor mum was only enjoying a little attention because she'd been cut off from the world. Sure enough, when Dad cottoned on to the tennis coach vibes, that was the end of that. No more tennis for anyone.

We weren't always the world's best behaved children and Mum had her hands full trying to discipline us. Such was our collective fear of Dad's ire that Mum would sometimes use it as a weapon. 'I'll tell your father when he gets home!' Mothers around the world say that all the time, but in our house it was a truly terrible threat. Mum hardly ever followed through because she knew the eruption would emotionally immolate all of us. She was as scared of Dad's outbursts as we were. More so, actually. I know that he abused her in multiple ways.

Ironically, 'hands-off' doesn't even begin to describe Dad as a family man. He never once kicked a ball with me. We never went for a bike ride together. He never took me to see a movie. He didn't push me on a swing or read me a book. None of that stuff happened. I can honestly say the only things my father ever taught me were how to cook and how to cheat.

After the Fantauzzo family cleared migration at Bonegilla in the late 1960s, my grandfather Vincenzo opened a pasticceria – an Italian specialty cake shop – in suburban Preston that traded for the next forty years. When 'Nonno' retired, his eldest son – my uncle Leno – donned the apron and took over the reins. Dad, who'd been working night shifts at the printing factory, decided to set up his own business with his other brother George. They rented the shop right next door to the cake business and fitted the place out using machinery, spare parts, tools and printing supplies Dad had stolen from his employer. He kept up his night shifts at the factory but during the day he and George filled orders at the shop in Preston.

The cake shop was a magnet for the large brood of Fantauzzo cousins. We'd hang out behind the buildings and around the local streets while our fathers worked inside. Some of my cousins would do graffiti and cruise the pinball parlours. I was still a bit young for that kind of free-footed delinquency so I didn't stray too far from the shops. Besides, I liked spending time with my cousin Enzo. He was much older than me and worked in the cake shop with Leno on weekends. Enzo was a lovely person who captivated me with his incredible ability to draw. When he wasn't too busy he'd sit with me in the shop and show me how to sketch cartoon characters like Batman, Spiderman and the Incredible Hulk.

As time went on my hot-headed father fell out with both of his brothers. Although Leno was a very decent man, Dad and George could be as bad to each other as they were to everyone else. Our families became estranged and I hardly saw any of them over the following three decades.

Dad kept the business going for a while and he continued to lie, cheat and steal his way through life. Even our Christmas presents were off the back of a truck. In Dad's eyes, everything in life had to be a shortcut or a scam. The one time he took me fishing, near the town of Bright in the Victorian High Country when I was eight or nine, was with a group of families from his swimming club. It was proposed the family that caught the biggest fish on the day would win the right to stay in the sole caravan at the campsite while everyone else had to rough it in tents.

CHAPTER ONE

We drove for three and a half hours to get there and Dad didn't even let me wet a line. Instead, he took me on a sneaky mission to a local trout farm where he bought the biggest fish they had in the fridge. It had already been cleaned and gutted so some extra subterfuge was necessary. On the way back to the campsite we stopped at another river where Dad rolled the trout in the dirt. His reason for the stopover was twofold – to make our 'catch' look authentic when presented to the other anglers as the winning fish, and to have a bogus location to cite should anyone ask where we'd hooked it. It was an awful deception. We might have slept in the caravan that night, but I never got to try fishing.

I'd be shocked if Dad ever paid a cent in tax. On trips to the supermarket he instructed us to swipe batteries and razor blades. Anything that was expensive and could fit inside a pocket we were encouraged to steal. I suppose he thought he was showing us his secret to getting ahead, or maybe he just wanted some batteries and preferred his kids risk getting caught for shoplifting than cough up the money. Whatever the reason, he schooled us in how to be dodgy.

The only worthwhile thing he did for me as a parent was show me how to cook. Dad was amazing in the kitchen and an expert in everything Italian. He made gnocchi, lasagne, cannelloni and all of the sauces and pizzas from scratch. The problem was he only cooked once a week, on Sundays. I think he did it partly to escape spending time with the family and, perhaps, to avoid contemplating his sins.

Although Mum self-describes as Irish-Catholic she's not religious at all. That didn't stop her forcing all of us to go to church with her, however. At the time I couldn't understand her motivation but as I got older I realised church was a place where she could have a social network that Dad couldn't destroy, and it was also somewhere for us kids to fit in. Despite not believing a word of the sermons, Mum helped the priests before and after the service and even handed out communion. So once a week we'd pile into the car and drive to a church in Essendon to pretend to be Catholics while Dad stayed at home with his ciggies, pots and pans.

The divine aroma of food when we came back through the door and the sight of my father busy in the kitchen is what spawned my lifelong love of cooking. It was tied to a fleeting, weekly glimpse of what family life could be like. I took every chance I got to join him in the kitchen where I watched and learned. I asked a lot of questions and came to know the recipes by heart. It wasn't because I wanted to be a chef or a food critic when I grew up, I just desperately wanted to connect with the man. For all his shiftiness and anger, I still loved my father, and I longed to impress him. I wanted him to notice me, to see that we had something in common and cherish it the way I did. I would spend the next thirty

CHAPTER ONE

years trying to bond with him, but he always pushed me away.

Even as a boy I realised human connection isn't about sharing experiences or the same house or the same kitchen, it's about shared emotions. Dad didn't know how to share emotions, and he certainly wasn't the type of person a child could go to with a problem. It's a great shame. Because I had some very big problems.

Otis invited some of his mates around after school one afternoon and as usual they started picking on me for sport. It began with, 'Why don't you fuck off you little cunt?' Then someone flung a piece of toast at my head. These guys were fourteen and fifteen versus my nine or ten. If I hated anything it was being bullied. I snatched up a knife from the kitchen and went for them. Furniture toppled and drinks spilled onto the floor as teenage boys dived out of the way of the little psycho with the serrated blade. I chased them all over the house as they half-shrieked, half-laughed but fully panicked. I was deadly serious and they knew I would stab them if I had the chance. What they could never have known is what made me that way.

There was one guy in Broadmeadows who wasn't the least bit put off by my violent pantomimes. He was five years older than me and he lived nearby. This person filled me with more dread than anybody or anything has before or since. He knew it and he leveraged that terror to make my life a living hell.

He always managed to corner me when I was alone. He smoked cigarettes and he forced me to suck on the wet dregs of the burning filter. 'Do the fucking drawback!' he'd instruct as my lungs spasmed against the poison. 'That's *your* fucking cigarette.' Then he'd spit in my face. Other times he'd burn me with the glowing tip and beat the shit out of me with a commentary that filled me with so much fear it ensured I'd never tell a soul. This was grooming 101. When he started sexually molesting me he knew his secret would remain safe. I spent years wetting the bed in fear of my abuser.

The anxiety and shame were so overwhelming I felt like I was dying inside. Eventually I decided it would be best to get it over and done with. I sat down with pencil and paper to write my note, careful not to cry in case Dad saw me. It was all there in black and white: the sadness, the abuse and the farewell to a cruel world . . . then the winds of chaos blew and life went on.

After a year of secret misery, the sexual attacks stopped. Predators leap on people who can't stand up for themselves, or who they know won't talk. As I grew older I sensed he reached a point where he saw his control slipping away. Maybe he was worried I'd tell someone, even though I didn't – not until now, save for my lovely wife.

My guess is my abuser went on to molest and violently attack others – a thought that makes me furious, heartbroken, ashamed and guilty all at once. Abuse messes up your head forever. Those dreadful moments, while relatively brief in duration, change the way you react to everything in life. Relationships are affected and beautiful moments become tainted. When I kissed a girl for the first time, when I fell in love, when I lost my virginity – long shadows fell over all of that. It's so unfair.

Abuse placed an explosive anger and burning sense of vengeance inside me. It made me hyper-alert to predators and instilled in me an instinct to destroy them. But surviving it has also caused me to cherish life and to take a great interest in humanity: how vulnerable we are and how special. How unique in good ways and bad. How beautiful and how terrible, too.

Dad eventually left the family and he barely looked back. I put my suicide plans on hold and kept trying my hardest to learn how to read and write and count. I might have felt stupid but at least I had one thing going for me, something Enzo had pointed out in the cake shop – I was really good at drawing.

There was a small window of time when our fortunes actually improved.

Mum was anxious to shield us from the worst elements of a Broadmeadows-Glenroy upbringing. That's why we attended church in Essendon. While it wasn't exactly Melbourne's most upwardly mobile postcode, to poor people like us, Essendon might as well have been Toorak. The twenty-minute drive south was a bold expedition to higher socio-economic terrain. Since we were already impersonating Catholics, why not fake being from the middle class, too?

The same demographic hocus-pocus lay behind Mum's decision to enrol us in a Catholic school in Essendon. St Therese's might have been a step up from the public institutions in Broadmeadows, but since I was Australia's dumbest kid, the upgrade was pretty much wasted on me. Mum dutifully drove us there and back in her faded yellow Ford station wagon every day.

I don't know if our illusory social status fooled the Essendon school community, but we definitely didn't kid ourselves – we knew we were little fish out of water. All the other students arrived in fancy cars and went home to nice houses in the afternoon while we piled into the Falcon and chugged back to our lesser lives.

The class divide became really obvious the first time I went to a friend's place after school. He lived in a large, beautiful brick home in Essendon that had a boat on a trailer in the front yard and a vivid blue swimming pool out the back. It was the loveliest house I'd ever been in. I explored the spacious rooms and was stunned by his parents' ensuite. I never knew such a thing existed. Everything was so neat, clean and stylish. When no-one was looking I crept back in there, popped the lid off what I thought was a bottle of coconut suntan lotion and inhaled deeply. 'Mmm.' I squirted a dollop onto my hand and rubbed it all over my face. When I woke up the next day my head and hands were stained orange. Had I been able to read I'd have seen 'fake tan' on the label.

Culture shock goes both ways. One year I invited some school friends to my birthday party. As each boy arrived, their faces mapped their discomfort at the blighted state of the neighbourhood and the overstuffed disarray of our home. Not even the novelty of a forlorn-looking Shetland pony in the weed-swamped backyard could soften the impact.

Around this time Dad's crooked printing practices started to pay off. Soon there were a couple of new cars parked in our driveway – a Toyota Tarago for Mum and a Mazda RX-7 sports car for Dad. Next, the seemingly impossible happened: he took out a mortgage on a family home. In Essendon! Although the place was a bit shabbier than my classmates' homes it looked like we might finally be getting somewhere.

Fantastic! I thought when I first heard the news. *Maybe this means we get to be like everyone else.*

Sadly, behind closed doors, I doubt we were like everyone else at all. Dad was as dodgy, explosive and abusive as ever. The slapping, smoking and seething never let up and, by the time I was twelve, Mum had had enough.

She'd been thinking about leaving Dad for a long time, a huge step that was not to be taken lightly. He could easily have gone nuclear and Mum fretted how bad the fallout might be. In the end her exit strategy was to surround herself with us kids as a kind of human shield. This meant everything happened in front of us: the announcement of the marriage ending, the awful arguments, the petty threats and the destruction of property.

After Dad's last reserves of anger had been expended, he finally accepted reality. Then he scorched the earth around him. Everything vanished: the cars and the house were sold, and we went from having sneakers to no sneakers again; from decent food to survival fare. The mortgage was so big that there wasn't a penny left over to help Mum support us. Dad quit his job and shut his business down to sacrifice his earning power on the altar of vengeance and giving us the hardest lives possible.

From then on our father contributed zero to our upbringing. He didn't pay for school uniforms or fees, he didn't hand over any child support or help with medical or dental bills. Financially he was a ghost. It was a strategy to punish Mum for ending their marriage in the hope we'd blame her for casting us back into poverty. Dad's message was clear: 'Fuck you! Not a cent for any of you. You want to do this to me? I'm out of here. See how you like it on your own.'

I hate to admit that it worked for a while. I liked the fact we'd been gaining ground. Ever since we'd arrived from England I knew I didn't want to live a lowly life. Despite our circumstances and the fact I couldn't read or count, I secretly dreamed of a big future. When the first sniff of one vanished overnight I selfishly held Mum responsible. I even asked her once, 'How could you do this?'

Of course I knew very well why she'd done it and I would have, too, had I been in her shoes.

Dad's next turn of the screw was to leave the country altogether to go and live in England. I was on the cusp of starting high school. Within a matter of months we had no house, no breadwinner and no father figure within reach. He might have been a terrible parent, but at least he'd always been somewhere nearby. Another significant shift in family dynamics occurred when Otis decided to leave, too.

Mum never quit on us. She quickly took out a lease on a small, two-bedroom place on the border of Moonee Ponds and Brunswick – the first in a series of low-rent dumps we'd call home over the next few years. Once again we were surrounded by unsavory characters. Mum had studied as a masseuse and had a long-held interest in homeopathic medicine and naturopathy. With Dad gone, she started a business from home offering therapeutic massage. Raising four kids on her own with a homespun income was a huge load, but Mum never once bagged out our father to us.

Money was extremely tight, even after she found work as a masseuse at a local chiropractor and other clinics in Glenroy. She slept on a couch by the front door so Michael, a cousin who had no place to go and I could share one bedroom while the girls slept in the other. She didn't dwell on our dire situation or let on that we were borderline homeless. Mum worked around problems and found solutions to try to make us feel secure, even though we sometimes had to play into it. For example, she'd dress up a frightfully thin meal with nothing more than a bit of hype and fanfare.

'Tomato soup tonight, everyone!' she'd announce in a sing-song voice.

'Yay! What are we having with the tomato soup, Mum?' I'd inquire.

'White bread!' she'd chirp. 'Dip it in there. It's delicious!'

The next night she'd trill, 'Mashed potatoes, kids! Come and get it!'

Baked beans on toast and fish fingers were other staples, as was bolognaise when Mum could afford to cook a batch. Stretching every dollar as far as it could go led to some dubious dietary decisions, such as buying jumbo-sized bottles of cola at discount. I don't think Mum was too fussed about the health consequences of all that sugar going into our systems, she just focused on getting as many calories into her growing kids as her purse would allow.

Today half of my teeth are missing at the back, and the ones I have left are full of fillings – the direct result of my childhood addiction to cola. As my teeth steadily dissolved or rotted away, the thrifty option was to have them removed because we couldn't afford to fix them. I still flash back to the Vietnamese dentist in Glenroy kneeling on my chest and prising a decaying molar out of my jaw with a pair of pliers. It's a good example of the things Dad could have prevented had he given a shit about us.

After a year in England he returned out of the blue in the hope Mum might take him back, but that ship had sailed. Mum was independent, and proud that she'd started her own business. She had no need for an abusive man in her life.

All of us were in bed and Mum was with a client in the living room the night Dad turned up and literally kicked the front door off its hinges. He charged inside, pulled Rachel and Marianne out of bed and into the living room. Next he yanked me off the top bunk and marched Michael, our cousin and me into the light. I was shocked at the way my father's rage had supercharged his strength. He'd lifted me clear off my bed with just one hand.

'Your mother's a *slut!*' he screamed, pointing a finger at her. 'She had her hands all over that guy!'

We were frightened and sobbing, but we knew how ridiculous and out of line he was being. Mum didn't give *that* kind of massage! Her poor client had leapt off the table and was halfway out the door. Dad chased him onto the street, leaving a torrent of expletives hanging in the night air (not exactly the relaxing remedial massage the guy had paid for). Dad stomped back into the house and hurled some more insults at our mother before marching out and leaving us with a busted front door. I knew it would be the last time he'd set foot in our house.

From an early age I'd been singled out and separated from my peers at school. At St Therese's I was eventually extracted from the mainstream and placed in a class with the special kids. There was a blind kid, a kid in a wheelchair, a deaf kid, some autistic kids . . . and me.

I couldn't understand why we'd all been excluded. None of us felt like we were better than each other, but we all knew we were in the too hard basket together. It was a weird position to find myself in. I was quite popular at school. I was good at sports, I could be charming and I made people laugh. I could draw great pictures, but teachers weren't interested in that. They only knew me as the disruptor who didn't do his schoolwork. From the primary grades right through until I left high school, I never passed a class. I didn't even get an E. I simply received no grades at all. I never read a book – not that I didn't want to – and I couldn't copy work from the blackboard into my exercise books. I never once did homework. I didn't even know the alphabet. Instead of the neat, comprehensible lines written in my classmates' books, mine were filled with unintelligible scribbles surrounded by cartoons, sketches and caricatures of the teachers.

I didn't tell a soul that I couldn't read, write or do basic sums. That was top-secret information that had to be protected at all costs. However, the moat that I dug around my shame left me feeling isolated and very, very lonely. It was better that I pretended to be too cool for schoolwork. If there was a class test, I became consumed with how I could get out of it. If there was any chance I'd be exposed as illiterate I'd act the clown or be naughty. I much preferred to get kicked out of class than be asked to stand up and read aloud. I hid everything from my teachers, my classmates, my mum and my brothers and sisters. No-one in the world but me knew how stupid I was. When school reports were handed out it was an opportunity for kids to doctor their grades. My friends would change a B-minus into a B-plus with the short stroke of a pen but I had nothing to work with. When they asked me to show them my report I always declined. 'I did alright,' I'd lie.

Being unintelligent was as perplexing to me as it was lonely. I recognised I was perfectly capable of taking in information verbally. I held rational thoughts and knew in some instances I was actually a few steps ahead of other kids on the common-sense scale. I watched a huge amount of television and movies to make up for the shortfall in understanding the world that would otherwise have come from books. I binged on anything celluloid – history, comedy, drama, epics, horror, love stories, action movies and documentaries. I rewatched it all until the VHS tapes broke. My guilty pleasure was kung-fu films, especially if they starred Bruce Lee. I had a very good vocabulary and could converse as well as anyone – I just had no hope of writing it down.

To this day I'm astonished that I was able to progress through year levels without anyone pointing out I might have been having a few problems, regardless of me keeping my secret. Back then, it seems that if someone had trouble learning, the simple solution was, 'Stick 'em in the special class'.

In the playground at primary school some kids called me 'retard' and received a crisp punch in the mouth in return. Ironically my willingness to be violent seemed to lend me some mystique. I became popular for being *that* kid, which gave me a misguided sense of confidence. I thought that if I couldn't be a good student, at least I could be good at being bad.

I appointed myself as a defender of the downtrodden, too. When I saw someone being picked on because of their handicap or their race, my hatred of predators and bullies flared. A very sweet boy in my 'special' class named Mark was a particularly easy target for teasing. A year younger than me, Mark had a severe learning disability and, I suspect, Tourette's syndrome. He humped poles out in the schoolyard and made strange noises while he was at it. Kids would crowd around and laugh at him, which Mark misinterpreted as approval and encouragement, so he humped and hollered even more. He might have been unaware of it, but I could see the gleeful cruelty of the mob and it infuriated me. The laughing stopped when I started swinging punches.

The same boys who tormented Mark were anxious to pick me first on their teams for lunchtime footy matches – not because of my prowess with the ball, because I didn't have much – but because they knew I'd be brutal and they didn't want to be on the receiving end. Given the disaster of my primary school years I have no idea how I was accepted into a private Catholic boys' high school, nor how Mum afforded it. I imagine she worked out a special deal with the church considering she was *such* a devout and attendant Catholic. At St Bernard's College in Essendon my abysmal academic career continued in tandem with my growing reputation as a brawler. Somehow I was still popular inside and outside of school, and girls seemed to like me despite my scary behaviour.

None of them knew the tough-guy image was a disguise – a cloak I wrapped around me to prevent people from seeing the dunce within. No-one knew I was a sensitive boy who wanted to be liked, loved and taken seriously. I was sentimental and strongly emotional. I wept when my heart was broken and my soul was bruised, and when despair fell on others, too. I experienced emotions physically. Waves of goosebumps rippled across my skin and the hair on my arms stood up at the memory of things that were beautiful, sad, deep and important. They still do.

While most of the teachers ignored me, one tried to sink me. Halfway through Year 8 someone broke all the handles off the classroom doors. It had nothing to do with me but this teacher insisted she'd seen me do it. We both knew she was lying but her word was believed over mine. I was removed from all of my classes and made to sit in an empty office by myself for the rest of the year. I had to take my lunch break at a different time from the other students and I was banned from doing sport. In effect I was in solitary confinement at school.

My social isolation deepened as word about the Fantauzzo kid got around among the parents. My circle of friends shrank as sensible adults forbade their children from associating with the violent class clown. Fair enough. I was trouble. It was richly ironic that the madman reputation I'd created to protect myself and my family ended up hurting me the most.

As loneliness, poverty and the strong currents of puberty swelled my sense of failure, I turned to drawing as an escape. Aside from sport, it was the only thing that came easily to me. I didn't consider myself an artist or anything so highbrow – after all, I'd never picked up a paintbrush. I drew with pencils and figured everybody did, so I was nothing special. In addition to sketching friends and teachers, I did larger works on the walls at home – dragons and characters from comics and picture books. When Christmas and birthdays rolled around I drew caricatures of my family and made intricate personalised cards. I also sprayed graffiti all over the local streets and alleys.

As time went on our housing situation grew even more unstable. Because she was over-extended with school fees and the cost of clothing and feeding us, Mum inevitably got behind on the rent. We fell into a system of packing up and leaving before real estate agents could evict us or seize our stuff.

It wasn't unusual for a sheriff to turn up looking for Mum. Others would try to repossess the car or take our TV. Since they couldn't legally serve papers to children we'd stand at the door and tell whoever was there, 'Mum isn't home.' Later on I bought a pit bull for back-up and called him Cujo, after the rabies-infected killer dog from the 1983 horror film of the same name. Part of his job was to help make ours an even scarier address to anyone who might think about robbing us, and to growl at big Samoan repo-men.

You can stall all you like, but eventually you have to get out if you're not paying the rent. Mum tried her best: she worked hard and long but, on a low wage with four kids to feed, reality eventually knocked sharply at the door. Before any creditors or evictors arrived we'd pack up the place, hire a van and scurry to the next rental Mum had hustled her way into, only to get behind on the rent again and have to repeat the process a few months later. This exhausting game of rental leapfrog went on for years, but we managed to stay one step ahead of homelessness. We moved at least twenty times.

Now and then we'd slip between the cracks and the five of us would crowd into one bedroom in an aunt's apartment while Mum looked for a new place to lease. We always had a roof over our heads but it was never *our* roof and it was never permanent. Even though the divorce had triggered massive upheaval and a dramatic change in fortunes for us

CHAPTER TWO

all, I was relieved Mum had broken free from Dad. She deserved to be happy.

Mum sometimes reminded me of one of those kids who is denied sugar their whole lives and when they're old enough to decide for themselves they go overboard. After my parents broke up, that's how Mum was with her friends. She went to over-forties nightclubs and her girlfriends came over for 'Mother's Club' most Saturday nights. They'd get smashed in our tiny kitchen, which pissed me off a little. As a boy I thought the rowdy, drunken women corrupted my mum, but the truth is she loved being corrupted. After living under Dad's yoke for so long, who could blame her? Although I wasn't the biggest fan of some of her buddies, I evened the ledger in my own way.

The Mother's Club saved money by partying in our kitchen before hitting nightspots by taxi and leaving their cars – and keys – at our house. While the ladies were out on the tiles enjoying themselves, I'd be out on the streets of Melbourne thrashing their cars. No licence. No insurance. No worries!

One of Mum's friends owned a nice new convertible Ford Capri Turbo. It became my vehicle of choice. I'd put the top down, pick up some reprobate mates and cruise around town. Sometimes I attempted stunts from my favourite car chase scenes in movies. One night I tried to put the Capri into a reverse spin manoeuvre but I only managed to smash it backwards into a steel street sign. I parked it back outside our house and went to bed like nothing had happened. When the owner came by the next day she ran inside and said, 'Oh my goodness! Someone's crashed into the back of my car!'

'Oh geez!' I said, feigning surprise and disgust. 'That's terrible!'

Increasingly unable to imagine much of a future for myself, and lacking any guidance from a father figure, I became quite the delinquent. Violence was a more regular feature of life, too. Fighting bullies at school was small game compared to the gang-related clashes that happened on the streets. Essendon railway station was a major arena for warring tribes – a crossroads where people from different schools and postcodes converged after the final bell to flex their muscles.

I didn't realise until much later that the parents of half of those kids were fruiterers, restaurateurs and members of the underworld. Still, their offspring feared me. If someone so much as looked at me sideways I exploded. I'd use a skateboard, a baseball bat or a fence picket. I'd stab people, I'd bite holes in them and rip their hair out. I'd smash glass bottles on people's heads – whatever it took to win, I would do it.

Unsurprisingly I was on a constant war-footing. Everywhere I went I scanned the terrain for weapons. In the newer suburban developments the nature strips were planted with straggly saplings supported by wooden stakes about half a metre long. I didn't need to carry a weapon when going into those neighbourhoods because they literally sprouted out of the ground. More than once those bits of wood helped me win the day, or night, and if there were no newly planted saplings around I could always kick someone's picket fence apart and arm myself with a sturdy piece of timber.

I once went to a party during Year 8 knowing some guys would likely start a fight with me. I didn't want to get jumped so I pretended I was injured and went along on crutches. My hope was that nobody would be so low as to attack a guy who was hurt but, if they were, the crutches would make a good weapon. All of this strategising was exhausting. You shouldn't have to think about those things when you're a kid.

I never picked fights and I never bullied anyone because I hated bullies and aggressors more than anything in the world. While there were a lot of gangs around, I wasn't in one – I hung around on the fringes of the various crews. If someone called me out, however, or if I was threatened, I never took a backward step. I worked out that in a street fight – that is to say, a fight in public – you only have to win for the first twenty seconds because it either gets broken up or someone gets knocked out.

Whenever there was trouble I looked for opportunities to work that to my advantage. Essendon train station played host to many a showdown between rival outfits: the Turks, the Lebanese, Asian gangs and Broadmeadows crews. One afternoon some of the Turks drove there to confront me. One guy in particular wanted to take me on and brought five mates with him. The primary fella was huge and the handful of friends I'd been hanging with took off on me. I considered doing the same until I spotted a cop car parked a little way down the road.

Conventional wisdom says you shouldn't fight in front of the cops, but in this instance their presence was a flashing green light. I'd recently taken up taekwondo and had clearly watched too many kung-fu movies because I ran straight at the big guy and launched a fly kick into his face. He fell hard and as his mates jumped in to help him I started fighting them off. Just as I'd calculated, the police arrived within seconds and broke it up. The upshot was people thought I'd taken on six guys. I hadn't, it just looked like I had.

My ability to avoid a serious beating boiled down to two things: first, I didn't hesitate and was willing to do things others thought unthinkable in order to survive unscathed. Second, my mind doesn't seem to race the way most people's do in fight or flight situations. For some reason I remained as cool as a cucumber on the inside, even while I outwardly acted like I was out of control. I could quickly calculate moves and plan what I would do each step of the way: *Okay, I'm going to headbutt this guy, then I'm going to punch his mate and bounce his head off that parked car, then those guys over there are going to break it up . . .*

For the most part, it went according to plan.

Although Dad went so far as to declare himself bankrupt to avoid paying child support, he picked us up on weekends, took us out for a coffee (he actually paid!) and dropped us back home again. That was the full extent of my relationship with him for most of my teenage years. Unfortunately some of his prior fatherly input had already left its mark on me.

Some of my mates from the neighbourhood were into shoplifting, and I was too. We'd go to the Victoria Markets or a shopping mall, put some clothes on in the change rooms and just walk out. For a lot of kids, stealing was all about the thrill. Some guys I knew robbed shops and even did break and enters. For them it was a test of who could push the boundaries the most. I stole out of envy and covetousness because I could never hope to have the things that others had. I'd see that everyone was wearing bomber jackets. *It sucks that I can't have one!* So off I'd go and pinch a bomber jacket.

Every time I stole, however, intense guilt and shame came calling soon after. I knew it was wrong and I could almost sense Dad watching on approvingly, ciggy in mouth and proud of the little thief he'd spawned. It played on my mind a lot.

I took other shortcuts simply so I could partake in whatever was going on socially. If my friends were heading to the Melbourne Show or the Moto GP, I'd tag along, say, 'I'll meet you inside,' then jump the fence. I never once paid for a movie ticket, either. Typically I'd go to the cinema with a couple of mates. They'd go in ahead of me before one came back out and handed me the other's ticket. Voila! Free movie! I felt bad about that, too, but I'd try to justify it on the basis our family never had the money to spare for such simple pleasures.

One year when the Melbourne Show was approaching I decided to make my own money – literally. Using very thin paper I photocopied both sides of a $50 note, glued them together, cut them precisely and – using pencils specially sharpened for the task – coloured them in with absolute precision. I scrunched up the finished product a little, shoved them in my pocket with some real fives and maybe a ten dollar note and suddenly I had a couple of hundred bucks to go crazy with.

My counterfeit notes weren't perfect, but the Melbourne Show hotdog stands are not manned by bank tellers or people from the Royal Australian Mint – they're run by teenagers and people throw money at them all day long. Those kids were never going to hold my dodgy notes up to the light. I'd hand over $50 for two hotdogs and, *pow!* I'd get $45 in change. Somebody would have cottoned on eventually but by then I'd be long gone with a full stomach and a bunch of showbags to take home for Marianne, Rachel and Michael.

It's kind of funny, but also sad, to think those fake $50s were my first works of art that had a monetary value.

By the time I reached Year 9 the days of my formal education were numbered. The fighting and clowning around grew even worse as my secret stupidity became harder to conceal. While most staff rolled their eyes and got on with teaching everybody else, there was one educator who seemed to recognise I wasn't a completely lost cause. He taught science and was a champion javelin thrower. I was sitting in the back of his class one morning when he leaned over and had a good look at a portrait I'd drawn of a classmate.

'That's amazing,' he said quietly so only I could hear.

'Thanks,' I replied, taken aback by the compliment. After eight and a half years of schooling he was the first teacher to ever give me one.

'Listen, I know you can't do science,' he said. 'I'll give you a pass, but you can just draw the whole period, okay? Just draw whatever you like.'

'Are you serious?' I asked.

'Yep,' he replied. 'Draw me if you like! No matter what, just keep doing what you're doing.'

From then on, my favourite class was science – just without the science part.

Halfway through the year a new kid arrived at our school and started mouthing off at me on the sports oval. He was much bigger than me and he didn't know or didn't care about my reputation. It was obvious he'd chosen me to make a statement about himself, so violence was inevitable. I realised if I fought him on the oval and we got into a wrestling match, his weight advantage could cause me trouble. I waited until we were in an environment I could control.

Sure enough the big dude sat behind me in the next class we had together and started making all kinds of threats about how he was going to bash me. I spun around and launched at him. We crashed to the floor and I punched him in the face three or four times before biting into his cheek. It would have appeared as a shocking and spontaneous attack but I had orchestrated it to end quickly with me having the upper hand. Sure enough the teacher broke it up within twenty seconds.

Biting another human being is a heinous, savage act. It causes excruciating pain and is psychologically devastating in a fight. That's why I did it.

It was the last straw. I was expelled from St Bernard's at fourteen. Mum wasn't thrilled by the news but she adopted a sanguine view. 'School's not for everyone,' she said soothingly. 'You might be better suited to an apprenticeship.'

I acted like I didn't care that I'd been kicked out of school but I was shattered and deeply dismayed about what was quickly shaping up to be an awful life. Dad had some typically pedestrian ideas about my future that he shared over our next weekly coffee. Thankfully I also took some guidance from a complete stranger who became an actual father figure. One I could look up to.

Just about everybody I knew was on drugs. Ecstasy, speed and marijuana were the vices of choice among my peers who wolfed them down alongside the river of alcohol that flowed through our teenage subculture. It's no coincidence that a lot of people I hung out with ended up in juvenile detention, jail or worse – inside the dreaded psychiatric ward where they babbled about being chased by witches and demons.

Suicide was epidemic, too. One boy I knew jumped in front of a train. Another friend hanged himself off a bridge and another kid did the same in his parents' garage. I wept for those poor boys and I empathised with them, not that my fragile mental health had anything to do with drugs. I became severely depressed after I was expelled and I once again questioned the need to stick around to see just how shit my life would be. I scribbled out another

CHAPTER THREE

incomprehensible suicide note but somehow found enough reason to make it to one more sunrise and then maybe another. If I'd fallen for the lure of drugs the way my doomed friends did, I might have found myself a speeding train or a lonely bridge, too.

That's not to say I didn't try drugs. My first experience – at my friend Glenno's house – was an eye-opener, and it underscored the different experiences I had when going to the homes of the fancy, private school crowd versus the poor neighbourhoods of my youth. Like me, Glenno lived in Shitsville and his dad wasn't around much, either. His mum was as rough as they come. She seemed to respect, even revere, violent males and was friendly with an extended family of Māoris who staged bare-knuckle fight nights in her front yard. She took a shine to me, too.

'Are you gonna teach Glenno how to fight or what?' she pressed me one afternoon when I dropped by to visit. 'I've given him a pocketknife but he's too bloody scared to use it. If you show him how to fight like you can, Vinnie, I'll make sure I look after you.'

Glenno and I went outside to talk shit and muck around in the yard, and I showed him some of the basics of self-defence. After a while his mum sang out from behind the flyscreen door, 'Come on in, boys!'

There was hardly any furniture in the house and some of the Māori guests were planted on the floor giggling like a cackle of hyenas, beatboxing and rapping freestyle. The whiff of dope hung in the air and the visitors looked mighty stoned. Glenno's mum came in from the kitchen with a warm, maternal smile on her face and a ceramic bong in her hand.

'Come here, Vinnie, look at this,' she said. With the demeanour of a woman who was making a batch of cookies she showed me how to heat up a block of hash, rub it into the tobacco and pack it into the bong without compressing it too much. 'There's a good boy,' she said, and passed me the pipe. 'Get that into ya.'

I'd seen people smoke bongs before so I knew in theory what to do, but when the warm, grey gasses surged down my windpipe I just about coughed my lungs out onto the dirty carpet. I wasn't sure if I got very stoned or not but at the time I thought the episode was pretty funny, and almost worth bragging about ('I smoked bongs with Glenno's mum!'). Today I see it for what it was. Child abuse.

In addition to pretending to be the most dangerous teenager in all of Melbourne, fitness became a foundation of my self-defence. I'd started doing taekwondo when I was twelve. A friend of mine was into it and, since I loved Bruce Lee, I became intrigued. I loved the discipline side of the sport but, mostly, I thought taekwondo might give me an edge on the street.

Training was held twice a week in a function room at the local RSL. Since we had no money to spend on sport I figured I could pay in kind. I arrived at the RSL early and stacked up all the chairs to clear space for the session. Once it was over I swept the floors, tidied up and put the chairs back in place. In return the instructor let me train for free. By the time I had a black belt two years later I realised I'd chosen the wrong martial art. To the untrained eye taekwondo might look like kung fu or karate, but it's more like dancing than fighting. It's a beautiful sport, but if you're looking for a means to protect yourself, taekwondo isn't it.

I had a few more encounters with weed after the motherly hash bongs at Glenno's, but cannabis never did much for me. While the kids around me slowly sank into the quicksand of drugs I stayed on solid ground – partly because I thought the chemicals would drag my fitness down but mainly because I'd made a promise that I really didn't want to break.

Unlike taekwondo, boxing *can* be handy when it comes to street fighting. As with martial arts, I was first attracted to boxing purely for self-protection. A far deeper love of the sport came through the exploration of it, and for that I have to thank Jack Rennie. Jack was a legend of Australian boxing who operated the old-school Marco Polo Gym in Essendon. He trained generations of top Australian fighters in the musty old joint, including Lionel Rose, whom he famously coached to a world title in 1968.

I was awed to think a bare-bones local gym in my 'hood could be a launch pad for a world beater, let alone the first Aboriginal person to ever win a world title. Not only was Jack one of the greatest Australian trainers in history, he was also an elder statesman of the sport who had co-founded the Australian National Boxing Federation back in the 60s.

I was still in school when I first showed up at his gym. Once again I offered to sweep the floors and clean the toilets if he'd let me train for free. Jack – who was a big, gruff bear of a man – nodded his agreement and I went there just about every day after school.

I fell for boxing the first time I laced up a glove. I received a floor-to-ceiling ball as a birthday present once and when I rigged it up to the clothesline in the backyard it became my happy place. The ball – tethered on a bungee – is all about timing and rhythm, and not many people can do it well. It entranced me. When my fists chased the wobbling leather orb through the air I could think about nothing else. Whenever the persistent waters of anxiety and depression climbed over my shoulders, boxing training was one of the things that kept me from going under.

I gave myself fully to the sport and grew even more obsessed with fitness. Like Sly Stallone in *Rocky* I swallowed raw eggs in the morning and smashed out a ten-kilometre run before training and sparring at Jack's in the afternoon. Real 'pinch me' moments arrived when the great Lionel Rose turned up now and then and gave me some tips.

Although boxing lifted my confidence and allowed me to feel less threatened, I still faced trouble on the street. Cujo and I went everywhere together and forged an intended reputation as a fearsome double act. People took note and word got around that we were to be avoided. Eventually it reached Jack Rennie. One day he pulled me aside for a talk. 'You have real potential, Vincent,' he said, placing a hand on my shoulder. 'You can actually box, son. I believe you can do something with it.'

For the first time in my life I glimpsed what that big future I'd always dreamed about might look like. While I couldn't seem to handle basic schoolwork, the man who coached Lionel Rose to world dominance just told me he believed in me. 'You keep turning up and putting the work in and I'll train you for fights,' he promised.

There were conditions, though. 'I don't care how good you are at boxing, if you take drugs, or if you smoke or drink – you're out,' Jack warned. 'Not only because that stuff will ruin you, but because I care about you.' The veteran warrior understood that in my strife-torn adolescence boxing had become my currency. Outside of drawing, boxing was the only thing I was good at, and my best chance for a better life. I wasn't going to risk losing it. Jack seemed to know that, too. I promised him I'd stay away from drugs.

Jack told me to write down what I wanted to become on a piece of paper and not show him but keep it in my wallet.

'I don't have a wallet,' I replied.

'Get one,' he said.

I did, and for years I carried that note around, and I referred to it nearly every day until the paper fell apart.

Outside of Mum, Jack was the first authority figure to treat me in a caring way. I had no boundaries growing up, aside from the ones I set for myself. Suddenly a male adult with wisdom and experience was in my life, and he disciplined me with a practical and moral purpose in mind – not just a smack in the mouth to make me stop crying.

Jack started inviting me to his house for dinner with his family. Afterwards we'd discuss plans for my boxing career. His dream – and mine – was for me to make it as a professional. As an amateur he thought I had a shot at qualifying for the Commonwealth Games. During these chats Jack was at pains to emphasise the difference between being a boxer and a fighter. 'Another rule,' he said to me early on. 'Pick fights outside of the ring and you're out.'

He knew where I came from and the local gang culture, and he understood the day-to-day realities I faced. 'I know you've gotta look after yourself and I have no problem with you fighting in self-defence,' he continued. 'But I'm telling you now, if you ever pick a fight or come the bully with anyone you can forget about training with me. Right?'

I gave him my word, even though I stretched the definition of 'self-defence' to include protecting my loved ones, which led to a bit more trouble than I should have been in. However, since Jack was the

CHAPTER THREE

first man to treat me the way I had always yearned to be treated – like a son – I vowed to honour his code.

Meanwhile our long run of quarterly house-hopping finally came to an end. My aunt vacated a Commission house in Aberfeldie and when Mum heard about it she hatched a plan to move us in. We were on a waiting list for public housing but since we were a big family, the options were mainly located outside of Melbourne, in rural Victoria, and Mum worried that a move to the sticks would isolate us. Knowing the place in Aberfeldie would be empty for a few days after her sister left, she hired a van, told us to pack and in we swooped. When a bemused government official showed up at the door, Mum folded her arms across her chest and refused to budge. 'I'm a single mother,' she said. 'I have four kids here who need a place to live and we're not leaving.'

We stayed for the next five years.

Aberfeldie wasn't as bleak as Broadmeadows, but we lived in a street full of Commission houses so some of the old ways prevailed. The place was more like a bunker than a house: a squat, cement cube with two bedrooms, a dining–living room, tiny kitchen and not much else. Just about every fitting was broken. As usual Mum took the couch by the front door and slept there for the next two thousand nights.

I shared a bedroom with Michael while the girls crammed into the other small room, but I soon decided I needed my own space and moved into the laundry. The Aberfeldie place might not have been fit for purpose but the rent was capped very low and we at last had some stability. The cruel heel of poverty, however, kept our ambitions in check. I couldn't have friends over because there wasn't the space and, besides, Mum's bed was in the living room.

Growing kids have growing needs and Mum could barely cover them. Dad still took us out for a coffee every week, and when he found out I'd been expelled he decided it was time to step in – not by way of a material contribution to my welfare of course, just by calling in a favour from some mates. 'I can probably get you a job with some people I know,' he said while sipping his espresso. 'They've got some restaurants.'

And so, at the age of fourteen, my lowly working life began. The men in question were a bunch of Lebanese brothers who ran a chain of Italian restaurants and pizza shops. As friends of Dad's, naturally they were dodgy. They promised me an apprenticeship as a chef and paid me $3.80 an hour over a seventy-hour week. Since I worked mostly at night – sometimes right through until dawn making great vats of Italian sauces – I waved goodbye to whatever dwindling social life I had.

It was more of an apprenticeship in crime than it was in cooking. The brothers regaled me with tales of their standover operations, bashings and the ins-and-outs of fraud. Like Dad, they loved to cut

CHAPTER THREE

corners, so they had no problem sending me out to deliver pizzas in the waitresses' cars, still underage and unlicensed, of course.

The payoff, however, was a boost at home. At last I could contribute and help my mum. My big sister, Rachel, had taken up triathlon and was becoming successful so I supported her as much as I could, too. In 1995 she represented Australia at the triathlon world championships in Mexico. It felt good to give some financial backing, like I was becoming an adult. I was very protective of my siblings, particularly the little ones Michael and Marianne. I loved them all, of course, but I had a special connection with Marianne based on our dark sense of humour and a shared penchant for mischief. While my pay packet certainly eased the pressure on Mum, there was nothing left over to save for a rainy day. We still lived hand-to-mouth, week-to-week.

Although I felt conflicted about stealing from stores and counterfeiting currency, I had no qualms about pinching food from Dodgy Bros. Inc. Now and then I'd pilfer a couple of steaks from the cool room just so we could have something a little more special for dinner at home. One night I was caught red-handed by the dodgiest brother.

'What have you got there?' he asked when he saw me secretively fiddling with a plastic bag in the kitchen.

'Just some lasagne,' I replied sheepishly enough to make him look inside it.

'Fucking arsehole!' he said when he eyed the steaks. 'I should sack you, you thieving dog.'

'Go ahead then!' I shot back. My face flushed with indignity. He had a hide paying me a pittance to slave through the night and then play the victim when I took what amounted to morsels for my family. He'd have never noticed the missing meat if he hadn't caught me. It wasn't like I'd stolen money from the till. I wouldn't stoop that low.

'You know what?' I said as my embarrassment hardened to anger. 'Don't bother sacking me. I quit! Fuck you!'

After a day or so we both cooled down and I returned to work. Temporarily.

An interesting quirk of my Dad's personality was that he always had to have a partner and a family around him. It didn't matter that it wasn't us – any human beings would do. He'd started seeing a woman who had a few kids of her own, including a son who was around my age. A couple of months after the steak incident I was put in charge of the pasta dishes. Although I couldn't comprehend the written menu, I knew all the recipes inside out and back-to-front. I was very good in the kitchen.

Feeling slightly more fulfilled, and with the owners happy too, my problematic life started to stabilise a bit. Then Dad turned up at the restaurant one night with his new lady friend and her kids in tow. I couldn't believe it was happening – the man whose contribution to my formative years was one coffee a week brought a replacement family to my workplace so he could treat them to a nice Italian meal that I had cooked for three fucking dollars eighty an hour.

I stood at the stove completely crushed. I weighed up whether to go into the dining room to let him have it when one of the brothers ushered Dad and his new brood into the kitchen. 'Hey, Vinnie,' he announced. 'Look who's here to say hello!'

I don't know what reaction Dad expected – whether he was trying to hurt me or was so lacking in empathy that he just didn't get it – but he seemed shocked when I threw every pot and pan in the kitchen onto the floor with a series of deafening crashes and a great splash of bubbling sauces.

'You can get fucked!' I seethed at my father.

The cacophony brought the other brothers running. 'You cunts can all get fucked, too,' I said, waving a finger at them. 'I quit.'

There was no going back a second time.

Not long after I left their employ the brothers tried to burn the restaurant to the ground. Another Italian eatery had opened nearby and the Dodgys started losing business. In their haste to cash in on an insurance policy they soaked the place in petrol in the dead of night, but instead of just lighting it on fire they blew it up. One of them died. Pretty dumb.

Trouble kept looking for me, too. Now free to socialise, I was out late one night with some mates in Moonee Ponds when a skinny guy took a dislike to me outside a kebab shop. I was blithely stuffing my face when he started to goad me. The next thing I knew he pulled out a butterfly knife (they were very popular among young gangsters back then) and twirled it in front of me. In a heartbeat his bodyweight shifted and he came at me with intent.

Jesus Christ! I thought. *This kid's going to stab me!*

My brain clicked onto autopilot fight setting. I threw my half-eaten kebab flush into his face and at the same time grabbed the wrist of his stabbing hand. I pulled him close, headbutted him in the face a couple of times and shoved his dagger arm behind his back. The blade sunk into his arse almost up to the hilt where, strangely, it remained stuck. I tried to pull it out but it wouldn't budge. I learned later that muscles can seize up and clench tight around an embedded blade. Apparently, you're supposed to twist and pull.

I began to worry because my fingerprints were on a blood-soaked butterfly knife protruding from another person's body. I let the guy go and his shocked mates took over knife retrieval duties. Everyone who witnessed it knew I'd acted in self-defence and the consensus was the knifeman had it coming. I disappeared before the police arrived and never heard another thing about it. No-one – not even the guy I'd stabbed – dobbed me in. A lucky escape.

In addition to boxing I still took refuge away from the streets in the meditative headspace my art provided. My cluttered mind was somehow able to make more sense of the world when I had a pencil in my hand. One day, on a whim, I got a hold of some paint and a brush, and gave painting a go. It was like the lights were switched on.

My first painting, which my mum still has, was a portrait of Albert Einstein. I didn't know who he was but when I saw a poster of him in a shop I was taken by his crazy hair, kind eyes and interesting face. There was a quotation on the poster so I pretended I couldn't see it properly and asked the friend I was with to read it for me.

'Imagination is more important than knowledge.'

That landed right in the middle of my heart. *I have imagination*, I thought. *I might not be smart but I can think as big as anyone else in the world and that's got to count for something.* I loved Albert Einstein after that.

I found I could paint easily and accurately straightaway without any practice, even though I painted Albert using acrylic paint which is harder to work with than oil. *This is incredible!* I thought as I conjured his likeness on a piece of masonite board that I'd pulled out of a chest of drawers. *If you make a mistake you just paint over it!*

Later, when I switched to oil, the process was even smoother. I painted Albert many times after that. I guess I liked the juxtaposition of a dumb kid painting a genius.

At sixteen, feeling excluded from the world, I decided I needed to return to school. Knowing I'd never get back into St Bernard's I enrolled in Buckley Park College, a public institution just down the road from Aberfeldie. I blagged my way into Year 11 by claiming I'd completed Year 10 at another school. At the time, Buckley Park had a bad reputation – kids smoked bongs on the oval and fights broke out every day. It was a proper bogan public school and a disturbingly large number of kids I went there with are now dead.

Still, it was a fresh start in a new school and none of the teachers knew me. I went there to succeed, or at least keep up and be like everyone else. It didn't take long for me to realise I'd made a mistake. The only schoolwork I could remotely handle was the practical side of art and although my art teacher was encouraging, all of the others seemed to wish I wasn't there. One came straight out and said it: 'Why do you bother coming to school, Mr Fantauzzo? Accept it, you're hopeless and you're going to fail in life.'

My street-fighter credentials followed me into the schoolyard far more than I expected them to. I was challenged almost every day and had to fight to prove myself. Guys from other areas even drove to the school at lunchtime to jump the fence and take me on. Then there was the extra-curricular combat at the train station afterwards. It was exhausting, completely out of hand and plain stupid.

After three months it was all over. If you can't read or write you're screwed. I walked out feeling like such a loser. I found out later that the girl I had liked wanted me to take her to the mid-year formal, but she went with someone else instead. I was shattered. I wondered what the other guy was like and what he'd do with his life. Maybe they'd fall madly in love, get married and have kids? Or maybe they'd find great jobs and travel the world together?

A few weeks later I was hanging out on the street in Moonee Ponds when my ex art teacher drove by. She parked her car and walked straight up to me. 'Hi, Vincent,' she said. 'It's such a shame you left school. You have such potential. Is there no way you'll consider coming back?'

'No, I'm good, Miss, thanks. School's not for me,' I replied, trying to act detached and cool even though I was dying inside.

'Well, it really is a shame because you have a talent. You should do something with it.'

As she drove away I wanted to cry.

I did, however, return to school one final time.

Marianne arrived home one day in tears. When it happened a second time I asked her what the problem was and she told me she was being bullied by some guys who went to Buckley Park College. This fell into the category of protecting my loved ones from harm, so I felt justified in suspending Jack Rennie's ban on picking fights.

A couple of days later I turned up at the school at lunchtime wearing a balaclava and carrying a baseball bat. I chased Marianne's bullies down, gave them a flogging with the bat and disappeared as fast as I'd arrived. Even by my standards it was pretty horrific and I wondered if it might make the news. It didn't, but the bullying certainly stopped.

In another act of pre-emptive family defence, I'd gotten wind that some bad fellas I vaguely knew of were planning to rob our home. They lived in a share house a few suburbs away so rather than wait for them to come to us, Cujo and I paid them an unexpected visit. They were sitting around in the loungeroom smoking bongs when – channelling my father – I kicked their front door in and charged inside with Cujo snarling and barking alongside me.

These guys had a reputation for being quite heavy so I went full psychopath. I upended their table and screamed at the top of my lungs as their bongs, beers and ashtrays crashed across the floor. I put my boot through their television screen and kicked a PlayStation across the room and into a wall. I had Cujo on a short leash but let him get close enough to my terrified foes to just miss mauling them. It was all over in about thirty seconds and – just like the baseball bat attack at the school – I was gone before they could process what was happening.

As soon as I was a safe distance away I collapsed, physically and emotionally spent as if I'd gone fifteen rounds in the ring. Mission accomplished.

So much for the sensitive aspiring artist.

For a while it looked like I might have a future in organised crime.

Mum started seeing a guy called Giuseppe Colombo. While I doubt he said much about his social circle when they first started dating, it became obvious Giuseppe had links to the underworld. Mum and her new beau appeared to get on just fine, though, and had a few things in common. For one thing, Giuseppe was also a single parent raising two little boys.

My next kitchen job – at Joey's Italian restaurant in Brunswick – came courtesy of Mum's new boyfriend. Giuseppe was friendly with the owners and vouched for me as a hard worker who was experienced for my young age. Working in that place was like being in the Australian version of *Goodfellas*. The owners and staff were all gangland guys with personalities and names to match. I became friendly with men named Spider and Tiny. Just like in *The Simpsons* episode when Bart meets the mob, the gangsters took a shine to me.

Giuseppe loved to bask in the notoriety of the place. His demeanour would change as soon as he walked in the door. One minute he was a suburban dad, the next he was a tough guy. I didn't really buy the performance, though. More than most people, I knew a pretender when I saw one.

Joey's was well-regarded so I had to bring my A-game to the kitchen. It was an extensive menu and there was a lot of pressure, but I quickly found my feet. The real action, however, took place in the illegal casino out the back. People in the know could slip through a secret door straight into the underworld where a who's who of identities from cops, doctors and lawyers to fruiterers, bookmakers and construction bosses congregated to gamble.

The casino was a soft-lit smoky den featuring a couple of roulette wheels, blackjack tables, a bar and leather sofas. The first time I went back there I was shocked to see loaded guns on the tables alongside those early mobile phones the size of house bricks. I loved the job from the start – not because I was necessarily impressed by guns or criminals, but because they embraced me and treated me with warmth and respect. They even gave me a nickname. As soon as I arrived at work each night I was no longer Vincent but Junior, the young boxer who made a mean penne arrabbiata.

CHAPTER FOUR

From what I could tell, the restaurant was three businesses in one. The dining part was a hands-down success – a very popular place frequented by crooks and civilians alike. A lot of money also changed hands in the casino but I suspect the main racket was drug distribution. Mid-level dealers regularly came in to pick up their gear before heading back out onto the streets. Joey's was the dealers' dealer and it wasn't long before I was brought into the loop, since it ran right through the kitchen.

Large amounts of drugs were stashed in the flour barrels and hidey-holes in the cool room and storeroom. We handled a lot of amphetamines and marijuana, although the weed wasn't as lucrative as the chemicals. Strangely there was no cocaine. Large bundles of cash were handed over in exchange for commercial quantities of illicit substances and I became a trusted in-house distributor. I'd be busy in the kitchen when a well-dressed dude would pop his head in, hand me a thick wodge of fifty- and hundred-dollar notes in exchange for the pre-packed pizza box that had been prepared earlier.

Some of the restaurant crew were fight promoters who ran the big amateur tournaments in Melbourne. They loved the fact I could fight *and* cook. Between work and play, just about everyone I associated with was doing something wrong and it nibbled away at my conscience. Okay, I still wasn't picking fights, drinking or taking drugs, but I doubt Jack Rennie would have approved of my new buddies and my bit part in the local narcotic supply chain, so I didn't tell him.

When I wasn't at work or asleep I was training as hard as ever. I started to rack up a few more wins in the boxing ring along the way. I'd also taken up kickboxing at another gym and had some amateur success in that sport as well, although it was a hell of a lot more punishing than boxing. I could hardly walk for two weeks after a bout.

Guys never show it in the ring but kicks to the legs are absolutely brutal. Post-fight, my legs would just about turn black with bruises. Despite the pain I started boxing less and kickboxing more, mainly because the fight nights were much bigger events. The promoters turned up the music and I strutted to the ring with Tupac rapping out of the PA and fireworks sizzling. There was always a big, noisy crowd in attendance and I'd think, *Am I a fucking rockstar or what?*

There's no prize money in amateur sport but I kept pulling good crowds to the kickboxing bouts so I got a cut of the ticket sales instead. It may have been more appealing on that level, but kickboxing was far less dignified and respectable. If you trained with Jack Rennie you had a chance to represent Australia at the Commonwealth Games or even the Olympics. If you hung out in the kickboxing scene you could have a corrupt fighting career surrounded by dodgy guys and drug dealers. As sad as it sounds, I found the latter more appealing at the time. I thought I *was* a fucking rockstar.

CHAPTER FOUR

The kickboxers I trained with promised me the world and a big career, and although I won my fights with them I knew they weren't particularly interested in my future or my welfare. Not the way Jack was.

Meanwhile my underworld training continued at Joey's. One day I was moving a couch in the casino when I detected a heavy object wobbling around beneath the cushions. I reached in and my fingers froze on the cool metal of what was unmistakably a gun. After a quick look around to make sure I was alone I pulled it out. It was a Colt .38 revolver. I shoved it down the front of my pants and went back to the kitchen where I transferred it to a pizza box to take home at the end of the shift. When I left work that night I was a bundle of jangling nerves and adrenaline. It's not every day you steal a gun from the mob.

For the next six months or so Junior carried a pistol. I was never going to pull the trigger but I certainly flashed it around on the streets where it did wonders for my reputation. I had it on me one night when – after making some kind of nuisance of ourselves – police chased me and a couple of friends through the backstreets of Moonee Ponds. As I bolted through a darkened car park I tossed the gun into some bushes where it thudded heavily onto the ground.

I found out later that a kid from another group saw me ditch it, so – just like I had – he claimed the .38 for himself. I showed a clean pair of heels that night but the cops pinched the other lad in possession of the deadly weapon. He served time in juvenile detention for it.

Like the kebab-and-stab incident, this was a sliding door moment when I could have been in serious trouble but wasn't. Even though I was occasionally picked up by the police I got away with everything as a kid. Sure, I was whacked with the White Pages a couple of times and flung around in the back of a divvy van, but I was never charged with an offence – luck that wouldn't hold forever.

Even though I could have stayed at Joey's for as long as I liked, I knew it wouldn't evolve into anything special. At every place I worked I ultimately hit a paper ceiling and could go no further. Because I was illiterate, I had no hope of ordering food deliveries, making a roster or getting more involved with the business. I could run a kitchen easily. I could handle stress and cook my arse off, but when it came to the technical and accounting side of things I was stuck at the stove. I was never going to be the manager and although I'd dipped my toe in the dirty waters of the underworld, I didn't want to be a criminal.

While I had lied and cheated and stolen from an early age, malfeasance never sat well in my heart. I didn't want to end up like the crooks, or a sly operator like my dad. Surely my life could be bigger, brighter and more upstanding than theirs? It wasn't as though I judged them. I'd become very close to the Joey's crowd. I'd virtually lived with them every day for a couple of years. After I gave my notice I embarked on a string of dead-end jobs in search of a legitimate way forward. Now and then, though, I'd poke my head into the restaurant just to say hello.

'Hey! Junior, ciao!'

Mum had been seeing Giuseppe Colombo for a couple of years when she'd begun to suspect things weren't as rosy as they seemed. She confided in me that she thought he was cheating on her. Giuseppe was due to take us all out for dinner at Joey's the following night and Mum planned to confront him. As a result I was hyper-vigilant when we all sat down at a large table as my old bosses fussed about, handing out menus and carrying drinks.

Giuseppe ordered a bottle of champagne and – completely out of the blue – proposed marriage to our mother right in front of us. She stared at him in silence for what seemed like forever.

'You *fucking* cunt,' she finally said.

'What?' Giuseppe said, looking shocked and guilty at the same time.

'You've been screwing around behind my back!' Mum said through gritted teeth. 'You want to get married? You can go and get fucked instead.'

Mum found out that Giuseppe hadn't just been cheating on her – he'd been living a secret second life with another woman and her kids. He spent half the week with them and the rest with us. Giuseppe should have crawled away with his tail between his legs but he opted to play the hard man instead. He started verbally abusing Mum but before he got too many insults out I dived across the table, knocked him backwards off his chair and repeatedly cracked him in the head in the middle of the restaurant. The guy had cheated on my mum then somehow thought he could talk shit to her in front of her family in public. Where I come from you can't do that with impunity. I was of a mind to kill him.

Maybe Giuseppe thought he was in his safe place surrounded by his mafia mates, but he had always been a fringe player. The owners dragged me off him and threw him out on the street where he was told to piss off and not return. I don't know if his exile from Joey's ever ended but we certainly never saw Giuseppe again. The only shame about it was his two kids were really nice guys. They'd become like little siblings and then – just like that – they were gone from our lives. I hope they grew up to be happy.

Most of my employment came through who I knew, not what I knew. When I first went to Centrelink for support payments I was put in the job network and sent to attend interviews. My first – for a storeman role in a factory – triggered the same anxiety and self-loathing I felt when doing an exam at school. I was ushered into a room with around thirty people to sit for what I imagine was a fairly basic test. I was the only one who failed. The realisation I couldn't even take the first step to get a job packing boxes was devastating, particularly considering some of the people who passed the test were clearly off their heads.

I gave Centrelink a wide berth after that. No amount of welfare was worth the ritual humiliation of interviews. Luckily Dad came out of the woodwork for a while and I fell back into the path well-trodden by those I knew. He was working in another printing business and organised an apprenticeship for me there. I had no particular ambition to be a printer but I instantly seized the opportunity to chase a relationship with my father.

What should have been a bonding experience was the complete opposite. Bewilderingly, Dad was a likable person at work. People seemed fond of him and thought he was funny. I looked on and thought, *Who are you?* I didn't know the popular guy who cracked jokes and held court in the lunch room. I felt like I was watching a movie about printers with Dad playing the charming lead role. I quickly came to resent the good-humoured stranger and stewed in silence as he performed his scenes.

'How about kicking a ball with me some time, eh?' I'd mutter under my breath as Dad made another joke. Or, 'How come you never shared this side of yourself with us?'

Still, the pay was better than in the restaurants and I managed to scrape together enough to buy a lowered 1971 Chrysler VG Valiant with fat tyres – a beautiful, loud, classic thug ride. As part of my apprenticeship I had to attend a technical college where I consistently bombed out but it didn't seem to matter too much at the factory, maybe because I was Claudio's boy. Then one day, and not for the first time in my life, he just quit his job and left me.

I stuck around at the factory for a while and became mates with a lovely guy who was a talented guitar player. He told me he was also about to quit the factory to concentrate on playing in his band full time. We were operating a large printing machine one day when he tried to make an adjustment. His hand got sucked into it and crushed between two giant steel rollers. He screamed and begged us to help him but we couldn't get his arm free. Eventually the fire brigade worked out how to reverse the machine to release my poor mate. I held his face to stop him looking at his mangled arm. I wish I hadn't seen it myself. His music career was gone, his dream was over.

After he was taken to hospital by ambulance the old, skinny factory owner cornered me. 'So how in the hell did this happen?' he wanted to know.

'There's no safety guard on the machine,' I replied. 'That's how it happened!'

I knew I was right. Dad had warned me the machine was supposed to have a safety guard in place to prevent the operator getting caught in it but, for whatever reason, it had been removed.

'He must have been doing something wrong!' the owner insisted.

CHAPTER FOUR

'No!' I dug in. 'There's no safety guard on the machine.'

Things got heated and I quickly arrived at the 'Fuck you!' stage. I stormed out, returned in my Valiant, reversed it up to the factory's open roller door, smoked up the tyres, sped off and never returned. As tragic as it was, that day taught me not to waste my life in a factory doing something I hated. Over the years I've often wondered if I'd have ever heard my mate's songs on the radio or gone to see his band play had he not quit that place sooner.

Depressingly, my departure didn't lead to a new dawn – just a series of false starts. I tried my hand at house painting, concreting and installing home security systems with a couple of criminals. Nothing lasted too long. Illiteracy always brought me unstuck.

Just as in school, I found that I had to lie and cheat to get by in the big, bad world – particularly if I didn't want people to discover I was stupid. At school I couldn't even spell my own address, never mind pass a test on new words once a week. I failed most of the time but whenever I didn't, it was because I copied someone's work. My friends didn't mind but just as many kids refused. They would put their folder up as a screen or hunch forward over their answers to block my view and remind me I was a hopeless loser. After a while I figured out if I sat on the left-hand side of right-handed students and tilted my head in a certain way I could sometimes copy without them knowing.

The stakes were a lot higher in the adult world where passing a test, for example, meant the difference between having a driver's licence and not having a driver's licence. The practical part of getting my learner's permit would have been a breeze – after all I'd been successfully hooning around unlicensed since I was fourteen.

Passing the VicRoads multiple-choice test, however, was impossible. I sat for it five times and failed. If I wanted to drive lawfully I was left with no choice but to cheat. I didn't want to, nor did I relish the challenge of beating the system – I'd have given anything to be able to read the questions and give the right answers. To me, cheating wasn't a shortcut, it was a necessity, not just to get my licence but to keep the sad, sorry, charade of my life rolling along.

During many failed excursions to the VicRoads test centre I noticed that people were sat next to each other to do the test, and I had always sat next to strangers. Obviously I couldn't cheat off them or ask them for answers. However I also noticed teenagers like me often arrived to do the learners' test together. Staff would say, 'Are you two kids both doing the test? Yes? Great, come and sit over here.'

Bingo! All I had to do was turn up with a mate and I'd be licensed and legally on the road in no time. I waited a few weeks until a friend of mine was going for her L plates and tagged along. Sure enough they sat us together. She knew I could already drive and when I told her I hadn't studied the booklet she was happy to whisper the answers to me.

I was a menace on the road. The Valiant was the first in a revolving fleet of fast cars and motorbikes I piloted around the streets as if greater Melbourne were my personal racetrack. I put people's lives at risk on a daily basis and it's a miracle I never caused a serious accident.

One night, after watching a famous video of a guy speeding through the streets of Paris in a Ferrari, I was inspired to set the land speed record between a mate's place and my home. I set sail in the Valiant around 2 am and reached terrifying speeds. I got airborne over train tracks and sped through every stop sign and red light. The mind boggles at my stupidity.

After I bought my first motorbike I went even faster. Dad had also been a fan of bikes but, as with everything else in his life, he never shared that passion with me. When I discovered two-wheeled machines for myself, I fell in love from the first kick-start: the freedom, the rush and the adrenaline that was available at the flick of a wrist was intoxicating. I leaned into corners at 200 kph with no racing gear on. I flew through intersections in 60 km zones at 150 kph and I taunted the police to chase me, which they did. A few of my mates and I rigged our bikes with a cable and switch mounted on the handlebars that allowed us to flip our licence plates horizontal so the cops couldn't see them.

When I reflect on that young kid today I feel sick. My near criminal disregard for other people's lives is something I can hardly comprehend now, particularly when I think about my wife and children out on the road. But I feel sorry for him, too. Driving with a death wish was the closest I came to suicide. Sometimes I convinced myself I wasn't going to live to be old, and that a note wouldn't be necessary if I died in a road accident. Perhaps the stupidest and saddest thought that played in my mind as I blew through red lights was, *At least if I die this way it'll be something special.*

Somehow I made it to eighteen, an adult in the eyes of the law. Feeling that the clock was ticking faster on my life I grew even more desperate to escape poverty. I wasn't naïve: I recognised the limits illiteracy put on my professional ambitions and it was clear I wasn't cut out to answer to superiors, so I went into business for myself.

For years my aunty had operated a laundrette and it always struck me as a fairly simple operation, something I could easily handle. On a whim I applied for a lease on a little shopfront in Buckley Street, Essendon, opened the doors and called it a laundrette (although I spelled it lundreet).

The whole thing was one big hustle. My first order of business was to phone an industrial dry-cleaning company. 'Hi there. Yeah, look, my mum's opened up this laundrette and I'm helping her run it,'

CHAPTER FOUR

I began. 'We're looking for someone to handle our dry cleaning at a commercial rate.'

No problem, they said, and we entered a simple arrangement. I accepted people's dry cleaning, the other operator picked it up every morning and dropped it off in the afternoon. I charged above the commercial rate I was paying and all of a sudden I was a dry cleaner. In reality I was just an empty shop.

Next I phoned a major newsagent, knowing they did deals with little shops in the area. I spun the same story, pretending I was part of a family business, not some teenager on the make: 'I'm helping my mum out,' I said. 'She doesn't speak English too well. We'd like to start a regular order for magazines and newspapers.'

By subbing as a dry cleaner and selling magazines I made just enough money to cover the rent on the shop and pay for my petrol and some groceries, which I considered a success. As with just about every aspect of life, I still encountered the paper ceiling but I learned to work around it. If someone came in with two shirts, a tie and a suit to be dry cleaned there was no way I could write that down on the order form. Instead I'd pretend to be too busy and say, 'Would you mind filling this out?' and slide the form and a pen across the counter. 'Don't forget to pop your name and phone number on there, too. Thanks.'

As for job satisfaction? There was none. With nothing to do most of the time I spent my days drawing. When customers came in they lingered over the pictures I'd Blu Tacked to the walls and paid me compliments.

'Oh my god.'

'That's amazing!'

'Did you do that?'

Some asked me to draw their kids, husbands, wives and girlfriends – even their pets. I also got to know a guy who dealt in sports memorabilia. He was a pretty shifty fella who was addicted to heroin, but he was entrepreneurial enough to go to footy training sessions and media events around Melbourne and ask famous sportspeople to sign photographs of themselves. He sold them – sometimes for quite decent money – and used the proceeds to keep his drug habit ticking over.

'Photographs and prints are okay but one-of-a-kind original drawings are going to be worth even more, don't you reckon?' I said when we got chatting one day.

He agreed they would.

'So how about I draw them, you get them signed and sold and we'll split the money?' I proposed.

Soon I was making more from the sports memorabilia side-hustle than I was through the lundreet front-hustle. It was easy money, too – just a matter of flipping through magazines and newspapers and knocking out lead pencil portraits of famous people. I drew a lot of AFL players, tennis stars, the late, great Shane Warne (we did quite a few of Warney) and even Muhammad Ali.

CHAPTER FOUR

I earned a few hundred bucks a week but, once again, I found myself dealing with some sketchy people. The sports memorabilia scene is a den of thieves. All kinds of stuff gets peddled as authentic when it's not, and half of the signatures are fake. Still, sometimes I'd lock up the shop at the end of the day and head home feeling like I was becoming an artist. I knew I was only copying pictures from magazines but people were still paying money for them.

Isn't that the definition of an artist? I'd wonder.

Most trainers and fighters like to know who they're going up against in the ring. My kickboxing coaches, for instance, gave me videotapes of my upcoming opponents' fights so we could work out a strategy and then train for it. Not Jack Rennie. He was old-school. He didn't even want to know the name of the next bloke I was fighting until it was absolutely necessary. 'This is amateur boxing,' he'd growl. 'You walk in there and you fight. Somebody wins. Full stop.'

We did prepare for my bouts, of course. Normally we spent two weeks training physically and mentally for a fight but one Monday afternoon Jack surprised me by saying, 'How would you like to fight on Friday night?'

'Okay, where?' I asked.

'Tasmania,' he replied.

I was stunned. 'How do I get there?'

'On a plane,' he said, looking confused by the question.

'I've never been on a plane!' I said, forgetting I flew halfway across the world when I was five.

'Well now's your big chance, Vincent,' he said. 'I can't come with you. There's not enough money so you're gonna have to go by yourself. I'll take you to the airport though and put you on the plane. It'll be fine.'

Mum was worried about me travelling so far away alone and didn't want me to go. Dad was off who knows where with some new woman. He had no idea what was going on in my life. I decided I would fly away to fight.

Boxing Victoria paid for me to travel to Hobart on the Friday afternoon and return to Melbourne on Saturday. As promised, Jack made sure I boarded the little twin-engine plane and bid me goodbye and good luck. The plane had arrived earlier in the day from Hobart and a Tasmanian newspaper was stuffed into the seat pocket in front of me. I don't know what masthead it was but on the back page there was a photo of a tough looking boxer posing with his gloves up. As far as I could tell the headline said something about a title defence. When I absently scanned the text underneath, a couple of familiar words jumped out at me: Vincent Fantauzzo.

The defending champion was an unsmiling thirty-year-old truck driver who was fond of tattoos. He was my weight and size but he looked scary. The

CHAPTER FOUR

fight was held in an RSL club somewhere in the suburbs of Hobart. The truckie's pissed, rowdy mates were in full attendance while a random guy from a local boxing club had been assigned to my corner. Amateur fight night at its best.

In Jack's gym I could spar with the top guys and go toe-to-toe, no nerves, no problem. When it came to fights, though, I got so anxious I almost made myself sick. It wasn't for fear of getting hurt – that didn't worry me at all. What terrified me was the thought of losing the fight and, therefore, a shot at a good future. I always calmed down once the fight started but by then I would already have zapped 30 per cent of my energy.

When the opening bell sounded the truckie came out strong, caught me a couple of times and cut my lip. I gathered myself and fell back on my strategy. I don't like getting hit so I tend to move backwards and punch. For the next four rounds I stayed long, made the most of my shots and won the bout. I was handed a trophy and the stranger in my corner bought me a banquet of Coke and a steak sandwich to celebrate. When I got home to Aberfeldie nobody said much about it. I put the trophy on a shelf and that was that. Interstate champion.

Although Jack and I thought I had a chance at a professional career, I also started to seriously contemplate how I might work as an artist as well. I thought being a newspaper cartoonist would be cool, or working as a book illustrator. My big sister

Rachel helped me write to the major newspapers, the *Herald Sun* and *The Age*, and major book publishers with examples of my art. I was mostly ignored but the few responses I received were all the same: 'Sorry, kid. We already have in-house illustrators.'

I continued to fight amateur bouts under Jack's guidance and won them. Increasingly aware he was training me for free, I decided to do a lead pencil portrait of Lionel Rose and present it to him as a gift. I arrived at the gym one afternoon and handed him the finished work, rolled up with an elastic band around it.

'What's this?' Jack asked with trademark bluntness.

'It's for you,' I said, nodding at it.

Jack unfurled the white rectangle of paper and took in my drawing of his old protégé.

'Wow,' he whispered as his tough demeanour softened. 'That's beautiful. Did you draw that?'

'Yep,' I said. 'I drew it for you. It's a thank-you.'

Jack didn't say anything for the longest time. He just stared at the drawing. Finally he cleared his throat and I looked up to see a couple of tears rolling down his cheek.

'You okay, Jack?' I asked.

'Yeah,' he croaked.

'What's up?' I pressed.

He choked up again.

'I know . . . I just know you're going to be alright now,' he finally said.

Relief was written across his face. He saw I had a talent for something other than fighting the world. Outside of my family, friends and a couple of teachers, no-one had ever seen my portraits, certainly not the ones I took seriously.

'Yeah, you're definitely going to be okay, Vincent,' he continued. 'The problem for me is I don't think you're going to be a boxer. I think you're going to be an artist.'

We kept training but almost immediately Jack steered me in another direction. After dinner at his place one night he produced a framed black and white photo of Lionel Rose sparring with Australian featherweight champion Johnny Famechon, another boxing buddy.

'Do you think you could paint this?' Jack asked.

'Yeah, sure.'

'They only ever sparred together once and this is the only photo of it,' he explained.

Jack was in the process of setting up the Australian Boxing Hall of Fame. He saw an opportunity to raise money for the cause and put some in my pocket, too. 'If you paint this I can get the boys to sign it and we can auction prints off.'

'Sounds great,' I said. 'How about I do it in colour?'

Once I finished painting the sparring champions, Jack had a stack of prints made. We took them first to Lionel Rose's place to get them signed and then to Johnny Famechon's so he could add his signature. It was a bittersweet day. Johnny had been hit by a car while jogging a few years earlier which caused him to suffer a stroke and left him with a brain injury.

He moved slowly and didn't have much to say about the painting other than, 'The pants are the wrong colour.'

I had no reference when transposing the image from black and white into a large colour oil painting so I'd taken licence and put him in a pair of green shorts. I thought they looked cool!

'Oh, I'm sorry, Johnny,' I said.

'Don't say sorry, just don't do it again,' he grumbled.

We were there for an hour or so as Johnny signed print after print. Every time I put another one in front of him he seemed a little put out. 'Oh sorry,' I said. 'Maybe I'm going a bit fast for you?'

'Don't say sorry, just don't do it again.'

He must have said it fifteen times that day, which shows what a slow learner I am. Johnny died in 2022, but he lives on in my home. Whenever my young sons apologise for screwing up, guess what I tell them?

The prints sold out. Jack raised some money for his Hall of Fame and gave me a decent payday, too. It was my first commissioned painting and the first proper financial reward I received from art. Although it was a nice feeling it was also both the beginning and what felt like the end of the road. I had no idea how to get more work doing paintings. I had no connection to the art world. I didn't know where art galleries were, let alone how to approach them. I didn't know how to go to art school or if people like me were allowed to attend. Hell, I didn't even have a high school education. And yet the potent knowledge that people had paid money for a print of my painting stuck fast in my mind.

Deep down all I really ever wanted to be was an artist. I believed Jack when he told me I was going to make it as a painter. I believed the handful of teachers who said I could have a future in the arts. I believed the friends and strangers who said, 'Wow! You're fucking amazing!' I almost believed in myself, too, and carried the words 'Be an artist' on the piece of paper in my wallet.

I knew in my soul that more than anything else on this earth, art was my best chance of being a success. I felt my portraits were good but I had always been too scared to back myself. Now that all of my other options and distractions seemed to have slid off the table I resolved to give painting my best shot. Unfortunately I still had no idea how to break into the art world. Ultimately I decided there was only one way.

I'd have to cheat my way in.

The law of averages meant the law of Victoria was going to catch up with me sooner or later.

In January 1998 my sixteen-year-old brother Michael went to a party with some of his friends and got jumped by a couple of older guys. When I heard about it I did some digging and found out they lived in a share house in Niddrie.

The following weekend I took Michael with me and went looking for them. I parked the Valiant near their house and started surveillance. Eventually two guys walked out, jumped in a car and drove off. I followed them along Keilor Road and as they approached a KFC outlet I ran their car off the street. I jumped out of mine – which was stopped diagonally across the lanes – ran to the driver's side window and carried on as if I was a cop.

'What's your name?' I demanded.

The guy looked scared and gave me some bullshit name like Bob Smith.

CHAPTER FIVE

'Show me your ID,' I barked.

'What the fuck? Why?' he protested.

'You jumped my brother,' I said.

Michael was out of the car, too, and I shot him a look. 'Is this the guy?' I asked.

He nodded. I was so pissed off. These two pricks were five years older than him and twice his size. So, bullies.

I dragged the driver out through the car window into the middle of Keilor Road where I laid into him with fists and feet. My *Starsky & Hutch* manoeuvre had blocked traffic and stopped a tram that was ding-ding-dinging away. With all those witnesses watching I ran to the passenger side and did the same to his mate. When I felt enough karma had been served, I jumped back into the Valiant and we sped off.

I was arrested at home in Aberfeldie the next day. Mum was beside herself. Two young officers put me in the back of a divvy van and drove me to Moonee Ponds Police Station where I was relieved of my shoelaces and belt, and charged with assault. I was terrified. At the time, Moonee Ponds served as a small jail as well as a cop shop. The whole place radiated danger. I was polite and cooperative with the officers and answered their questions with 'Yes, sir' and 'No, sir'. Good manners counted for nothing in that place.

'Listen, you little cunt, do you see that?' one of the officers said as he pointed to a CCTV monitor showing a live feed from the lock-up. It looked like a mental hospital bristling with malevolent grown men yelling and shaping up to each other – no place for a fresh-faced twenty-year-old who was almost in tears. My Starsky persona from the previous day was nowhere to be seen.

'That's where you're going, boy,' the copper continued. 'And guess what? Because it's Friday afternoon you'll be in there until Monday. You'll be lucky if you don't get hepatitis or an STD.'

Usually when someone is charged they're taken before a court – which in my case was literally next door – where they're bailed (or not) and given a return court date. Although I'd been charged with a violent crime, it was my first offence and I'd just turned twenty so I'd have almost certainly been granted bail. My arresting officers had other plans.

'You won't be seeing a magistrate today,' I was told. 'So get ready for a very long weekend, dickhead.'

They left me alone in the interview room on the verge of a nervous breakdown. Ten minutes later an older sergeant walked in. 'What's the deal with you?' he asked. 'You look pretty fit and healthy. What's your story?'

'I did an apprenticeship as a printer and I'm training as a boxer,' I said. 'I just had a fight representing Victoria.'

'Where do you train?' he asked.

'With Jack Rennie in Essendon,' I answered. 'I might make it to the Commonwealth Games.'

'Where do you live?'

'With my mum.'

'Alright,' he said and left the room.

A couple of minutes later he returned with my arresting officers.

'So, you think you can lock this kid up with those fucking scumbags for the next three days?' the sergeant berated them in front of me. 'And for something that hasn't even seen the inside of a court? You're not the fucking judge and jury. You don't even know what he's done! Get your arses into that court right now and you'd better come back with the means for this lad to be released on bail today.'

I walked out of the police station that afternoon on bail feeling relieved and enlightened. I'd grown up believing cops were the enemy – this was just the stupid code of the street in my neck of the woods. That day I realised they weren't all out to get me. Still, I was facing serious charges and the police had a tram full of witnesses.

At my next court date I pleaded guilty and, ten months after the assault, I faced a sentencing hearing in Moonee Ponds Magistrates' Court. I dressed in the smartest clothes I owned – my old grey school trousers and a carefully ironed white school shirt. I didn't have a jacket or tie. Unable to afford a solicitor, I was represented by a guy from Legal Aid. I met him for the first time that morning, so he was virtually useless. I had a sinking feeling: maybe I was destined to be a crim after all? The prosecutor read the brief of evidence detailing my rampage in Niddrie and I had to admit, when he spelled it out like that, it sounded pretty bad.

All I had was a reference from the only important person I knew – a cardiothoracic surgeon who was married to one of my aunts. As the magistrate studied the document I noticed the slightest flicker of change in his flavourless demeanour. When he finished reading it he addressed me directly.

'Mr Fantauzzo, do you wish to say anything to the court about your actions?'

I took a deep breath and told him the truth, and some lies. I said I'd never been in trouble before (sort of true). I told him the assault was out of character (lie) and I felt terrible about what I'd done (lie). I said I had only stuck up for my little brother because my victims had jumped him (true). I explained how I happened to see them on that fateful day (true-ish – I omitted the bit about stalking them) and agreed I reacted poorly.

'I made a terrible mistake, Your Honour, and I deeply regret what I did.' (True.)

I received a lecture about how I must never take the law into my own hands. The magistrate remarked on how reckless my behaviour was and how serious the consequences could have been for my victims – and how they might still be for me. 'The maximum penalty for summary assault in Victoria is two years in prison,' he said. 'You need to understand that it's within my power to give you a custodial sentence.'

Mum and Dad on their wedding day, and at the beach.

Nonno with Dad and my uncles Leno and George.

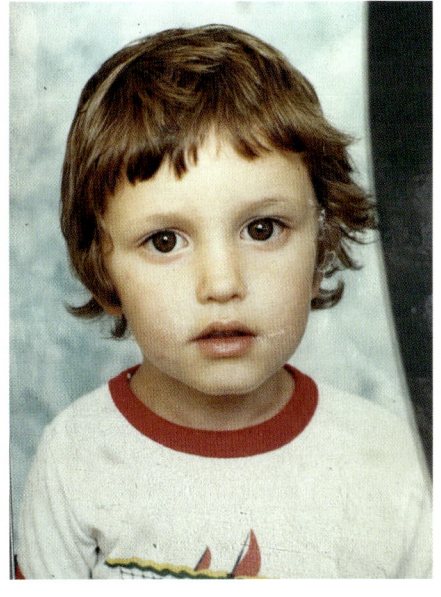

An infant Vincent.

Pretending to be a good Catholic boy.

With Marianne, Michael and the Ford Falcon.

(Left to right) Michael, Marianne, Vincent, Rachel and Otis.

Playing in the Broadmeadows backyard.

Growing up, I was very protective of my younger siblings, especially Michael.

Cooking offered the possibility of connection with my dad.

I couldn't afford a taekwondo uniform and paid for my training by preparing and cleaning the space we used at a local RSL.

By my mid-teens I'd worked out that you only have to win a street fight for the first twenty seconds.

Above: Michael, Marianne, myself, Rachel and Otis.

During my brief return to high school, at Buckley Park College. After three months it was all over.

With Michael during our time as hydroponic crop entrepreneurs.

At work in Hong Kong during the Thirty Portraits in Thirty Days project.

And taking the project to New York, where I spent time with Marc Freeman.

My exhibition in Vietnam, with *Inner Conflict* behind us.

My portrait of Chanel Iman from the NYC iteration of Thirty Portraits in Thirty Days, and *below*, with her and Michelle.

My photo of Ezekiel on his Chelsea basketball court, and him inspecting my handiwork at the opening night of my exhibition at the National Arts Club.

Rashad and N'fa.

Rashad and Aaliyah.

Heath and N'fa during the making of N'fa's film clip that Heath directed.

Baz does not live life by half. *Anticlockwise from top* In front of my 2011 Doug Moran winner, and the night before it was due for judging as me and Mark Heydon picked off grit and strands of hair from the canvas; one of my Gatsby paintings I created to help Baz convince Leonardo to join his movie; with Baz and Brandon Walters, whose portrait won me the Archibald People's Choice Award in 2009.

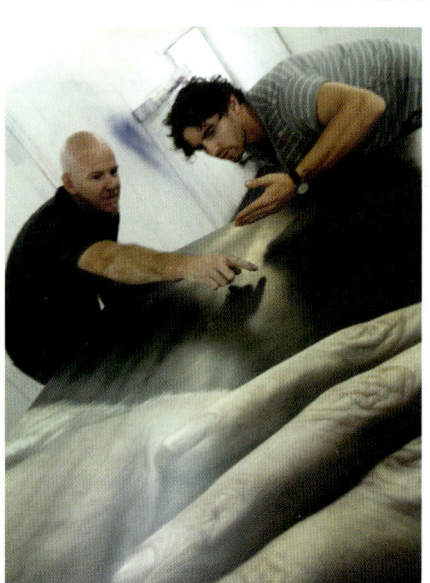

The elaborate set of *The Creek*, 1977.

I was amazed by the scale of Baz's ambition for our project.

With the finished canvas.

On the road in Rajasthan.

Top left: There's nowhere quite like India.
Bottom left: At the hotel in Mumbai from where Baz and I rode our Royal Enfields all the way to Delhi and back.
Right: Amitabh Bachchan, the most hospitable Bollywood legend.

With James Tobin.

Above: Riding a motorbike has always represented freedom to me.

Sharing my love of bikes with Luca.

Outside Harley House Bar and Grill on a Ducati Monster.

The laneway was briefly the largest canvas I'd ever worked on, before the council came and sandblasted my painting away.

I am extraordinarily grateful for the experiences *Last Contact* afforded me. With Tommy Watson on one of the trips I made to Central Australia, and my portrait of him.

With Gloria Petyarre.

Ken McGregor opened my eyes to an Australia that most of us never get to see.

A young Valentino and me working on my portrait of Kudditji Kngwarreye.

Below: With the canvas Kudditji painted for the triptych.

My portrait of Linda Syddick Napaltjarri flanked by a landscape I painted *(left)* and one she created *(right)*.

I won my fourth consecutive Archibald People's Choice Award for this portrait of Luca.

Arriving with Matt and Matt . . .

. . . which went on to win the Archibald Packing Room Prize.

I've spent my life getting to know people from all walks of life, be they former prime ministers (at the unveiling at Parliament House of my portrait of Julia Gillard), trailblazers and executives (New York Fashion Week founder Fern Mallis), or professional gamblers and champions of the art world (David Walsh).

I was first attracted to boxing purely for self-protection. Jack Rennie was instrumental in getting me competition ready, and I've continued to make time for the sport for my own physical and mental wellbeing, whether that's training alone or with friends.

CHAPTER FIVE

Oh my god. Am I going to prison?

Time seemed to stand still. In a one-in-a-million twist of fate I only found out about later on, my then uncle the surgeon (now divorced from my aunt) had once saved the life of the magistrate's wife. He could never have imagined that in doing so he'd save my life, too.

'I'm familiar with this doctor,' the magistrate said as he held up the reference. 'I put great store in his judgement and if he says you deserve the leniency of the court and a chance to redeem yourself then I will take it into account. It is your lucky day, Mr Fantauzzo, but if you come before this court again there'll be no such consideration given.'

I was handed a two-year suspended sentence with no conviction recorded. He also placed me on a good behaviour bond and ordered me to complete six months of community service. I'd been given a get-out-of-jail-free card and wasn't going to waste it. Chastened, relieved and grateful, I aimed for the stars and applied to art school.

I got completely lost navigating the sprawling campus of the Victorian College of the Arts in Southbank. The place reminded me of the 80s TV series *Fame*, and the students chasing dreams at New York's High School of Performing Arts. As I blundered around the VCA in search of the visual arts department I ran into people wearing leotards and dance tights, was almost knocked over by a guy carrying a trombone and had to step around actors practising their lines in a corridor – all preparing for interviews in their chosen fields. The *Fame* theme song started up in my head, minus the optimism. I didn't really feel like I was gonna live forever or learn how to fly (high!) – I was back in a place of learning which meant I felt about half an inch tall.

After a year in the laundrette, I'd amassed dozens of pencil drawings (mostly portraits) that represented my first large body of work. I knew I could call this collection a 'folio' and that a folio was necessary if I wanted to get into art school and, by extension, the art world. Rachel had helped me apply in writing to the VCA and I was surprised and nervous when they wrote back to invite me to an interview.

When I finally found the right location on campus, a dozen or so high-school graduates and a handful of mature-age applicants were already waiting. A few of the kids seemed to know each other from school. They chatted easily about art theory and this painter and that painter as they compared folios. I eavesdropped and stole glances at their work, and I knew straightaway my bundle of portraits from the laundrette wasn't going to cut it. I began to worry my fraudulent paperwork might not stand up to scrutiny, either.

Since I didn't have a Victorian Certificate of Education, a friend who was a wizard at making fake IDs had helped me forge one. It was pretty

CHAPTER FIVE

straightforward: we got our hands on a former Buckley Park College student's certificate, photocopied it, substituted his name for mine and awarded me some respectable marks. We didn't go overboard and make me a straight-A student – just a solid performer, but a high achiever in art.

They barely glanced at my fake VCE and the interview flew by in a blur of anxiety and embarrassment. Two weeks later I received a rejection letter in the mail.

I underwent another round of degradation a week later during an interview at the Royal Melbourne Institute of Technology. It wasn't like *Fame*, more an episode of *Australian Idol* when the crew interviews budding performers before the auditions and you discover some of them can't sing. Just like at the VCA, the high-school graduates arrived with excellent folios. They'd had the benefit of making one every year since Year 10, within a formal curriculum and with the support of interested teachers. They'd studied art history and could talk about it with confidence. Meanwhile I sat off to the side clutching drawings of Warney I'd copied out of *Black + White* magazine and a study of somebody's cat. Very much the contestant who couldn't sing.

The RMIT interview was another disaster. Even though they tried to hide it, I could tell they were laughing at me. I received another rejection letter to add to the growing collection of knock-backs from newspapers, book publishers and other art schools.

I limped back to the banality of the laundrette and the sports memorabilia scene. My social life, on the other hand, took some exciting new turns. I left home and moved into an apartment above a shop in Ascot Vale with an old school mate, Matt Pillios. When we could afford it we hit the city bars as young men do. One evening I was at Metro nightclub with my old Moonie Ponds crew – Leon, Dippa and the twins Rob and Remo – when I got chatting to a lovely Malaysian girl who was studying design at Monash University. Although she was very shy and quiet, we clicked. One thing led to another and we became an item.

Latifah wasn't your average international student, though – her father was a billionaire and her uncle was a senior minister in the Malaysian government. She drove a brand-new Audi, had a different designer handbag for each day of the month, carried a platinum credit card and lived in a luxury apartment in Toorak. Having learned to masquerade as a middle-class Catholic back in Essendon, I happily slipped into her gilded world.

My life could not have been further from Latifah's. I only had enough money to pay the rent with Matt and a few dollars left over for baked beans on toast, mashed potatoes and the occasional skinny night out on the town. Suddenly I was being driven around in a $50,000 car and taken to the best restaurants in Melbourne. I even ate caviar once.

Ever the chameleon, I never let on that I was a poor boy who couldn't read, write or get into university. I split my life between my messy bachelor pad with Matt and Latifah's five-star lodgings and never the twain did meet. I don't know if she'd have liked me any less, but I figured what she didn't know wouldn't hurt her, or me.

When Latifah moved to England to continue her studies at Norwich University of the Arts, I went with her. I stayed in her room on campus but I didn't have a job so to pass the time I found a local boxing gym where a lovely old bloke took me under his wing. (Trainers get excited when they think some new talent has walked in off the street.) He really wanted to train me up but I already knew I wasn't going to be in England for long. After I won a couple of amateur fights he asked me if I wanted to work as a security guard.

I knew I was wasting my time pretending to be a university student and I felt like a freeloader because I wasn't contributing financially to my life with Latifah. She was very intelligent and kind, and we really liked each other's company. Deep down, though, I didn't imagine we had a long-term future since Latifah was Muslim and a full commitment to her would require me to convert to Islam, which is something I'd never do for insincere reasons – only if I meant it. Meanwhile everyone around me was getting an education while I was a squatter. I didn't think England, the land of my birth, was for me but I was dead sure about one thing – I didn't want to be a security guard.

I returned to Melbourne and applied again to the VCA and RMIT, knowing I'd be better prepared this time around. I upgraded my folio to look like the ones the high-school graduates carried the previous year. I included some life drawing, conceptual art, a bit of observational drawing and I cobbled together some abstract art, too. Since it was my strong suit I still kept a lot of portraits, self-portraits and – because it was always willing to sit for me – drawings of my hand.

The VCA was still unimpressed and rebuffed me for a second year running but in late 1999 I was invited to begin a Bachelor of Fine Arts in Painting at RMIT in the new year. I think I got in mainly on technical ability, but my capacity for bullshitting my way through the interview no doubt helped. I merely regurgitated parts of conversations I'd overheard about history and theory out in the waiting room. I had essentially impersonated an amalgam of art students. Maybe I could have tried out for the acting course?

While I should have been elated to finally have my foot in the door, I felt overawed and hopelessly unqualified, like an imposter. I also felt a nagging guilt over the fact I'd had to weave yet another latticework of lies just to get by in life. When university started in the new year, reality hit almost immediately. Art history class was the worst. I still hadn't been to an exhibition, let alone paid a visit to the National Gallery, and I had no understanding whatsoever of

CHAPTER FIVE

art history – a major sticking point that would come back to haunt me.

To make matters worse my history teacher rubbed me up the wrong way. She leaned very hard on her lofty British accent and constantly corrected people on how they spoke – 'It's aitch, not haitch!' she'd intone. She was absolutely obsessed with art history, too, and would have just about died on the spot if I told her I didn't know who Picasso was.

While I recognise it's really significant – and it matters a great deal to many artists and the art establishment – you don't need to know anything about Pablo Picasso or art history to be thoughtful as an artist, or to practise as one. Some of the greatest musicians of all time can't read music, they don't understand theory or know where their inspiration comes from, but they *can* play and write, and they have conquered the world with their art.

After one month at RMIT, however, I knew I wasn't even going to conquer the first semester. Familiar feelings of dread and anxiety swept in. Something had to give. Confessing that I had next to no education, was virtually illiterate and had faked my way into art school was out of the question. Far better that I acted like I was too cool for university, the way I'd always done when I couldn't cope at school. Before I was even halfway through the first semester I up and quit.

When friends and family asked me why I'd bailed out I casually brushed their inquiries aside and pretended, ridiculously, that I was above a tertiary education. 'University is full of wankers,' I told anyone who'd listen. 'You've got no idea what goes on there. They draw pots all day and do life drawings, and they talk utter bullshit about it. I don't need any of that. I already know how to draw.'

After another despondent year of treading water and going nowhere I was determined to return to RMIT and do whatever it took to get a degree. I'd already cheated my way *into* university so I decided I would go all out and cheat my way *through* it. It was either that or grovel around at the bottom of the socio-economic ladder as a low-level chef or a hack artist drawing portraits of superstars from magazines while other people drove Audis, owned houses and ate in good restaurants.

That's not to say I didn't work hard when I arrived at RMIT for the third time in 2001. I hardly missed a day and I painted my arse off. Since I was incapable of any written work I convinced other people to do it for me. I flirted with girls and asked them to help me, and I used my sports memorabilia earnings to pay willing classmates to write my essays. When it came time for exams I sat to the left of a right-handed student and tried to copy them. I bombed a lot of the history exams but I still managed to pass the units on the technical strength of my painting and the essays written by others.

Although I put in long hours and painted a lot – sometimes into the night – I found the practical side of my studies relatively simple. I was never more at ease in the world than when I had a brush in my hand, and I sensed my lecturers and fellow students recognised I had real ability. I was a couple of years older than most of the other first year students and word somehow got around that I was a rich kid mature-age student. I never let on that I came from the precise opposite side of the tracks.

A lot of kids in art school hail from wealthy backgrounds: they have trust funds and maybe their relatives own galleries. They grow up around exhibitions and have accounts at the art store. I noticed many of them mimicked their favourite artists. Some wanted to be like Tracey Emin or Brett Whiteley, while others tried to be Andy Warhol. Not surprisingly there was a lot of pretentiousness afoot in the hallways of RMIT. While there are some very dedicated, kind and honourable people to be found at art school, my bullshit detector flashed red almost non-stop with the number of wannabees I encountered.

I became fascinated by one kid in particular who was very popular with a clique of lecturers, thanks to his thespian flair. I thought his art was terrible and his ability limited, but he somehow managed to tick the university's clubby little boxes. At that time the hot trend was to be experimental. If a student experimented – no matter how bad the result – the teachers loved them for it. To my mind that was absurd. If you applied the same approach to a creative writing assignment, for instance, and you used a crayon to scrawl a bunch of gibberish sentences, your experiment would be laughed out of the room. Not in the art world!

I saw straight through the kid. I knew he was playing a role and the silly establishment was all too happy to fall for it. When he started pretending to be homeless, I looked on with amazement. He even asked if he could sleep in the studio. Naturally his cheer squad at RMIT let him. I imagine he fit their noble ideal of the struggling, tortured artist. I was tempted to tap him on the shoulder and call him on it: 'Hey mate, cut the act, will ya? I saw your mum drop you off in a Mercedes on the first day. I've seen you in the art store. You have an account there! You're not fucking homeless.'

The next year the kid got himself a drug habit. I rolled my eyes but many of our peers clearly thought this made him edgy, dangerous, creative and cool. Meanwhile I was super naïve in thinking the only art that mattered was something I could understand. As a result my paintings were very realistic, even hyper-realistic. My practical output earned top marks but I didn't know how to articulate my work – a frustrating limitation in group sessions. We had to sit in a circle of seven or eight students, plus a lecturer, and put our work up for critique. I had no idea how to analyse or discuss an artwork so I didn't venture much in those classes, but anytime someone had something critical to say about my work I didn't know how to defend myself or explain what I had done.

CHAPTER FIVE

When the faux tortured-homeless-art-genius put his latest experiment forward for critique, however, people tilted their heads, stroked their chins and gushed with solemn appraisals: 'It's so childlike. What was your journey in creating such a vulnerable piece?'

Nowadays I realise there's a place for that kind of art and I like it as well, but at the time I was far more impressed by the kid's audacity than anything he put on a canvas. I regularly walked out of classes thinking, *I consider myself a good liar but this guy is the king!*

Although I didn't admit it then he was nowhere near my league when it came to impersonation and deception. Whether I thought it was rubbish or not, at least he submitted his own work. I was fraudulently paying people to do a lot of mine for me. So, who was the bigger bullshit artist really?

Now that I'd stepped inside it I found the 'art world', in many ways, to be a giant circle-jerk populated by overblown, pompous snobs. An artist could stick anything on a wall and if someone said 'It's great' then it was great, and not only that – it was worth x-amount of dollars, too.

Once again I found myself in a city nightclub, having a few drinks and trying to chat up a woman at the bar. I thought I was doing okay until competition arrived in the form of a tall, suave and handsome African American guy who'd pulled up a seat next to us.

'Damn!' I cursed to myself as my new rival seemed to draw the woman's attention. We both pulled out all the stops to impress her but after five minutes she stood up and walked away without saying a word. My extremely cool-looking nemesis and I sat in silence and watched her go. We turned to look at each other and burst out laughing at the same time. We've been great friends ever since.

Rashad Haughton is an American writer, screenwriter, film director and one of the nicest people I have ever known. He arrived in Melbourne in the back end of 2000 while his younger sister, Aaliyah, was in town to film the lead role in the horror movie *Queen of the Damned*. I'd never heard of Aaliyah before I met Rashad at the bar that night, but I soon found out that aside from being an up-and-coming actress she was a bona-fide R'n'B superstar.

Rashad and I got on like a house on fire from the get-go and I hit it off with Aaliyah, too, when he introduced us a few days later. Rashad is my age and Aaliyah was just eighteen months younger. They were extremely close and went everywhere together. The film studio put them up in a huge, amazing apartment in Port Melbourne while Aaliyah was shooting her scenes. After a night out clubbing with them, brother and sister invited me to move in there, too. Unbelievably kind people.

Almost overnight I found myself starring in a Melbourne version of *Lifestyles of the Rich and Famous*. Aaliyah's star was rising ever faster. Film roles

CHAPTER FIVE

were pouring in, including for *The Matrix Reloaded*, and her music was charting around the world. I was gloriously swept up into their glittering galaxy and carried a million miles from Broadmeadows. I loved it. I loved *them*.

Coming from where I did, it was surreal to suddenly be riding in limousines to nightclubs with a full security detail. The time I spent with Latifah had often been fancy, but this was on another level. Whenever we went out, brawny private security guards were secretly planted in whatever nightclub we happened to be in. Usually the only disturbance involved fans swamping Aaliyah for autographs. It could turn into mayhem but it was never ugly.

Aaliyah returned to the US when her movie wrapped but Rashad stayed in Melbourne to hang out with me. When we weren't hosting wild parties at the glam apartment in Port Melbourne we were out clubbing. Rashad's mum, Diane Haughton – a singer who is Motown royalty (Gladys Knight is Rashad's aunt) – regularly called him and begged him to take security with him. She always worried that her babies' profiles might draw the wrong kind of attention.

'Mom, I'm fine!' I heard him explain over the phone more than once. 'You worry too much about me. Everything's cool over here.'

One evening after classes at RMIT we headed to a club in the city that was hosting a Latino night. To our minds that equalled two things – dancing and girls. It turned out that Rashad would have done well to take his mother's advice.

That particular club was a popular haunt for a couple of Melbourne's South American gangs. Rashad, being awesome, was a magnet for women on the dancefloor and they tended to throw themselves at him. I felt uneasy in the club and sensed trouble before it broke out. One gangster objected to Rashad dancing with his ex-girlfriend and took a swing at him. I jumped in straightaway and an ugly brawl erupted.

Rashad can look after himself, but I got lucky. If you hit someone clean in a bare knuckle fight you're probably going to knock them out. On Latino Night my punches were clean and I knocked three guys out in quick succession. Rashad looked at me wide-eyed and open-mouthed, 'Goddamn, Vincent!' he boomed. 'You're Jackie fucking Chan!'

If we'd had our own security, things would have ended there. The DJ stopped, the house lights came on and the club's bouncers broke things up. They'd seen what happened and knew we weren't the aggressors. Still, there was a heavy feeling in the place and one of the bouncers offered to let us leave through a back door. We had no way of knowing he was friends with the gang we'd just fought.

Rashad was the first to step into the darkened laneway where a dude was waiting with a set of knuckledusters. He cracked Rashad hard in the face and split his lip from just under his nose right down to

CHAPTER FIVE

his mouth. It was a horrible thing to do to someone and the cowardly assailant was gone in a flash. I helped my poor friend hold his torn face together while someone called an ambulance.

At St Vincent's Hospital I advocated for Rashad, knowing he'd want the best plastic surgeon in Melbourne. I tried to convince the medicos he could afford it, too. Meanwhile his mum was on the phone offering to send a surgeon from New York. In the end an amazing local plastic surgeon delicately sewed Rashad's mangled face back together. He flew back to America not long after and had a couple more procedures to help mend his lip. Today he has a faint scar but still dines out on the story.

It had been an awful experience, but far, far worse was to come.

Aaliyah's new album *Aaliyah* – which she partly recorded at Sing Sing Studios in Melbourne – took off around the world and in August 2001 she was booked to shoot a video for her single 'Rock the Boat' in the Bahamas. Rashad, who had filmed a few of her prior videos, was going to tag along but at the last minute I convinced him to come and hang with me in Australia instead.

While he was in the air en route to Melbourne, news broke that the light plane Aaliyah had boarded to fly from the Bahamas back to Miami had crashed just after take-off. As I waited for Rashad's flight to land I was in a state of shock and deep sadness.

When he came through the arrival gate Rashad had already heard the terrible news but he refused to believe it. He was also yet to receive confirmation that all eight people who were on the flight had died. After an excruciating six-hour wait as he frantically tried to make contact with his parents and Aaliyah's team, Rashad finally received a call from her manager. No-one had survived the crash.

That night I held him in my arms as he went through nine circles of hell. I had never seen anyone so broken or tortured. It was the saddest, most traumatic twelve hours of my life so I couldn't begin to imagine Rashad's pain. The next day I put him on a plane back to the US where a funeral and a hurricane of grief awaited him.

As I drove home from the airport I could not stop crying. I cried for the loss of Aaliyah, for Rashad and I also wept with bitter frustration that I couldn't go with him. The intensity of our time together had brought us extremely close and I knew that I should have been alongside him on his long flight home. I was not from that world, though, and I couldn't afford it.

When I lived with Rashad and Aaliyah I had to hustle hard to keep up with the clubbing, the drinks and assorted A-list outlays. I cut corners, skipped the expensive meals and sold a few extra drawings here and there. Rashad would leave $100 out each week for the cleaners and sometimes I got so desperate I'd call up the cleaning company, cancel the appointment, clean the apartment myself and pocket the money to buy food and put some petrol in my car. I have carried a lot of guilt about it but I justified it on the basis I did a better job than the cleaners. It was semantics; I'd still swindled a mate. I even used to check down the back of the couches for loose change that fell out of Rashad's pockets.

Aaliyah and Rashad's goodness and generosity rubbed off on me and so did Latifah's. As much as I was an outsider in her world, I was grateful to learn how to hold my knife and fork properly. It's surprising how glad I was to change some of the unrefined things about me. I see people holding their cutlery like cavemen today and it kills me, even though it's no big thing. I want to show them how to do it properly, the way others showed me. Maybe that would be a bit too much and a potential humiliation, like someone correcting my grammar.

Latifah opened the door but Rashad and Aaliyah – through their friendship, warmth, love and the mastery of their respective art – showed me there was a road ahead to a life less ordinary. I realised I admired successful and talented people and I was determined to become one myself. I was fairly certain I had a gift, but I knew the life I wanted wasn't going to be handed to me. I would have to go out and get it for myself.

I just didn't expect I'd wind up a drug dealer in the process.

It took me more than a year to scrape together enough money to visit Rashad in New York City. After I paid for my ticket I only had about $800 left for spending money. I didn't know how long that would last in the Big Apple but since I'd be staying with Rashad I'd at least save on accommodation. He was supposed to meet me at the airport but when I landed at JFK he was nowhere to be seen.

Suddenly stranded with nowhere to go, I fell in with some Swedish guys I'd met on the plane. When Rashad's phone kept going to voicemail they invited me to join them at a backpackers' hostel they were booked into in downtown Manhattan. It was December, it was snowing and I was freezing my arse off so I jumped into the taxi with my new buddies from Stockholm.

The backpackers was a dump. The first New York native I had a meaningful encounter with was a large rat. As darkness fell I considered leaving it until the next morning to contact Rashad, but a night spent in a bunk bed with snoring Swedes and a rogue rodent on the loose didn't hold much appeal. I went downstairs to an internet café and emailed my errant friend. He replied straightaway. 'SORRY!'

I gave Rashad the address and forty-five minutes later he turned up in a massive black SUV driven by some crazy rapper friend of his. Rashad wrapped his arms around me, apologised some more, threw my luggage in the back and the car dived into a river of traffic. Rap music blasted at full volume as Rashad's mate threw the big machine into corners with tyres screeching and pedestrians scurrying out of the way as he blasted the horn.

'We're going to a party, man,' Rashad explained with a laugh. 'He doesn't want to be late.'

First we had to drop off my bags at the accommodation Rashad had arranged uptown. We rolled to a stop outside a skyscraper on Fifth Avenue that had a huge atrium entrance and big gold letters out the front. When we walked into the lobby a tall man in a dark suit greeted us. 'Rashaaaad!' the man boomed and shook my friend's hand. 'So nice to see you.'

'Donald. It's always a pleasure,' Rashad replied. 'This is my friend Vincent, he's just arrived from Australia. First time in New York.'

'Welcome to Trump Tower,' he said, and shook my hand.

I didn't recognise the guy at all, or know he owned the building, or that he'd one day become the most polarising president in American history. As he chatted with Rashad at a counter in the lobby, Jay-Z – who was and remains one of my idols – materialised from out of nowhere and joined the conversation. Donald ushered us into a lift that whisked us up to a spectacular suite that Rashad had booked for the next four days. 'Let me know if you need anything,' our dapper host said before departing.

After I quickly changed clothes we rode the elevator back down to street level and piled into the rap-mobile. Our next stop was a nightclub where another friend of Rashad's was throwing a birthday party. It was only a small venue, but Rashad told me it was very exclusive. Glancing around the crowded room I was struck by how many people looked vaguely familiar. The first person who spoke to me was a very friendly, tallish white guy with a big face and a hat on his head.

'I know that accent well,' he said as we exchanged pleasantries. 'I've been to Australia. I know a lot of people there. I was in Sydney a few years ago for work. I love the place.'

'Next time you come you need to check out Melbourne – it's even better,' I said. 'I'll tell you what, though, I'm loving New York. I'm excited to be here.'

As the guy chatted away I kept looking over his shoulder to the bar and decided I'd had enough small talk. 'You know, all the girls are at the bar, mate,' I said. 'I'm sorry but I've gotta grab a drink and go talk to them.'

He looked at me with a double-take and laughed. 'Okay,' he said, smiling. 'Say hi from me.'

I pulled up next to Rashad at the crowded bar, ordered a drink and checked out the guests.

'So you met Leonardo DiCaprio?' Rashad said.

'What?' I said and spun around to face him. 'Leonardo DiCaprio's here? Where?'

'You've just been talking to him for five minutes!'

I've been known to struggle with faces and this was one such occasion, even though I was a massive movie fan and I'd seen all of Leo's films. It turned out we were at the after-party for the premier of Martin Scorsese's *Gangs of New York*. Leo had decided to make it his belated birthday party, too. A lot of the famous faces started to fall into place. Leo was dating Cameron Diaz who was also at the bar and chatting to Naomi Campbell who was chatting to Rashad who told me other impossibly beautiful looking people in the room were Victoria's Secret models. They didn't look like they were being very secretive to me, though.

Over the next two weeks, most nights were spent in a similar fashion. After four days in Trump Tower we relocated to Rashad's apartment in some funky part of Manhattan. He took me to some of the world's hottest nightclubs, invited me to Usher's birthday party where I watched the great man of R'n'B dance on the bar, and I even went on a double date with Nicole Richie and Paris Hilton.

Rashad was seeing Nicole at the time. She was at the height of her fame alongside her best friend Paris. It wasn't a real double date because I wasn't dating – nor did I have any hope of dating – Paris Hilton, but the four of us went out together when the girls hosted a party in yet another New York nightspot. We met them in a hotel where they were getting ready. It was like an episode of *The Simple Life*. Nicole and Paris looked and sounded the same way they did on their TV series, but they were a *lot* smarter than people gave them credit for. They weren't ditzy or lazy – they were highly organised, professional, savvy and they knew exactly what they were doing. I immediately understood why they were becoming pop culture icons.

In that world, $800 will only get you so far. After a fortnight pretending to be a prince of the city that never sleeps, all that remained was my plane ticket home. Stretching my meagre bank balance had required constant corner-cutting and a huge amount of hustle. Rashad was a very generous host but I hated the thought of being a penniless passenger so I ate around spending money the way I had done my whole life.

If a fancy restaurant was factored into the night's plans I'd throw up an alternative: 'Let's get a fried chicken instead and meet them at the club afterwards.' Or I'd say, 'I'd love to experience an old-school New York diner,' and then spend $9.50 filling up in some shitty little eatery. That allowed me to pay my way, buy some drinks for people and not feel like a cheapskate.

Having seen The Big Life up close I flew home just before Christmas 2002 to get ready to face my final year of university. I've never been more grateful for an in-flight meal.

Early in the first semester I experienced an unexpected hiccup. The usual suspects I'd been paying to write my essays either grew tired of helping me or worried what might happen to them if I was caught cheating. At any rate, they decided to end the arrangement. I had to find someone new.

I approached a student whom I'd never really clicked with for some reason I couldn't quite put my finger on. He was a quietish, slightly aloof and very academic young man who had a major thing for art history. In his world everything had to reference history: if you couldn't explain your work in that context then the work didn't matter. *Perfect*, I thought. I offered him $500 to write my next paper.

'You'll be able to whip something up in an afternoon, won't you?' I said after we sealed the deal.

He assured me he could and slipped the money into his jeans, but instead of whipping up an essay he ripped one straight off the internet. When he gave it to me a couple of days later I was extremely grateful. 'Thanks so much, mate,' I said, pretending to quickly scan it, not realising it was a ticking bomb that was about to blow up my academic career. 'That's awesome.'

I submitted the paper confident it would pass muster. The guy was an art history brainiac and I'd paid him well so I was guaranteed a decent mark. Besides, I'd been getting away with it for years. I could practically see the end of my undergraduate days and all the wonderful possibilities that lay beyond. Maybe I'd return to New York and try to paint portraits there?

A couple of days later I was summoned to a meeting with the course co-ordinator, a lecturer and well-known abstract artist named David Thomas, with whom I had a hot and cold relationship. When I walked into his office I was surprised to be met by a woman from student services and my history teacher, too. History with an aitch. I took a seat and David gestured at my latest paper on his desk like it was a handcuffed co-conspirator who'd already given me up.

'Tell us about this essay,' he said.

Oh. Fuck.

Ever since I was a little boy my brain has functioned nimbly, rationally and at lightning speed in a crisis. It's perhaps the reason I was so effective as a street fighter. In a split second I can evaluate a range of options in any high-pressure situation and follow what almost always turns out to be the least damaging course of action. I still had no idea my history-buff classmate had lifted the essay straight out of Google but I knew there was a major problem with it, otherwise I wouldn't be sitting there, half an inch tall again. Three possible answers to David's question quickly flashed up for consideration:

1. 'Okay, I plagiarised it.' – The problem with option one was I'd be unable to explain from whom or where I'd plagiarised the essay when my interrogators inevitably asked.
2. 'Look, I paid someone else to do it because I'm lazy. Sorry. Can I do it again?' – This would never fly because I couldn't 'do it again' if I tried. And they would watch me try.
3. 'Guess what? I can't even read or write. I have no idea what this essay says and I can't even understand the questions.' – This was the most horrifying option by far. It would require me to tear off a mask that had been stuck to me for so long it might as well have been my skin. All manner of ugliness and shame would spill out. It would also expose me as a serial cheat because, if I couldn't read or write, the stony-faced trio would want to know who'd penned the other essays I'd claimed as my own.

'Tell us about this essay . . .'

'Umm, look, I can't read or write,' I said as tears pooled in my eyes. I was surprised I'd become emotional, but after twenty years of holding it all in a dam started to give way inside me. 'I don't know what this essay says,' I continued. 'I don't even know what the question was because I couldn't read it. I can't even fill out a form to get a bank account.'

There was a long, uncomfortable silence. Then my art history teacher spoke.

'So, you've been cheating for *years*?' she asked accusingly.

Rightly or wrongly I'd imagined that being completely honest and more vulnerable than I'd been in my life might buy me some understanding, if not a sympathetic hearing. Perhaps a reaction like, 'Oh, you can't read? I had no idea! What's happened in your life that you never learned how to read or write?'

There was none of that. I was speechless.

'That's correct, isn't it, Vincent? You've literally cheated for years,' she persisted, obviously happy to apply the blowtorch. 'If you can't read or write you must have plagiarised every essay.'

'Yes,' I confessed in a near whisper.

I wasn't a fan of hers beforehand, far less so now. The shame and embarrassment burned, but I was also overtaken by a feeling of sadness. I put my face in my hands and cried. No-one outside of that little room knew the depth of my secret – not my closest friends or loved ones, not even my own mother. There I sat, owning up to the biggest lie of my life – the lie that *was* my life – and it was in a hostile environment. I'd never felt more alone.

CHAPTER SIX

Mrs Aitch wanted to move quickly against me. She proposed forcing me to repeat every year of art history, re-sit tests and write my own essays. This was code for 'kick him out' because I was incapable of doing any of that. Thankfully David Thomas didn't seem to agree with her. I certainly didn't, either.

'That's a bit unfair,' I protested.

'Why?' she asked. 'Everybody else has to write their own essays.'

'Because I think I might be dyslexic.'

There. I said it.

I'd heard the word plenty of times but I'd never been able to look up its meaning for myself (I thought it was spelled d-i-s-l-c). To me dyslexia had always been a nebulous term that got thrown around to describe people who were bad at spelling. My mum had even raised it with me once or twice: 'That's not how you spell it, Vincent. You might be a bit dyslexic!'

In the back of my mind I often thought I might be suffering some kind of mental defect but I opted for outright denial because I didn't want to be labelled the 'special' kid or worse, a grown man with a learning disability. I had pushed the spectre of dyslexia deep down below the mask but now that I'd taken it off, the word was one of the things that tumbled out among a lifetime of lies.

'You're dyslexic? Have you been tested to determine that you really are?' David asked, using a far more sympathetic tone than his uptight colleague.

'I can't even spell the word,' I replied. I lifted my eyes to meet his and I could tell he wanted to help me. 'No, I haven't been tested.'

'If you can prove to us that you *are* actually dyslexic then there are things we can do to help you, but we can't just take your word for it,' David said. 'You're going to have to find out for sure.'

A few days later I was in the Carlton offices of an organisation called SPELD Victoria, specialists in testing for, and supporting people with, learning difficulties. The dyslexia test didn't come cheap – about the same cost as two weeks in New York. I had to sell a mountain bike and some other minor treasures to come up with the $800 fee. A psychologist led me through extensive testing and evaluation, and at the end I was presented with a thick file that I couldn't read (and still can't) that apparently explained everything.

I discovered that dyslexia is indeed a learning difficulty, mostly related to problems with reading and writing but it can also impede understanding of mathematics and affect memory. I was heartened to know it has nothing to do with intelligence, hearing or vision impairment. The severity varies and there is no cure but when it's identified in early childhood, dyslexics can progress well through school with support and tutoring. I missed that boat long ago.

The headline news from SPELD was that dyslexia significantly affected my literacy, numeracy *and* my memory. I'd got the trifecta. Conversely, I scored

CHAPTER SIX

high for spatial awareness and problem-solving, so I took the good with the bad. Mostly bad, though. The diagnosis explained a lot of things and at least I was able to tell myself with certainty, *You're not dumb. You have dyslexia.*

And yet I didn't feel any great unburdening or sense of relief because in the next moment I'd think, *You have dyslexia. That makes you 'special'. It's considered a disability. You're disabled.*

Soon, new loops began to spin in my mind:

You're never going to be what other people can be.

Wave goodbye to your dreams.

Maybe I would have to, but I figured dyslexia would at least save my arse at uni.

When I presented RMIT with the results from SPELD, David Thomas got right behind me, as promised. 'It's quite clear that you have a learning disability,' he said. 'You're entitled to some assistance and I'll make sure you get it.'

I cringed when he said the word 'disability'. The cat was really out of the bag now.

I was introduced to the university's disability liaison team – an equally embarrassing academic summit – and I was paired with a staff member who'd help me accomplish future written work. Somehow I wasn't questioned anymore about the multitude of other times I'd cheated. Thankfully the university – no doubt guided by David – seemed prepared to let that slide.

I had to complete the previously Googled work and the final art history essay the following semester under my own steam. A feeling of dread that stretched all the way back to primary school rose up and grabbed me like an old foe. My disability liaison was lovely and she tried her best to help me. She read me the question (something about a particular movement in art) and sat poised at a laptop ready to tap out my responses: 'Take your time, Vincent,' she said, 'and tell me what you want to say.'

It wasn't as easy as having a stenographer on standby to record my thoughts, because my thoughts on complex issues like movements in art throughout history were a big part of the problem. I'd listened closely to dozens of lectures and tutorials, and I struggled to make sense of most of them. Supported or not, I still couldn't produce an acceptable essay.

The dyslexia cavalry that was absent for the entirety of my education had arrived far too late with far too little to assist me now. So I kept cheating. My liaison helped me get the essays started and I then took them away, paid someone else to finish them, brought them back and handed them in.

In 2004 I was conferred with a Bachelor of Fine Arts in Painting and even earned a distinction. It was my first ever qualification and the only thing I had completed up to that point in my life. I'd worked hard for it and done my best within my obvious limitations. I'd been aided in large part by the fact that – art history aside – the degree was visual-based. The truth is I really owed my graduation to David. We didn't always get along during my early years but when others wanted to throw me out of the university he knew I was dedicated, capable, and – most importantly of all – he knew how much it meant to me.

Art history largely remains a mystery to me. It's fair to say that one of the biggest things I learned during my years at university was that there was something fundamentally wrong with me. It would be years before I came to accept my dyslexia, let alone value it like I do today. I told Mum and one or two others close to me about the diagnosis but mostly I kept it under wraps. I slipped the mask back into place and pressed on with life.

To my surprise, RMIT invited me to complete a Master's in Fine Arts, a real endorsement of my painting ability. I was in my mid-twenties (getting on a bit for a student) and after a quarter of a century living extremely sparsely I was fed up with being broke. I knew I'd have to pay people money to cheat on my written work again and I wanted to afford a social life, too. Rashad was due to return to Melbourne to complete his Master's in Film and Television at the VCA and we'd made plans:

1. Share an apartment.
2. Party.

All my life I had watched people make easy money dealing drugs and I decided to do it, too. I didn't want to involve myself with anything evil like heroin or ice that kills people and ruins lives. At the time I considered marijuana no worse than alcohol and I knew it was easy to secretly grow hydroponically.

I leased a spacious four-bedroom house in Essendon and hired a dodgy electrician mate to illegally wire the place so I could steal electricity from the grid. This saved me paying for power and I knew police pored over unusually high power bills in their hunt for growers. I invited another friend, who knew all about hydroponics, to join me in the enterprise. He rubbed his hands together and said, 'When do we start?'

I sold my motorbike to bankroll hydroponic lighting and watering systems, heat extraction fans, pots, soil and fertiliser. We blacked out all the windows and sealed all other nooks and crannies to prevent telltale shafts of light escaping from our little operation.

Almost every square metre of the place was dedicated to covert agriculture: the bedrooms, the living room, dining room, the study and the laundry housed dozens of plants. I was amazed at how fast the stuff grew. Stepping inside was like plunging into a steamy jungle and the sweet, sappiness of cannabis thickened the air. Our DIY electrical work and the incessant heat from the grow lights made for a massive fire hazard. The house would have glowed like a furnace on infra-red.

CHAPTER SIX

I don't smoke marijuana and didn't even know what the plants were meant to look like, but according to my partner in crime ours were the greatest specimens that ever existed. The males were all dispatched and the remaining females were pregnant with thick buds that were so heavy they bent the branches. When they brushed against my skin they almost stuck like glue.

After we processed and sold the first crop the reviews came in, and we were told it was dynamite product. I knew a few people who could take it off our hands in bulk, including a girl I'd gotten to know at uni. She was a lovely person, a great artist, a major pothead and an established dealer. She ended up taking most of what we produced. I could hardly believe money literally grew on our little trees – thousands upon thousands of dollars. My first order of business was to buy a new motorbike.

Since we couldn't be at the house twenty-four-seven we needed someone to babysit the crop when we weren't around. All my life I'd been extremely protective of my younger brother, Michael. Because my dad and oldest brother weren't around I was more like a father figure than a sibling to him. Even if Michael swore too much, I'd tell him off. He had to do his homework and he had to stay in school. I busted his balls and there was no way in the world he was allowed to take drugs. For whatever messed-up reason, I asked Michael if he wanted the job of hydro crop caretaker.

When the next crop was ready for harvest I ferried it to my uni friend's house where we dried it out and bundled it up into different weights for sale. One evening I was riding to her place along Punt Road with a backpack stuffed with about 20 kg of weed. A woman pulled into my lane without looking and skittled me onto the road.

It hurt but I checked my vitals and quickly realised I could move my arms and legs. As I struggled to my feet, the woman got out of her car and rushed over to me in a flap. 'Stay down, stay down. I'll call an ambulance,' she said in a high, panicky voice. 'I'm so sorry. Oh my god, are you okay?'

'Yeah, yeah. I'm fine,' I insisted, waving her away in case she got a whiff of my backpack. 'Seriously, I don't need an ambulance.'

A pedestrian who'd witnessed the crash was next on the scene. He put his hand on my shoulder as I hunched over and tried to collect myself. 'Are you alright, mate? Do you want me to call the police?' he asked.

'No, no, no. It's fine, really,' I virtually pleaded with him. 'Don't ring the cops. I'm alright.'

'But your bike's damaged,' the woman wailed.

It was as if they wanted me to get busted! Like me, the bike was a bit banged up, but it started straight-away. I got back in the saddle and took off, leaving them dumbfounded by the side of the road. I was in possession of a *lot* of drugs. My good behaviour bond had expired years earlier but the assault charge remained on my record like the ever-watchful Eye of Sauron. Had I been arrested that day I doubt I'd have been granted any favours from the court – just like the magistrate had warned me.

Rashad, who'd been through a terrible time after losing Aaliyah, finally returned to Australia as planned. We rented a great apartment in Arden Street, North Melbourne – not quite in the thick of the action, but close enough to the city that when it called our names we could always answer.

He wasn't the only person who came back into my life. I hadn't seen Dad for about a year. He was living 300-odd km away in the western Victorian town of Horsham, which I liked to call Horseshit. He phoned me to say he was in Melbourne, so we arranged to meet in a café.

'So, what have you been up to?' my father began.

'Well, I've been growing marijuana and selling it,' I said. 'I've got this whole crop set up inside a rented house. It's like a marijuana factory and I'm making heaps of money.'

It was a half-brag, half-dare for him to say something about it, but what I really wanted was for Dad to tell me to stop. Deep down I was crying out for him to say, 'What in the hell are you doing? You could throw your life away selling drugs! You could go to jail!'

Instead, Dad calmly sipped his espresso, took a drag on his roll-up cigarette (the only kind he could afford by then) and looked me square in the eye. 'Marijuana, huh?' he said. 'Give me a look at how the setup works and I'll do it myself in Horsham.'

It was like staring across the table at a reflection of my worst self. I didn't see an artist, or a family man, a good brother or a friend – I saw a greedy drug dealer hell bent on cutting corners and fucking people over for money. In my father I saw what not to be.

What killed me most was the fact I had put Michael – who I love so much – in the middle of a criminal enterprise and exposed him to drugs. I was meant to protect him and I turned him into a drug grower instead, just because I wanted some easy money. I was ashamed that I had betrayed his trust so much and I don't know if I ever earned it back, although I've tried. Putting him in that house is something I have cried about many times.

The next day I went to Essendon, ripped up every last plant and binned them. I gave all the equipment away and never sold drugs again. My old life was over. I wanted a new one.

It's fitting that my art career began in a hospital. After all, childhood illness and endless injuries from fights, motorbike accidents and combat in the ring left me with a medical file an inch thick. I was no stranger to bedside vigils either, be it visiting drug-damaged friends in psychiatric wards or blood-spattered visits to emergency with fallen comrades, like my trip to St Vincent's with Rashad on Latino Night. When I returned to the same hospital in 2005, however, my clothes were smeared with paint instead.

The directors at St Vincent's set aside an abandoned wing of the hospital for an artists in residency program whereby up-and-coming painters were given free studio space in exchange for some works to hang in the corridors of healing. Although it was a pretty weird place it was also a hoot, and I was super grateful to be accepted. The wing could have doubled for the set of a Stephen King movie:

whitewashed walls, shiny linoleum floors and dilapidated beds on wheels scattered about the old wards like abandoned cars. When I wasn't painting I wandered the haunted hallways to investigate decommissioned hospital equipment, look through old medical files or nap on a gurney in my little room.

I'd held a small exhibition at the Jackman Gallery in St Kilda after I finished my master's degree that featured paintings I'd done at university. It didn't exactly set the world on fire. Standing in front of a blank canvas in my hospital studio I struggled to find inspiration for what to do next. Since I was fresh out of art school and self-conscious about my rookie status in the art world I found myself a hostage of the academic obsession with history. I second-guessed what people might say about my work and decided to pretend I knew something about history, too.

(I'll say it here, since it needs to be said somewhere: I have painted a lot of crap over the course of my life. Many of my choices have been cringeworthy and some of my output has been fairly average – particularly in the early days. None of that stuff made it into exhibitions, of course, but it's important I acknowledge that it existed.)

Although the series I ultimately painted in the hospital was technically very good, my so-called inspiration for the collection was embarrassing. In my desire to come off like an art history aficionado I contrived a contemporary take on characters from Greek mythology. I cast Aphrodite, for instance, as a young woman at a bathroom sink gazing at herself in a mirror on the wall. I rendered Narcissus as a male model reclining in a suit while a magazine cover on the table next to him reflected his image, and I painted myself as Icarus tumbling from the sky, shirtless and in a pair of blue jeans. While I was proud of the paintings, it was a totally inauthentic exercise – just a cover for my insecurities about my lack of historical knowledge. I wanted to fool potential buyers and critics into believing I knew more than I did. In doing so, I showed them a side of myself that didn't exist.

During my final years at university I had familiarised myself with some of Melbourne's bigger galleries. Following in the footsteps of RMIT graduates who'd gone before me I approached a number of the leading galleries in the hope they'd exhibit my work. After all, the conventional wisdom for painters in Melbourne was:

1. Try to convince a gallery to show your stuff.
2. If they agree they promote it, stage it and bring in potential buyers.
3. They take 50 per cent of whatever you make.

Fifty per cent sounded outrageous to me. Some even wanted 60 per cent! Who was I to complain, though? I toured the galleries with my folio from university and was told to run along and not waste their time. The Dianne Tanzer Gallery in Fitzroy was the only one that gave me the time of day. When I showed up on her doorstep, Dianne was much more open-minded and encouraging. Hers was a fairly prestigious gallery and she had a good reputation as a specialist in contemporary Australian art. Instead of shooing me out the door Dianne took her time to look closely at my work. When she finished she gave me my first real break.

'It's not perfect,' she said, 'but I think you have something we could work with.'

I went back to my studio at St Vincent's and completed my Greek mythology series, which I called The Nature of Fate (cringe again). Dianne agreed to stage a solo exhibition in 2007. Each piece carried a price tag of $9000 and the collection sold out – a very welcome payday for a struggling new artist, especially considering I was about to get married.

Michelle had my full attention from the moment we first met. After a day at the Australian Open in 2005 we wound up at the same restaurant in the city with a big group of mutual friends. We got talking over a few drinks and by the end of the night I was mesmerised. For one thing Michelle was stunningly beautiful. Sri Lankan/Indian by descent, she'd been raised in Perth but had moved to Melbourne to work as a doctor. She was willowy with enormous dark eyes and a perfect smile but most of all I was attracted to her charisma, sense of humour and the fact she was very, very cool.

CHAPTER SEVEN

We swapped numbers, followed by flirty text messages and phone calls. After two or three dates we dived headfirst into a serious relationship. I soon moved out of the North Melbourne pad I'd been sharing with Rashad and into a nearby apartment with Michelle. I was in awe of her. Michelle had graduated high school with a 99.5 score, studied medicine and worked in a city hospital. I admired how smart she was, particularly considering that I didn't feel like I was smart at all. And yet there she was, in my life and in love with me, too.

Michelle ticked another emotional box for me: she embodied my lifelong attraction to ambitious and successful people. She worked hard and I could tell she admired doctors who'd built high profiles through the media or reality TV, and I sensed maybe she had ambitions to head in that direction, too. She wasn't a workaholic, though, and we had a blast together. Michelle was a lot of fun in a real buddy kind of way. She was one of those people who is up for a bit of mischief and someone I could have an adventure with. Socially we had an interesting dynamic going as the artist and the doctor, and she slotted right into my fairly fast-moving world where much was going on.

I first met N'fa Forster-Jones through Rashad. N'fa had played a small part in *Queen of the Damned* alongside Aaliyah but his day job was frontman of the Melbourne-based hip-hop outfit 1200 Techniques. We became firm friends and, along with Rashad, spent a huge amount of time hanging out in the hip-hop nightclub scene together. I have literally lost count of how many 1200 Techniques shows I've been to. Rashad took his devotion to the band a step further when he appeared on a track from their album *Consistency Theory*.

Although he'd been born in England and his dad was a Sierra Leone Creole, N'fa – like Michelle – had been raised in Perth before moving to Melbourne to pursue his career. During the days when I lived with Rashad in North Melbourne, N'fa shared a house in St Kilda with his childhood friend Trevor DiCarlo, another Perth native who was also a part of our tight little crew. It was through N'fa, Trev and another mate named Tony Engelman that I became friends with the actor Heath Ledger. They'd attended school with Heath in Perth and Trev had been his best mate since kindergarten. They were like the Perth ratpack, and I adored them.

At the time Heath enjoyed a lot of success in Australia and was on the verge of becoming a major star in the US with the Ang Lee film *Brokeback Mountain*. Whenever he came to Melbourne though, Heath was all about N'fa and 1200 Techniques. The band was all over the radio and had won a bunch of ARIA awards. Heath was always at their shows and directed some of their videos, too.

When N'fa stayed at our place for a period Heath would pop in to visit. We clicked over a shared passion for film, photography and art. We came up

CHAPTER SEVEN

with a great concept for me to paint thirty portraits in thirty days in different cities around the world and discover the people and the culture in the process. We talked about me painting his portrait, too. He was a bit wary to begin with. Plenty of artists had asked Heath to sit for them and he had always declined. He promised me that when the time was right, he wanted me to be the one to paint him. He was also adamant that when we did collaborate on a portrait, I had to enter it in the Archibald Prize.

We talked about it for years but our problem was finding the time because, once he earned an Oscar nomination for best actor for *Brokeback Mountain*, Heath's schedule tightened like a drum and he spent most of his time in America.

Meanwhile my other West Australian connections (i.e. Michelle's parents) weren't as supportive of my chosen career as an artist. When we visited them together in Perth, one of the first things her father – a very stiff accountant – said to me was, 'If the ship is sinking you need to know when to get out. Tomorrow I'm going to take you somewhere special.'

The following day he drove me to some framing shop in the Perth suburbs that was owned by one of his friends. As they showed me around the place the unspoken message was loud and clear: 'Forget about making art, you can frame other people's instead.'

I imagine Michelle's parents – who'd no doubt encouraged their only child to work hard, excel and make a stellar career for herself – were alarmed that she had fallen in love with some poor loser wannabe artist. I left Western Australia thinking how good it was that he wasn't *my* father, and that we lived 2700 km away.

Nonetheless, when Michelle and I tied the knot in 2007 we did it in Perth. N'fa was my best man and I dressed up in traditional Indian formal wear. I flew my family over from Melbourne for the occasion but I still didn't know half the guests who were from a series of extended Indian families. It was a huge night and a great wedding and I was head over heels in love.

By the time our son Luca was born two years later, my lot as a poor loser artist had changed dramatically. I'd had two more sellout solo exhibitions with the Dianne Tanzer Gallery, an exhibition at Hong Kong's renowned 10 Chancery Lane Gallery of thirty portraits I'd painted in thirty days in that city, and I had twice won the People's Choice Award at the Archibald Prize. Art was beginning to pay. Down the track a little I even scored some work as a brand ambassador.

I moved out of the hospital and rented my own small studio space in Brunswick, then Michelle and I put down a deposit on an apartment in Docklands. That's where she fell pregnant with Luca.

I'd wanted to be a father from a young age but when the lines on the test stick confirmed the news

I was at once overjoyed and terrified. As much as I yearned to be a father, I had no references or role models for how to be a good one. I couldn't exactly look to my dad for any useful cues on how to raise a child. All I could think to do was somehow be the opposite of everything he was. Still, there were many days early in the pregnancy when I felt very anxious. With no-one else to turn to I phoned a friend who'd become a father a year or two earlier.

'Don't be nervous, Vinnie,' he reassured me. 'You'll know what to do and don't worry about how things will work out – it just does when you do it with love.'

He reckoned fatherhood wouldn't detract from my life or career either, only enhance it. 'Being a dad hasn't slowed me down but sped me up instead,' he explained. 'It's given me something to work for and a greater reason for being. Trust me. You'll see.'

I settled down a bit after that, partly because I got it in my head that Michelle and I were going to have a girl. In my mind, raising a girl would be a lot easier because it wouldn't be complicated by the paternal relationship – or lack thereof – that I'd had. I figured Michelle would dress her and do her hair while my role would be to give her cuddles, take her to soccer or dance lessons and put the fear of god into her boyfriends.

At twelve weeks we found out we were having a boy. I knew then that a huge responsibility was going to fall on me. Not that it would have been any less if we were having a girl, but because my relationship with my dad strangely came into play. All I could do was heed the words of my mate and just go forward with love.

I took a photo of Michelle's growing tummy every day so I could show our boy the love he was made with. The closer he got to being with us, the less anxious I became, and I couldn't wait to meet him. Because he was delivered by C-section I was the first one to hold Luca and I didn't want to let him go. I was enchanted by his heartbeat showing through the fontanelle gaps on the top of his head, by his tiny fingernails, the warmth of him and his beautiful smell.

As I cradled him in those first minutes of his life I knew I would be a father he could depend on. I had a strong sense that if everything in the world went wrong, Luca and I were going to be together forever. At the same time, I felt as though I had completed my life's mission, even though we had the rest of our lives ahead of us.

'I will never leave you,' I whispered to him.

And I knew that no matter what happened, I would never be alone again.

The first thing people ask any Australian portrait artist is, 'Have you been in the Archibald Prize?' The august and famous contest, hosted by the Art Gallery of New South Wales since 1921, is woven into the national fabric and these days winning it is akin to taking home a Gold Logie, an ARIA award or the Melbourne Cup. The current $100,000 first prize is a big deal in any artist's book, but the lifelong adornment to the winner's career is even bigger. As cynical as I was about the art establishment, my obsession with winning their most prestigious award proved that deep down I craved their validation and acceptance.

My desire for Archibald glory boiled down to fear, as things often do when you feel like an imposter. Although I'd started to rack up some career wins, whenever I held a successful exhibition, sold a collection or booked a commission I worried it would be my last, and that I'd never sell another painting as long as I lived. If Jack Rennie thought I was going to be okay in life because I had artistic ability, I reckoned I was only going to be okay if I won the Archibald Prize.

My first Archies entry, a painting of N'fa in 2005, was rejected by the prize's trustees, as were my next two attempts – portraits of indie rock legend Tim Rogers and the artist Charles Blackman, whom I painted in 2006 and 2007 respectively. Three strikes from three but I was still desperate to bust down the door of their club and make them *please* notice me. Just before Christmas 2007 I got a phone call from Heath Ledger. He was home in Perth on a break from filming in London. 'I feel like it's time we did that painting now,' he said. 'What do you think?'

We had kicked around the idea of me painting his portrait for three years. He was always busy and I suspect Heath felt a bit like I did when I started this book – nervous and unsure if he was ready, or if it was the right time in his life. But on the phone from Western Australia that day he sounded excited. The only caveat was the tiny window of opportunity we had before Heath had to head back to England for work a couple of days later. I grabbed my camera and jumped on the next plane to Perth.

That night Heath and I went to a big beer barn in the city to compare notes on life and discuss what we wanted the portrait to convey. I'd only been married for a few months but there were already some concerning fault lines in my relationship that dated back to my earliest days with Michelle. Heath was a sympathetic ear and while I loosened up emotionally with plenty of drinks, he stuck to water. When he opened up about his life I was surprised to learn just how much shit he was going through.

Only two months earlier Heath had split from his partner Michelle Williams, the American actress who'd co-starred with him in *Brokeback Mountain* and was the mother of his three-year-old daughter, Matilda.

Heath was vulnerable that night but he was in a strong headspace, too. He'd just come off six long, hard months in Chicago filming his now famous portrayal of the Joker in *The Dark Knight*. He'd gone to some dark places to conjure that performance but the young man who sat across from me at the pub in Perth was bright, positive and super healthy, albeit thinner than usual. Heath put his low body weight down to his role in *The Imaginarium of Dr Parnassus* that he was filming in the UK. 'People are worried that I'm sick but I'm just immersed in this role,' he assured me.

Although Heath was in the midst of a stellar professional run, he revealed that he, too, often felt like an imposter. The saddest thing he told me, however, was that his increasing fame had made him unsure of who his friends were or why people even spoke to him. I saw it first-hand that night: the punters staring at him, sneaking photos and calling out his name. One guy even slapped him on the back as he stood at the urinal. 'Hey, Heath Ledger!' the stranger boomed as he was trying to have a slash. 'How ya going, man? What are you doing here?'

'That's nothing,' Heath said of the encounter as we returned to our table. 'In showbusiness there are people like that everywhere, all day, every day. They're constantly at you with this request over here and that favour over there, and they're all pretending to be your best mate.'

'So how do you handle that?' I asked.

'I just give them what they want,' he said with a half shrug. 'But I always know it's just a matter of time before they tell me what they *really* want from me and why they're *really* there. It makes you wonder, Who are my friends? Do I have any friends? It's hard to know.'

The conversation echoed in my head when I fell into bed drunk at my in-laws' place that night. The reality was that I wanted something from Heath, too, even though we were in it together. During the course of our night the theme of the portrait had taken shape. There's no doubt he'd shared his woes, but Heath talked excitedly about the future with his daughter, his career and other artistic collaborations we could do in the years ahead, including Thirty Portraits in Thirty Days in New York. Heath's challenge was working out how to balance the complex, competing voices in his life and manage the demands of a clamouring world. Who did he let in and who did he keep at arm's length? How much

CHAPTER EIGHT

of himself should he share, and what parts should he protect? Ultimately that's what the portrait was about.

In the morning I arrived at his mum Sally's house a little hungover but excited to work. Sally made us a coffee and any lingering misgivings Heath had about a portrait in years past had totally disappeared by the final sip. 'Grab your camera, Vincent,' he said as he rose from the kitchen table and motioned for me to follow him out onto the back verandah. Wearing just his pyjama pants, Heath planted a garden chair on the floor, sat down on it and – without saying a word – launched into an impromptu performance that had to be seen to be believed.

First he sat perfectly still and stared at me while I shot frames from different angles. In the next moment he was on his feet, leaning in and cupping a hand to whisper something to himself as if he was still sitting on the chair. Then he was around the other side, yelling at his invisible self. I took dozens of photographs as the fervent one-man drama unfolded but I wish I'd set up a film camera as well because what he did was extraordinary and it was almost wasted on an audience of one.

At one point Heath dropped to the ground and lay motionless on his back before he dragged himself up onto his knees, bent over where he'd been lying and screamed at himself to 'Get up! Get up! Get up!'

The intensity was like nothing I'd seen before. It was a full bodily expression of what was going on in his head and I saw vivid reflections of the things we'd talked about the night before: the sense of being under siege in a celebrity blitzkrieg. When he finished twenty minutes later he reverted to the smiling, jovial chap who'd welcomed me in his PJs an hour earlier – just Heath in the sunshine for Christmas with his family.

Before I left for the airport that afternoon I sketched an outline of how I planned to compose the portrait. 'I love it,' Heath said as he tilted his head to examine the drawing. 'I can't wait to see it finished.' He gave me a bear hug, waved me goodbye and sent me on my way with one parting thought. 'This painting,' he said, 'is going to change our lives.'

I worked like a man possessed for the next three weeks. I didn't waste time commuting to my studio, I just stayed in our apartment in Docklands and painted day and night. When I wasn't asleep or eating I was working on the portrait. I'd known Heath for years but after our intense meeting in Perth I felt strongly bonded to the man. Knowing we understood each other and the project, and appreciating how much it meant to him gave me a drive that I hadn't felt before. I wanted to honour him with the best painting I had ever done.

My whole world during that period was Heath Ledger. I pored over the photos from our sitting and plucked out the tiniest minutiae from his expressions, body language and the changes in emotion and energy behind his eyes. In the process I understood for the first time the value of meditating over the subject. Heath was in my thoughts constantly and, as strange as it might sound, I tried to put myself into his mind, too. However, I never once picked up the phone to call him or text him. I wanted to surprise him with the completed work. When I was just about finished, I was too excited to wait any longer so on 22 January 2008 I emailed him a photo of the painting – an oil on canvas study of Heath in three poses. Then I fell into bed exhausted.

When I woke the following day I reached for my phone and saw that Heath hadn't yet opened the email. I went into the living room-cum-studio and switched on the TV as Michelle readied herself for work. The painting was right alongside our flatscreen because I'd been loading my photos of Heath onto it for reference. A 'breaking news' banner slid across the bottom of the screen. I turned the volume up and heard the anchors talking about the awful news that was grimly circling the world: Heath Ledger had been found dead in his apartment in New York.

I was numb for a minute and kind of glitched as I struggled to take it in. For the best part of a month that television monitor had projected a hundred different faces of Heath and suddenly someone else's face was on it telling me he was dead. My heart broke as reality sank in. In a state of gathering shock, I fumbled for my phone. N'fa was driving when I got through to him. He sounded chipper when he answered so

I knew he had no idea. It was devastating to be the one to tell him Heath was gone.

As I wept for Heath and the people who loved him, I thought about Rashad and what he'd been through when Aaliyah died so suddenly and young. Heath was very young, too, only twenty-eight years old. Now his little girl would grow up without a dad. His parents would never again get to hug him, and the likes of N'fa and Trev would never revel in the warmth, laughs and secret codes that lifelong friendship brings. Just like Aaliyah's family, Heath's loved ones were about to endure a media storm and a very public fixation on the unbearable loss of their beloved boy.

The press started calling me almost immediately. The fact I'd been painting Heath for the Archibald Prize was already out there: his friends and family knew and, evidently, so did people in the media. My phone rang off the hook with calls from newspapers, magazines and TV stations. I had never experienced an intrusion like it.

As it happened, phone calls were flying back and forth among Heath's friends and family to figure out how best to handle the media onslaught. I never knew how full-on the press could be after a shock death like Heath's. Hundreds of them swamped family, friends and associates for angles, information, insights and any kind of twist they could find. They were exactly like sharks in a feeding frenzy. I have no idea how they got my number, but multiple outlets wanted to use my painting in their reporting.

CHAPTER EIGHT

At that time I hadn't met Heath's father, Kim, so I didn't really know what to say to the poor man when he phoned me a couple of days later to assure me that if I wished to speak to the media about the painting and Heath, I had the family's blessing.

Ultimately I decided that Heath had been excited for the world to see it so I acquiesced. Soon *Heath* was published in newspapers and television bulletins across Australia and around the globe. Wide exposure, but I felt a great sorrow and a deep unease that the portrait had become instantly and famously synonymous with the passing of a beautiful, brilliant man.

'Are you still going to enter it in the Archibald Prize?'

I must have been asked that question one hundred times in the days after Heath passed away. The cut-off date for entries was due the following week. Once more, Heath's parents Kim and Sally encouraged me to proceed with the entry because, in their words, it was exactly what Heath would have wanted. I booked a flight to Sydney and when I turned up at Melbourne Airport with a 106 cm x 140 cm painting some staff at the Qantas check-in recognised it from news reports and said they'd make extra sure it was given VIP treatment in oversized luggage.

In Sydney I caught a cab to the Art Gallery of New South Wales on the eastern fringe of The Domain and handed *Heath* over in person. The packing room staff at the delivery dock were warm and welcoming.

They told me they'd been expecting the painting and assured me they'd take good care of it.

A few weeks later I received a phone call from the art gallery to inform me that *Heath* had been selected as a finalist in the Archibald Prize. A week after that I was back in Sydney on the eve of the big day for a special lunch at the gallery with the thirty-nine other finalists. It was a huge moment. I felt included, validated and blown away that the art establishment had literally invited the dumb kid from Broadmeadows to their place for lunch. I had never thought I'd be part of that scene, but there I was with other artists who not only recognised me, but said some lovely things about my painting.

Still, there was an underlying tension in the room because everyone wanted to win the glittering prize and the $50,000 that went with it that year. Our paintings were hung in the various rooms of the gallery and I learned that the curators moved the works around before the prize was announced to make sure no-one could guess the winner based on positioning. If you weren't hung in the main room, I was told, traditionally you had no hope of winning. *Heath* was hung in the main room.

After lunch, all of the other finalists started heading home for what promised to be a fairly sleepless night. I was just about to do the same when Edmund Capon, the art gallery's affable and well-dressed director, put a hand on my shoulder.

'Vincent,' he said. 'Come with me.'

CHAPTER EIGHT

I followed him upstairs and Edmund showed me into his office where he pulled out an expensive-looking bottle of vodka and filled two shot glasses.

'*Salute!*' he said, and raised his glass and tipped it down the hatch.

'*Salute!*' I replied, and did the same.

'Congratulations, Vincent,' he said. 'Tomorrow you're going to win the Archibald Prize.'

'What?' I just about shouted.

'You've won it,' he said and poured us another shot. 'Congratulations.'

I was speechless.

'You can't tell anyone yet, of course,' he continued. 'Not a soul until tomorrow.'

'Yeah, of course not,' I agreed.

'It's going to be a very big day. There'll be a lot of media and you'll be doing a lot of interviews,' Edmund continued. 'You've 100 per cent got to be here for the press announcement, yes?'

'Yeah, of course,' I assured him.

After a couple more shots and some warm words from Edmund I headed into the gathering dusk in The Domain feeling on top of the world. Elated doesn't even begin to describe my state of mind. That night I finally passed out on a futon on the floor of my good mate Michael Gracey, then an up-and-coming filmmaker who went on to a successful career in Hollywood. I struggled to fall asleep, not only through excitement but also guilt and sadness that Heath wouldn't be there to share the moment.

I was awoken in the morning by a courtesy call from the gallery, reminding me to be there on time. A couple of hours later I felt a little dissociated as I approached the building's towering Roman pillars, as if I were outside myself and watching on. *You're about to win the Archibald Prize!* I marvelled, as the curly-haired young artist stepped inside the gallery. *This is going to be one of the happiest days of your life.*

Sure enough, *Heath* still hung in the main room along with a dozen or so other finalists. After a bit of mingling and small talk the big moment arrived. Before crowning the winner, however, it was announced that the judges would also be naming a 'highly commended' painting – essentially a runner-up.

'Highly commended in the Archibald Prize 2008 is Vincent Fantauzzo for *Heath*.'

Cue applause.

You fuckers! I thought as I smiled and graciously accepted second place. I could not believe it.

'And the winner of the Archibald Prize 2008 is . . .'

History shows that Del Kathryn Barton won that year for an exquisite self-portrait with her two young daughters, and Kiwi artist Martin Ball took out the Packing Room Prize for his striking painting of Neil Finn. *Heath* and I went on to win the Peoples' Choice Award. All three were excellent paintings that could have won on the day. The only wrinkle for me was that I supposedly already had.

CHAPTER EIGHT

There was no vodka and backslapping when I spoke privately to Edmund Capon between media interviews after the announcement. 'Look, I'm very sorry,' he said. 'It was out of our hands. There was a last-minute problem with the sponsor.'

According to Edmund, the powers that be at the prize's major corporate backer had expressed alarm at the judges' decision when the trustees gave them a heads-up the night before. 'They felt it was too controversial and they made a commercial decision. It's as simple as that,' Edmund said. 'But don't worry, your time will come. I promise.'

'Yeah, thanks,' I said. 'Whatever.'

There was nothing to be done, though. It wasn't my prize and I had no say over what they could and couldn't do. I wasn't about to have a tantrum or make a scene. I didn't complain about it to anyone. I mention it here for the first time – seventeen years later – because I'm writing a book about my life and that is what happened.

On the day, my initial feelings of disgust and betrayal quickly morphed into acceptance that then made room for some pride and happiness. I received a lot of media attention, congratulations and professional kudos that day, and in a way it felt like I *had* won (sans the $50,000 that I really could have used).

That night Michelle and I attended the winners' dinner at the gallery, along with Del Kathryn Barton and Martin Ball. Throughout the night Edmond kept assuring me it would only be a matter of time before I took home the Archibald Prize. 'You're young, Vincent,' he said. 'You've got big things in front of you.'

That year the Archibald exhibition was attended by more people than ever before, and a great many of them went to see *Heath*. The painting attracted more votes in the People's Choice Award than any other in the prize's history. I received some big-money offers for *Heath*, too, but I decided to give it to Heath's mum, Sally, instead. Sally, bless her, said she'd feel guilty if she kept it for herself. 'Why don't you and I donate it to the Art Gallery of New South Wales together?' she proposed. 'That way people can go there and pay a visit to Heath whenever they like.'

It was a beautiful idea that was typical of a proud and loving mum, and it was only let down by the fact the gallery removed *Heath* from public view at the end of the 2008 Archibald exhibition and haven't hung it again since. In 2017 Heath's parents borrowed it for the exhibition Heath Ledger: A Life In Pictures that showed in Canberra and at the Art Gallery of Western Australia. Following that, Kim told the Art Gallery of New South Wales that if they didn't intend to hang *Heath* he'd happily buy it from them (even though we'd donated it in the first place). They decided to keep it instead and today it's still packed away in a storeroom at The Domain.

Not only did Heath give me the opportunities the painting brought but he also gave me some incredible people. Today I am close to his family. It's a

CHAPTER EIGHT

beautiful connection and I'm humbled by the way they have embraced me.

Kim Ledger and I have developed a particularly close relationship in the years since Heath left us, and has allowed some of his fatherly sunshine to fall on me. I can't fathom the pain of losing a son, but Kim has shown amazing resilience and a perspective on life that blows me away. When Michelle and I started having marital problems he gave me advice that was never one-sided and was kind to all of the human beings involved. A very special man.

Kim has passed down wisdom, compassion and business advice, as well. He found me a studio to work from in Perth and helped me stage an exhibition at the Art Gallery of Western Australia when I was going through some hard times. We have hung out a lot together and he never once asked me for anything in return for his great acts of kindness. Kim is as dear and instructive to me as Jack Rennie was, and I feel blessed to still have him in my life. Hardly a week goes by when he doesn't phone me, 'Just to say hi, mate. Just checking in.'

Often I feel as though Heath is conspicuous by his absence. I've been able to enjoy my life and my career – and a special bond with his dad – and I doubt any of it would have played out the same way were he still alive. On the day he sat for me at Sally's place I asked him to tell me about his tattoos. I was particularly interested in the concentric circles inked on his right shoulder. At a glance it looked like a target. 'That one signifies that what you give out is what you get back,' he told me. Today I have the same tattoo stamped onto my left wrist to remind me of how much Heath has given me. I can't give anything back to him, but I will never, ever forget.

I have entered the Archibald Prize almost every year since 2005 and been accepted as a finalist five times. After *Heath*, I won the People's Choice Award on three more occasions, in 2009, 2013 and 2014 – more than any other artist. I also won the Packing Room Prize in 2011.

I'm well aware I have allowed a large chip to develop on my shoulder about the Archie and it's probably past time I flicked it off. Last year I was in New York for meetings about some possible projects in the US and had timed the trip to coincide with that of an old friend, the Melbourne entrepreneur and property developer Larry Kestelman. Like Kim Ledger, Larry is excited by the arts and has become a big supporter of mine. We gatecrashed each other's meetings in the Big Apple: I sat in on Larry's high-powered business engagements and he tagged along to my appointments that were all about art. At one get-together, some stakeholders were looking through my catalogue when one of them, an Australian, remarked, 'Oh wow, you've won the Archibald Prize?' Before I could say I actually hadn't, an American in the meeting asked, 'What's the Archibald Prize?' Larry grinned at me across the table as if to say, 'Well, there you go.'

CHAPTER EIGHT

Out on the street afterwards he said, 'See? You don't have to let all that Archibald stuff define you when most of the planet hasn't even heard of it. You're better off making your own path in the world instead.' He was right. While for me the Prize had once represented validation, acceptance and an antidote to the fear of imminent failure, it doesn't anymore. I've accomplished a lot of things on the world stage that are important to me and that I'm proud of, but I remain grateful for the exposure the Archie has given me and the opportunity for my art to connect so widely.

I didn't go to Heath's funeral – not because I didn't love him, but because I hate funerals and I have a thing about avoiding them. A few months later, however, in July 2008, I accepted an invitation to attend the premiere of *The Dark Knight* in New York with Heath's friends and family.

It was at once awful and amazing to see his most famous performance on a massive IMAX screen in a theatre full of superstars. Although Heath stole the show as Gotham City's most memorable villain, I couldn't shake the feeling I was at the funeral I'd been so desperate to avoid. I cried as I watched the riveting portrayal that earned Heath a posthumous Academy Award. I didn't see him as the Joker on screen, instead I saw my friend at the top of his professional game that should have lasted another fifty years. That night I thought about how his life might have evolved in fifteen years' time or twenty years' time and the incredible body of work he would have created. I saw an imaginary future in which he was a famous director and his beloved Matilda was in her thirties as she fussed over him at Christmas lunch in Perth. I had to stay in my seat to compose myself as every last one of the credits rolled.

I'd be lying if I didn't admit *Heath* was the painting that opened the door to the rest of my career. Although I'd already started to sell out exhibitions and I was getting shown in other art prizes, the prestige of the Archibald lifted my profile like no painting before. I'd be lying, too, if I didn't acknowledge that Heath's untimely death was tragically entwined in the painting's success and, therefore, my success. I still have complex and painful thoughts about Heath and *Heath*, and I probably always will.

Galleries big and small are part of what I consider to be the art establishment – the collective gatekeepers of the fortunes of people like me. Other sentries in this cloistered world include art dealers, curators, art historians, buyers, art school lecturers, art prize judges and critics. After spending too much of my life trying to break into their club, now that I found myself kind of in it, I wanted to break straight back out.

Still, I owe a lot to Dianne Tanzer and others, although my attitude at the time prevented me from seeing it. From my final days at art school I was more or less aligned with Dianne's gallery for the first five years of my career. I showed with her at the Melbourne Art Fair, which attracts galleries from all around the world. It was Dianne who introduced me to Katie de Tilly, founder and director of Hong Kong's 10 Chancery Lane Gallery, and it was Katie who gave me my first break overseas.

When Heath and I conceived the Thirty Portraits in Thirty Days project, we had New York in mind. The idea was to meet, shoot and paint someone in twenty-four hours and have them introduce me to the next subject and so on in a cascading domino run of portraits. The result, we imagined, would be a unique exhibition featuring an eclectic mix of subjects. Heath had promised to show me around his adopted home city, introduce me to the right people and help me get started.

A year after he died I was invited to be an artist in residence at 10 Chancery Lane so I decided to do our project in Hong Kong instead. It was before we'd fallen pregnant with Luca, and since Michelle had to stay in Melbourne for work I spent a month exploring the Pearl of the Orient and painting its people. My subjects ranged from a butcher, a student and a monk to a security guard, a gangster and a socialite from China. It was an intense and exhausting feat of creative endurance. Generally I shot each subject before lunchtime each day and painted into the night in an apartment the gallery had provided for me in the city's posh Mid-Levels. Often I'd rise before dawn after a few hours of sleep to finish off, before heading back into the cacophony and chaos of Hong Kong to connect with my next instant muse. The exhibition was a huge success and, naturally, I worried it was going to be my last.

Thankfully a bona-fide muse had entered my life. I'd first met him on the night of my maiden Archibald

Prize appearance with *Heath*. After the official dinner had wrapped at the Art Gallery of New South Wales, Michael Gracey invited Michelle and I to join him at the Ivy, a highfalutin' bar in Sydney's CBD, where he was hanging out with one of his filmmaker buddies. I'd a had a few drinks at the dinner and after a few more at the Ivy I felt pumped.

At one point I found myself at a table with a group of people including Michael and his film director pal who, I noticed, had quite a few strident things to say about art that put my nose out of joint. I was perhaps a bit defensive given the day's proceedings and was up for a debate more than usual. I didn't have a clue who the opinionated fellow was – I'd never heard of him or seen his work – so when he held forth on subjects close to my heart I told him to get fucked.

'Come again?' he said, looking bemused.

'I said "Go and get fucked, mate." You don't know what you're talking about.'

He stood up. Then I stood up, and the table fell silent as it looked like fisticuffs might break out in the middle of one of the country's swankiest bars. In a throwback to a noisy nightclub with Rashad eight years earlier, the film director and I saw something in each other's eyes that made us erupt with laughter. That was the moment my great friendship and collaboration with the legendary Australian filmmaker Baz Luhrmann began. By the end of the night we'd grown friendlier – and messier. When it was time for Michelle and me to call a cab, Baz threw an arm around my neck. 'I'm gonna come and see you in Melbourne,' he breathed boozily into my ear.

'Yeah sure, Hollywood guy,' I said. 'You're talking shit. You're not coming to see me in Melbourne.'

Baz was adamant. 'You just fucking watch me come to Melbourne,' he said.

'Nup,' I snorted. 'You're full of shit.'

'Alright,' he said. 'I'll bet my watch on it!'

Baz removed an expensive-looking timepiece from his wrist and thrust it at me. 'That's Chanel,' he said. 'Karl Lagerfeld gave it to me. I'll see you in Melbourne.'

I slipped the thing onto my wrist and it flew home with me the following day. A week later I was in the studio when my phone rang. It was Baz Luhrmann. 'Vincent, I need my watch back,' he said. 'We need to organise a courier.'

'Nah. I'm keeping the watch,' I replied distractedly, like I was busy with something else.

'That's a one-off watch,' he said. 'You can't just keep it.'

'Yes I can,' I replied. 'You made a bet. I'll give it back when you come to Melbourne like you said you were going to.'

Then I hung up.

Three months later Baz finally came to town. He booked into Crown Melbourne and invited me over. By that time, my life had already undergone a serious transformation. I'd become friends with people from a world far beyond my beginnings. I'd hung out with

CHAPTER NINE

the New York A-list, I'd worked in Hong Kong, I'd been feted in the media and I was used to meeting rich, famous and powerful people.

Nevertheless, ascending to the Chairman's Villa in a private elevator at Crown Melbourne to meet up again with Baz was a rocket ride into the celebrity stratosphere. The opulence and exclusivity of Baz's accommodation was off the charts. The villa (where he apparently always stayed) is essentially a shimmering marble and glass five-bedroom luxury house that hovers at the top of the Melbourne skyline.

Amid all that space and sumptuous splendour sat Mr Baz Luhrmann. Since our last meeting I'd managed to break one of the links on his treasured Chanel watch so I handed it to him in a plastic bag. He laughed, but was so relieved to get it back he didn't even complain. 'So, what are we going to do now, Vinnie?' he said.

I took him to a couple of bars and we had dinner in the city – not the flashiest night he'd ever had but we quickly realised that we got on really well together. Telling Baz to get fucked had, evidently, been the perfect icebreaker. After an introduction like that there was no point in us having any pretensions. We found that we had intersecting interests, too: I'm a massive fan of film and cinema while Baz is a devotee of the fine arts and visual media. Publicly he has a huge personality and he doesn't mind putting on a big show (and neither do I, it turns out), but there's a very humble and thoughtful person in there as well, and I was delighted to connect with that guy straightaway.

Baz was in the white knuckles stage of preparing for the release of his big screen epic *Australia* – then the most expensive film ever made in this country. Over a few more drinks he filled me in on the artistic and commercial pressure he was under. He also talked excitedly about the young star of the film, an eleven-year-old boy named Brandon Walters who played a character named Nullah, a member of the Stolen Generations. 'If you're looking for someone interesting to paint,' Baz said, 'this young kid is amazing.'

Brandon was born and raised in Broome, Western Australia, and had never acted before he was cast in *Australia*. A talent scout had spotted him while he was swimming at a local pool with his dad, Paul, and although he was extremely nervous he ultimately agreed to accept the role of Nullah. Six months after I returned his watch to him, Baz called to tell me Brandon was going to be in Sydney with his parents for a promotional visit and would I like to meet them to discuss the possibility of painting Brandon for the Archibald Prize.

When I arrived at the apartment where they were staying the following week, camera in hand, I was struck by how shy the Walters were, particularly Brandon. 'This is Vincent,' Baz said to his young star. 'He'd like to paint your picture if that's okay with you.'

Brandon didn't say a word, he just looked up at his dad who in turn looked at the floor. 'Don't worry about all that, Baz,' I said, sensing their discomfort and also understanding what Baz must have gone through while directing the boy. 'I'm happy to just hang out instead.'

Coming from poverty and being dyslexic allowed me to develop other parts of my personality that compensate for my shortcomings. For one thing, I'm particularly good at making new friends. We sat in awkward silence for a few more moments and – not wanting to freak Brandon out – I made some conversational inroads with Paul, instead. When he told me he was a musician we suddenly had a lot to talk about. Brandon listened to us chat and saw that his dad had begun to trust me, so he opened up a little more, too. After I deployed a bit of humour – some dad jokes and making fun of Baz – Brandon became a totally different kid.

I shot stills of the whole family that day and captured some beautiful, candid images. By the time I was getting ready to leave a couple of hours later, Brandon wouldn't stop high-fiving me. He made me piggyback him around the flat and wrestled me all over the floor. He gave me a huge hug goodbye and an innocent look of trust that still makes my hair stand up whenever I think about it.

I painted several portraits from the sitting: Brandon with both of his parents and one with just Brandon and Paul. The painting I submitted for the Archibald was a head and shoulders of Brandon in shadow, save for a diagonal shaft of light across his face.

The painting was largely based on a handful of images I'd taken while he was in transition from being wary of me to bonding with me. It distilled the vulnerability of a boy in an uncertain moment.

He returned to Sydney with his parents the following year when *Brandon* won the People's Choice Award at the 2009 Archibald Prize. Baz showed up for the occasion, too. Although he was still a little shy, Brandon was clearly excited by the buzz of the lights and cameras, and seeing a two-metre-wide painting of himself hanging on the wall. I was told it was the second time in two years my Archibald Prize entry received more votes from the public than all the other People's Choice votes combined. Quite a big deal, but Baz and I decided it was probably best not to go to the Ivy to celebrate.

Although bummed again not to win it, another popular success at the Archibald gave me more confidence in my solo exhibitions. My third showing at the Dianne Tanzer Gallery consisted of a huge single painting 4.2 metres wide and 2.5 metres high. It was the first time I made a short film to accompany a painting. The self-portrait *Inner Conflict* featured six images of me physically attacking myself inside my dingy little Brunswick studio. While my previous solo exhibitions, like The Nature of Fate, had been an attempt to fit in conceptually, *Inner Conflict* was the real me. It touched on a theme of borderline self-destruction in the pursuit of pleasure: knowing something is bad for me but doing it anyway – like riding a motorbike through red lights at 170 kph. The painting was a big turning point. After a run at the Dianne Tanzer Gallery I exhibited it in Hong Kong and sold it for a bunch of money.

Back then my work wasn't overly expensive by today's standards but this payday still represented a big windfall, and I wasn't happy that half of it went to someone else. The fact is the gallery system is set up to make money for gallery owners.

In the back half of 2009 a tall, handsome Australian-Indian friend of mine decided he was going to try to make it in Bollywood. He booked a trip to India and asked me to go along to film him at castings and studio meetings for a mini documentary about his quest for success.

We stayed at Hotel Le Sutra in the affluent Mumbai suburb of Khar and one evening I got chatting to the owner in the bar. 'What brings you to Mumbai?' he asked.

I told him I was making a short film about my friend who had stars in his eyes.

'So you're a filmmaker?' he said.

'Not really,' I replied. 'I'm actually a painter.'

'A painter?' he said brightly, and suddenly gave me his full attention.

'Yeah, a painter,' I said. 'I paint portraits, mainly.'

He googled me on the spot and made a big fuss over my work, particularly *Heath* and *Brandon* – probably because they'd had the most press.

I didn't know it at the time but he was in the process of turning Le Sutra into the country's first art hotel. 'Do you want to have an exhibition at the hotel while you're here?' he offered with his palms turned towards the ceiling.

'I don't have any paintings with me,' I said, laughing.

'We'll just do an exhibition of prints,' he replied.

Within a few days the staff had organised large prints of a dozen of my paintings and hung them in the hotel. They attracted the local press and some real-life Bollywood personalities to their pop-up exhibition. I was amazed at how quickly they pulled it off and how much attention they were able to generate. All of the prints sold and I flew home with a pocket full of rupees.

A couple of weeks later the people from Le Sutra called to ask if I wanted to return to India and stage a proper exhibition at the hotel. I phoned Baz to ask his advice and I could almost hear his ears prick up at the other end of the phone. 'Here's a thought,' he said. 'Why don't I come to India with you?'

When I told the guys in India Baz Luhrmann might be involved, too, they lost their shit. That's when things started to get crazy. The hoteliers in Mumbai were friends with the owners of India's Royal Enfield motorcycle company. As luck would have it, the motorbike manufacturers were looking for someone to launch their latest model. India is home to a huge film culture and the thought of having a celebrated

CHAPTER NINE

Hollywood director launch their new bike was a dream come true.

Although he was keen, Baz was anxious to use the trip to focus on some social issues as well as have an adventure. 'I can't just do something completely self-indulgent,' he said. 'It'd be nicer if we could raise some money for charity while we're over there.'

There had been some very nasty, well publicised and politically destabilising attacks on Indian university students in Australia at the time. Baz wanted to treat the trip as a peace mission – an outstretched hand of friendship to India on behalf of the Australian film industry. Meanwhile the guys at Le Sutra told me they were already connected with a charity called Deeds that supported hearing-impaired children, which would be only too happy to benefit from the fundraising opportunities of our visit.

By the time we boarded a plane for India in January 2010 the initial idea of an art exhibition had ballooned somewhat. Now we were to ride Royal Enfield motorbikes across Rajasthan, document our travels and visit communities along the way to help raise money for Deeds. Baz would do his bit to promote peace and harmony between our two nations in the local media. We'd stage a charity exhibition of our photographs from the road trip and finish back in Mumbai with a showing of my paintings that had been shipped from Australia.

When we touched down in Mumbai it was clear the trip was going to be bigger than *Ben Hur*.

We were met by a huge welcoming party at the airport and whisked to the Le Sutra where press and TV cameras awaited. Once we settled in, our hosts sat us down and rattled off a list of commitments they'd arranged on our behalf: 'Tomorrow, you're on this TV show and the next day you're on that TV show and then A.R. Rahman is going to come to visit you . . .'

A.R. Rahman is a legendary musician, composer and a giant of Indian cinema who also happens to have won a couple of Oscars and Grammys. Baz was a huge fan, so meeting him was quite the honour. On the flipside, a roll call of Bollywood filmmakers and actors wanted to meet with Baz, the venerated director of *Romeo + Juliet*, *Strictly Ballroom* and *Moulin Rouge*.

On the art side of things the hoteliers decided to kick our visit off by having Baz and I paint a mural on the outside of the hotel. *No worries*, I thought. *A bit of street art will be fun.* When we walked out to get started we were directed to a giant, two-storey-high brick wall. 'Here it is!' they said. 'The cranes are arriving in a couple of hours and we have a few people coming to help you.'

The project looked like a major construction site. They gave us twenty assistants, a truckload of paint, cherry pickers and a crane with a cameraman to film the whole thing. Baz came up with the theme of celebrating dance in cinema and we used stencils and spray paint to cover the wall in images of stars dancing – Elvis, Fred Astaire, Ginger Rogers and

Michael Jackson. I learned that one of Baz's favourite sayings was, 'A life lived in fear is a life half lived,' so we painted that on the wall in Hindi, too.

After a few days doing media appearances and meeting with Bollywood's best we picked up our brand-new Royal Enfield bikes and set off across Rajasthan towards Delhi. One minor concern was that Baz hadn't ridden a motorbike since he was a kid and had only received his licence a few days before we left Australia. Fearlessly, however, he climbed aboard and went for it.

Deeds did a great job of publicising the trip because as soon as we chugged into each new town, swarms of kids appeared and chased us along the road. In each community we played with hearing-impaired children, took photos and did some street art with them. Afterwards, in a bizarre disconnect from needy children, we were taken to all manner of parties in the palaces of the rich and famous. Mostly our hosts had Bollywood connections. They dressed us from head to toe in Indian clothing and threw banquets complete with dancing girls and traditional ceremonies.

A highlight of the trip was visiting the home of legendary Bollywood actor Amitabh Bachchan, the living god of Indian cinema. After we passed his armed guards at the front gate we were shown to an elevator. As we ascended past each floor we could see through the lift's glass door that each level of the residence was lined with artworks of Amitabh.

When we reached the top level we were greeted by the man himself. He treated us to a beautiful lunch and afterwards – as we were having tea and chatting about art and film – he excused himself, walked to a window and opened the blind. A massive roar erupted from below. Baz and I rushed to the window to see several thousand people cheering and waving from the street. Every day, whenever he was home, Amitabh would wave to his fans – just like the Pope at the Vatican, only one hundred times cooler. I took some photos of him and painted his portrait when I returned to Australia. Baz went one better and cast him as Jewish gangster Meyer Wolfsheim in *The Great Gatsby*, giving Amitabh his Hollywood debut at the age of seventy-three.

In contrast to the A-list trappings of our odyssey, riding motorbikes through Rajasthan was a dirty, bone-shaking, harrowing business. The air pollution was as thick as smoke and there were accidents, cows and chaos everywhere. We even had to ride around dead people on the road. After one especially long day, Baz removed his goggles and I was amazed to see his face was black with soot and filth, save for two white circles around his eyes.

Not surprisingly, the stress of the road occasionally boiled over. Towards the end of the trip we were due to have a charity exhibition of the photos we'd sent along the way. After a particularly torrid time on the road we arrived at the hotel venue about 3 pm with black faces and aching muscles, only to be told the event was kicking off at 6 pm. The photos had already been hung in the ballroom and there was going to be a huge media presence. Baz got really stressed about it. 'How do we know the exhibition's going to look right?' he said as we stood in the lobby. He turned to the guy at the front desk and said, 'Get me some food and the best wine that you have and send it to my room.'

We went up to our rooms and after I freshened up I joined Baz in his suite for an early dinner. We cracked open the very expensive bottle of vino but rather than chill out, Baz kept going on and on about how shit the exhibition was going to be. After we'd downed half a bottle each we started to argue.

'You're being a fucking diva,' I told him.

'Well, you've got no idea,' he fired back.

Then we really got fired up, Ivy style. I threw my plate of curry at him and he launched his dinner at me. 'Fuck you,' I said and stormed out of the food-spattered room. 'You're doing the exhibition by yourself.'

I sulked in my suite for the next two hours. Like an old married couple, Baz expected me to go back while I imagined he'd come to me and apologise. As the sun started to set the anxious organisers knocked on Baz's door. Now he was stressed because he didn't want to let people down. He came to my room but I wasn't done sulking. 'I'm not coming out!' I said in probably the most childish outburst I'd made in years.

We eventually ended up going down to the ballroom together where we had a massive night, a great exhibition and saw our photos sold to raise good money for Deeds. We laughed about the curry fight and made up. The next day we climbed back on the bikes for our last leg of the trip back to Le Sutra in Mumbai for the exhibition of my paintings.

As usual I rode a little ahead of Baz. As the more experienced rider I was protective of him. When I turned my head to see how he was doing I was alarmed to discover he was no longer in my wake. I doubled back and found Baz trying to wheel his twisted bike away from a road accident, clutching his left hand to his chest.

On more than one occasion our hosts had warned us that a road accident in India can easily become a riot. If witnesses believe you're in the wrong and if you've hurt someone, a crowd can turn against you and suddenly you find yourself in a very dangerous situation. Neither of us knew – until it was too late – that buses in India don't stop to let passengers alight: they slow down just enough for people to jump off. A guy had stepped off a moving bus and straight onto Baz. This accident clearly wasn't Baz's fault but the hapless bus commuter had a broken leg. A couple of locals at the scene told us to get out of there quickly. I swapped bikes with Baz and managed to straighten the bent handlebars a little. Somehow we limped back into Mumbai where we went straight to a medical centre.

CHAPTER NINE

As we sat in the overcrowded waiting room I felt very proud of Baz. He'd only had his motorcycle licence for two weeks and already he'd ridden through India with filth all over his face, swerving around corpses and all sorts of animals on the road. Then, after being injured in a bizarre prang, he got straight back on the bike.

Still, he was used to getting VIP treatment from hospitals in the West. He had no such sway in Mumbai, though. The waiting room was a crazy carnival of sick and injured people moaning, their loved ones yelling and staff scurrying about. After two hours of waiting, Baz still hadn't been seen by a nurse. To pass the time I pulled out my camera and flicked through photos from our trip.

I came across a nice shot of Baz and me with Amitabh Bachchan. Unbeknown to me a young woman was looking over my shoulder and when she saw that photo she yelped like she'd seen a ghost. Suddenly the people next to her wanted to know what was on the camera screen. I showed them and someone grabbed it off me. Soon it was passed around the room and people started to freak out: 'Oh my god! Oh my *god*! They know Amitabh Bachchan! *They know Amitabh Bachchan!*' The waiting room filled with screams of disbelief and delight, which brought the doctors out of their rooms. When *they* saw the photo, Baz was taken straight in for priority treatment – and not a single waiting patient complained.

Poor Baz had broken several bones in his hand. Once he was patched up we were virtually carried out of the medical centre like stage-diving rockstars in a mosh pit. People brushed our hair and fawned over us all because of our fleeting association with the god of Indian cinema.

The next night we hosted my exhibition where we enjoyed another round of Bollywood glitz and glamour before returning to Australia exhausted. After a few days back in the relative calm and order of Melbourne it almost felt like the trip had been a dream. Several weeks later, however, the people at Royal Enfield shipped the motorbikes to us – gleaming relics of our surreal jaunt across Rajasthan.

Not long after that trip I received a call from a Vietnamese art collector who'd bought some of my paintings in Hong Kong. She suggested I have an exhibition in Vietnam. 'Absolutely,' I said, immediately thinking how cool it would be to ride around Vietnam with my mate Baz.

I rang him immediately: 'If you're not sick of motorbikes, I'm going to have an exhibition in Vietnam,' I said. 'I hear you can buy a bike there and just hit the road.'

'I'm in,' he said.

Baz does not live life by half.

Apart from being a unique and brilliantly creative filmmaker, Baz has reached the top of his profession by being dedicated and focused. I guess you have to be in order to shoulder the responsibility of mega-budgets and work with the biggest stars in the world. As a result his life, to me at least, can look very serious and hyper-organised. My life, on the other hand, is the complete opposite. Dyslexia means I constantly lose things – phones, wallets, passports and even paintings – and I forget appointments like they never existed. Unlike Baz I don't have a plan or, to be more accurate, I *can't* have a plan. I get blown along by the wind instead, and the result is usually chaotic. There's a fifteen-year age difference between us, too, but for some reason our adventures just seemed to work. We're more similar than people would expect.

Our next collaboration actually drew on Baz's younger days. Having grown up in the shadow of a petrol station run by his dad on the Mid North Coast of New South Wales, he came up with a story called The Creek, 1977 about a family that was loosely based on his. In the saga three boys, including one who is very close to his mother, all live together with their ex-army father at a petrol station near a narrow road bridge that leads into a country town. The bridge is an accident black spot and the family is constantly going to the aid of people who run off the road and into the creek. One night they rescue a young man who crashes his car off the bridge and take him to their home to recuperate. The guy prolongs his stay in the town and causes havoc among the family and the townspeople.

It was a dark subject and Baz wasn't quite sure what to do with the story. After many discussions about the crossover possibilities between painting and film we came up with the idea of combining the two mediums as a piece of art. Baz said the drama in Renaissance paintings had always struck him as being like stills from a film or a play. The idea of *The Creek, 1977* was for me to paint a still from a movie not yet made. It sounded awesome. I didn't know it then but I was about to get a taste of production Baz Luhrmann-style. 'Come to Sydney,' he said. 'We'll set up a photoshoot.'

The following week Baz picked me up from Sydney Airport and drove me straight to Fox Studios where he'd taken over a soundstage. I was amazed by the scale of his creation. He'd found a smashed-up Holden Kingswood that he'd had flipped onto its roof. There was scaffolding, ladders, lighting rigs, costume and make-up. Baz had hired half a dozen professional actors, including Claudia Karvan, to play the roles of the driver, the family and a cop at the scene of the accident. The central character – the driver – had been chosen by a casting director. It was para-cinematic and very exciting.

Ultimately Baz wasn't happy with the actor who'd been cast as the injured driver and convinced me to step in and play the part instead. When Baz finally had things set up to his liking we spent the next few hours enacting the scene of a driver being pulled out of a rural car crash by torchlight in the middle of the night. Baz had a cameo as his petrol station owner dad.

CHAPTER NINE

Over the next few months, as I brought the images we'd created to life on canvas, Baz built an installation in which to show it. Since it was a confluence of art and cinema we didn't want to simply stick it on a wall, so Baz designed a darkened space, about the size of a shipping container and evocative of a theatre, that slowly illuminated as people entered. He commissioned a musical score which played alongside sound effects from a car crash and rescue operation as the painting was gradually lit by candles and torchlight, revealing the characters and car wreck before fading to black again.

We received an invitation to show it at the Hong Kong Art Fair. Baz flew down to Melbourne on the eve of our departure for Hong Kong and we had a few drinks at his customary digs in the big villa in the sky before I called it an early-ish night around 11 pm.

Downstairs I climbed onto my motorbike (which I really shouldn't have done) and as I took off a taxi did a U-turn right in front of me. The impact sent me to the ground hard and I knew immediately I'd hurt myself properly. My left shoulder burned with pain and it didn't seem to work anymore. The taxi driver took off but a Crown staffer came to my aid and helped me get my bike off the road. I tried to call Baz but he didn't answer. I couldn't assess the damage to my shoulder because I still had my leather jacket on, but I had a feeling I might have dislocated it. Hotel reception buzzed Baz and I took the elevator straight back up to the villa.

'Ah, I've had an accident,' I said as he opened the door.

Baz took me inside, undid my jacket and yelled, 'Fuck!'

I'd snapped my collarbone and one half of it had speared gruesomely through my skin. Baz called an ambulance as I sat down and tried not to faint. The next thing I knew he had a camera in his hand and was filming, complete with front-line commentary. 'Okay, we're meant to go to the Hong Kong Art Fair tomorrow and Vincent's had a motorbike accident,' he narrated in his best TV reporter's voice. 'An ambulance is on its way because there's a broken bone sticking out of his shoulder. It looks to be a very nasty injury. How does it feel, Vincent?'

The ambulance arrived quickly and gave me the green whistle pain relief. Baz grabbed it and had a few hits, too, but he kept filming and commentating. The paramedics thought it was hilarious. I had surgery early the next morning to have the bone screwed back together and the wound sewn up. We postponed the trip for just twenty-four hours after Baz somehow convinced the surgeon to let me catch a flight to Hong Kong the following day.

Because Baz was a Qantas ambassador we were upgraded to first class – a milestone that should have been pretty special but that I have absolutely no recollection of today. I was fairly doped up on painkillers and the last thing I remember was slipping into complimentary first-class pyjamas and being handed a glass of wine. Ten hours later, as the plane descended into Hong Kong, I stirred from what I thought was a little nap.

'You alright?' Baz asked, grinning.

'Yeah, I'm good,' I said. I looked around my little first-class nook, which seemed to be in a bit of disarray. I noticed I had wine stains all over my nice new jammies, too.

'You were a fucking crazy person!' Baz said. 'You were throwing your wine around, making speeches, singing and toasting everyone.'

I'd been prescribed oxycodone, a powerful opioid that I'd never had before and have avoided like the plague ever since. (A word of advice: if you ever have to take it, don't drink alcohol under any circumstances.) I was still medicated to the eyeballs as we took part in multiple interviews, including live breakfast television. 'You did really well,' Baz remarked afterwards. 'Maybe you should medicate yourself more often.'

When we arrived at the art fair, Baz was dismayed to discover the carefully specified plans he had sent to organisers to build our installation had been ignored. He insisted they rebuild the entire thing before the opening night. It was a good lesson in artistic perfectionism. 'You've got to follow through your projects to the very end,' Baz explained. 'Don't ever think that what you're seeing and describing as a creative person is what someone else sees. You can be as specific as you like – "It's gotta be black walls and two feet by four feet and separated by two inches and blah blah blah" – and you get there and someone's had a better idea, only it's not.'

We received mixed reviews for *The Creek, 1977*: some critics thought it was kitsch and commercial while others raved about it. For me the most exciting thing was the huge line that snaked around the art fair because the installation could only accommodate a couple of people at a time. Seeing people queue up for art made the whole thing worthwhile.

We brought the installation back to Australia where it showed at Sydney's Sofitel Hotel, and a smaller painting I completed based on the concept went on to win the Metro Art Award. The icing on the cake, however, came a few months later when an art buyer from Singapore offered to purchase the original painting I'd created for the installation. I discussed it with Baz, since it was our collaboration. 'Do whatever you like with it,' he said, encouragingly. 'It's your painting.'

I sold it to the guy for six figures.

In the early days of my career, just as I began to exhibit paintings, a rich Australian art collector threw his support behind me and a few other young artists who were also on the way up. He was an older, married guy and maintained a position of influence in the art world. He knew we were pretty broke youngsters – me in particular – and he was generous with his money, time and attention. 'Come out to lunch!' he'd say, or, 'Let's go out to dinner!'

The collector would send a car and deliver me to fancy restaurants where we'd wine and dine as he talked excitedly about how much he loved my art, how he was going to introduce me to this person and that person, and how he was going to make me a star.

'You're very special, Vincent,' he said. 'You're going places.'

With that kind of backing I certainly felt special, and very lucky to have a man like him in my corner. It's a shame his interest was all about something else. I was a long-term project and I didn't even notice it was happening. As with a lot of the Me Too cases that were exposed years later in Hollywood, the art collector *did* help me professionally. There was ten grand for this painting over here, a nice commission for a portrait over there and introductions to powerful people all over the place. After I racked up some success and had a few career breakthroughs, his posture changed from, 'I love your art and I want to help you' to 'You can't do this without me. Look at what's just happened, and at what will be happening next. It's all because of me. You need me!'

The difference between me and a lot of the Me Too victims was that I didn't feel threatened by the man. Yes, I was manipulated, but I wasn't scared or physically intimidated, and he never got what he wanted. Psychologically, however, it was awful.

'If you want all this to continue, I need you to do things with me,' he told me out of the blue over dinner one night. 'Don't worry. Everyone does it.'

I was gutted. I hadn't realised until that moment he was a predator. It was a wicked mind game and I was even more appalled when he tried to weaponise my childhood disadvantage as a means of satisfying his sexual urges. 'Don't forget where you've come from and look at where you are now,'

CHAPTER TEN

he continued. 'I'm offering you all of this and more. All I need is for you to go along.'

I felt worthless as the sordid penny dropped. I didn't cause a scene, I just sat there thinking, *So for all these long months while you introduced me to people and told me how good my art is, all you wanted all along was to have sex with me?*

After a long pause I said, 'Okay, well, fuck you then.'

I never saw him again, but it wasn't my last experience with the Harvey Weinsteins of the art world, of which there are many. A few years later someone else tried to pull the same crap. She pressured me for sex for months on end, all the while controlling major decisions about the direction of my career. I dodged and danced around it, and rebuffed her over and over again until I could extract myself from any connection to her but I suffered some professional setbacks as a result.

The worst parasites have their hands on the levers of power that make the art world turn. Those two people tried to weaken me by convincing me I was entirely dependent on them if I wanted to succeed. It made me question my ability as an artist. If their appearance in my life was nothing more than a charade to get into my pants then I had to ask myself, *Are my paintings really any good? Is it me or my art that's interesting?*

When it came down to it, I doubted they cared about the creative output of the people they surrounded themselves with and traded on. Nowadays I wonder: if there wasn't any money in it for them, or the promise of sex or some other advantage, would they even bother looking at a piece of art?

I have no doubt my experiences are fairly common – there'd be a lot of artists who'd back me up, although predators manipulate different people in different ways depending on what they can get from them. It called to mind Heath's words to me at the pub in Perth: 'It's just a matter of time before they tell me what they *really* want from me . . .'

I was fairly young when these things happened and it took a long time before I felt like my paintings were truly good, and that I was an interesting and worthwhile person. Fortunately I was blessed to have a lot of beautiful people come into my life to help me realise that.

Like a lot of Australians, Michelle and I became swept up by the cresting wave of reality TV cooking shows that broke in the late noughties. I was enchanted by the recipes, ingredients, techniques and presentation while Michelle was more into the personalities and the drama of competition. I liked that side of it, too, but if you asked me to name a single celebrity chef I'd have drawn a blank. Michelle was fond of a show called *The Chopping Block* and, in particular, the famous Sydney restaurateur who helped struggling eateries turn their businesses around.

CHAPTER TEN

Early on the same night that I went home with Baz Luhrmann's watch, Michelle spotted *The Chopping Block* star, Matt Moran, in the crowd at the Ivy and marched straight up to him. 'Hi, Matt. My husband is a huge fan of yours!' she outright lied. 'He's an artist and he's just over there. He really wants to meet you.'

Suddenly Michelle appeared in front of me with a burly stranger. 'Darling, this is Matt,' she said. 'Matt's a very famous chef and he's on TV.'

'Hello, chap,' I said and stuck out my hand.

Matt shook it and we exchanged a few pleasantries and wisecracks before he mentioned that Michelle had told him I was an artist.

'So, what kind of artist are you?' he inquired.

'The most recent thing I did was a painting of Heath Ledger for the Archibald Prize,' I said.

'Oh my god! My wife loves you!' he said, beaming.

'I reckon that makes us even then,' I replied.

Before parting ways we swapped phone numbers and a bromance began. 'If you're in Melbourne hit me up and I'll show you around some places,' I promised.

Several months later Matt buzzed to let me know he was in town and proposed a night out. And, boy, did we have a night out! I found out chefs behave more or less like you'd expect rockstars to carry on.

I also discovered Matt was always the first to get up in the morning, long before everyone else. By the time you drag yourself out of bed he will have been to the gym, had breakfast and be ready to smash the day ahead. It wouldn't matter what he'd gotten up to the night before, because as soon as the sun rose he was unstoppable. Matt's boundless energy spoke to his hard-won, self-made success. He grew up on a dairy farm in Sydney's west and left school at fifteen to follow his dream of becoming a chef. He opened his first restaurant at just twenty-two and now runs a food empire that includes some of the country's best restaurants, farming interests and a high-profile media career.

We quickly became good mates. Whenever I was in Sydney I'd hang out with Matt and when he came to Melbourne he'd look me up and give me another night to remember. To see him ply his trade in the kitchen was inspiring, and he was good enough to take me with him when he appeared at the Melbourne Food and Wine Festival.

Matt has a disarming personality. He tends to own the room and is always telling a story. I can't put my finger on why it is, but people seem to feel like they can get right up in his face and give him a hug, slap him on the back or rub his bald head. He can be a beast, though, and often gives it straight back by putting someone in their place with a sharp quip. At his core he's a very lovable guy.

While he'll gladly lead me down the path of staying out all night, Matt would never take me down the wrong road in life. Time and time again I find I can rely on him. We make fun of each other

CHAPTER TEN

but if I ask him a serious question, he'll always give me a considered answer. That instantly made him a person of influence in my life.

Since my father left us hanging without any support, it's no mystery to me why I was attracted to strong male role models like Jack Rennie, Kim Ledger and Larry Kestelman. Because he's much closer to me in age I saw Matt more as a big brother figure. It was Matt who I called for advice when I found out I was going to be a father for the first time.

As much as Michelle and I loved one another, our relationship was under incredible pressure for reasons that will always remain private. In 2010 I looked for a way to shake off some of the issues we were facing as a young family and proposed a change of scenery. 'Why don't we go and live in New York for a while?' I suggested.

Michelle loved the idea and felt it would be a good opportunity to have some extended mum time with Luca, since she couldn't practise medicine in the US. I was determined to execute thirty portraits in thirty days in New York City just as Heath and I had first envisaged. Meanwhile Baz had taken up residence in Manhattan's famous Plaza Hotel to write the screenplay for *The Great Gatsby*. 'Come to America,' he said. 'I'll hook you up.'

We managed to jag a three-month lease on an amazing loft apartment that doubled as a studio in downtown Manhattan. When we settled in, one of the first people I looked up was Kane Manera, an actor who'd been childhood friends with Heath and who'd lived with him in New York for a time. Nowadays he's a highly successful Manhattan real estate agent but back then he was in between jobs. Baz had suggested I make a documentary of the Thirty Portraits project and Kane put his hand up to be both cameraman and my personal guide and fixer in the Big Apple.

On day one we took a drive through some of the grittier suburbs of midtown Manhattan where we spotted an extremely cool-looking little kid playing basketball on a neighbourhood court in Chelsea. His name was Ezekiel. He was five years old, wore sunglasses and had his afro hair pulled back into a mad ponytail. I chatted with his mum and learned that Ezekiel's dad was a gang member who was locked up in jail. She was a lovely woman and a loving mother, and she invited us to meet the rest of her family in a nearby high-rise housing estate. It was a humbling experience to get a first-hand glimpse of what a hard life in New York City looked like. Little Ezekiel was only too happy to pose for photographs and he became painting number one of thirty.

Over the next four weeks I rode an artistic rollercoaster that took me from the basketball courts of Chelsea all the way to the uptown catwalks of New York Fashion Week. I painted everyday citizens, including a park artist and a waitress, and also found a bunch of high-profile people like the legendary

CHAPTER TEN

heavyweight boxer Lennox Lewis, DJ and musician Mark Ronson and expatriate Australian model Jessica Hart.

The project was even more exhausting than it had been in Hong Kong because in New York I not only had Michelle and Luca with me but the likes of Kane and Baz inviting us to endless parties, openings and dinners. One night we met Mick Jagger and some of his kids and on another occasion Baz introduced us to the iconic *Vogue* editor Anna Wintour. We scored invites to Fashion Week and sat in the front row with Beyoncé and Pharrell Williams.

My day job, however, was a gruelling, non-stop exercise in concentration. I'd take fifty-odd photos of each subject and then paint into the night and again in the morning to complete each portrait. Sleep was at a premium and often I painted with little Luca cuddled up to my chest in a baby pouch. Whenever we went out at night we had a babysitter look after him before Michelle's mum flew over from Perth to help us manage. Somehow I was able to get every single portrait painted within twenty-four hours. One of them, however, looked like it might run off the rails before I even began.

I was overjoyed when Fern Mallis – the powerhouse American executive, Brooklyn native and founder of New York Fashion Week – agreed to be part of the project. She was hard to pin down but finally found time in her tight schedule to sit for a photoshoot. Kane and I passed through security and by a phalanx of sleek supermodels before being shown into Fern's luxurious office. This lady was all business.

'Okay, gentlemen, let's get started,' she said. 'What do you want me to do?'

It was a huge moment for me. This woman had almost single-handedly created New York Fashion Week and over the years had rubbed shoulders with some of the most famous photographers in the world. While I loved photography and considered myself fairly capable, I was no Mario Testino.

'Alright, Fern, where you're sitting now is just fine to start with,' I said. 'There's nice light coming through the window.'

Part of me died when I went to switch on my $10,000 Canon camera and realised the battery was flat. *Fuck!* It was another one of those crisis moments when a list of options instantaneously appeared in my mind for consideration:

1. Say, 'Oh, no! My battery is flat. Can we reschedule to a time when I have my shit together?'
2. Ask Fern if she had any batteries and could I please borrow them?
3. Shoot her using my iPhone.

Option three was the only way forward that wouldn't waste her time or cast me as an idiot. I raised the dead camera to my eye and started directing Fern like I would in any normal artistic shoot. I snapped away as if the memory card was

CHAPTER TEN

filling up with amazing images. I even pretended to change settings on the Canon and focused the lens manually. 'That's it, Fern. Great. Can you look up a little bit? Perfect. That's lovely!'

It remains the only photoshoot I have ever done where I didn't take a single photograph.

'Can I see some shots?' the queen of Fashion Week asked as I was winding up.

'Ah, no,' I said with a cheeky smile. 'No-one gets to see the shots – it'd spoil the surprise!'

When I finally finished the ridiculous charade I said, 'I'm just going to take a couple of reference shots on my phone and then we'll be done.'

I whipped out my iPhone and shot five more photos. 'Okay! We're finished, Fern,' I said. 'Thanks so much for your time. It's been a real honour.'

Although I'd hustled my way past what would have been a fairly embarrassing episode, I also realised that it's not necessarily the camera that helps support and inform my paintings – it's the moment: the time spent between me and the subject. When I went back to our apartment and painted Fern that night I took as much inspiration from what I learned about her personality that day as I did from the handful of pictures on my phone.

When I completed the thirtieth painting (of renowned music photographer Mick Rock), Baz and Kane used their connections to help me stage the exhibition at the historic National Arts Club in Gramercy Park. I'd already had some good publicity while the project was in full swing, including an appearance on American ABC News and I was written up in a couple of the New York newspapers, too. We got great press on the opening night at the National Arts Club and just about everyone I painted turned up, including my first and possibly favourite subject – little Ezekiel from Chelsea, who breakdanced his way across the dancefloor and into everyone's hearts.

Later on we moved the exhibition to where Baz was holed up at the Plaza Hotel and had another opening there. I got an insight into his creative process during our time in New York. The reason he'd ensconced himself at the Plaza to write his Gatsby screenplay was because the grand old building had featured in key passages in F. Scott Fitzgerald's book.

I spent many hours watching Baz work alongside his co-producer, music supervisor and good mate Anton Monsted. They'd set up a giant whiteboard that was covered in notes, diagrams and sketches. They sat around telling stories, improvising scenes, trading ideas, discussing casting, taking notes and updating the whiteboard as their vision took shape. They recorded everything they said and played it back later while Baz slowly sculpted a screenplay out of it all.

After two months immersed in New York's rich and vibrant artistic scene, things went tragically downhill in my marriage. Michelle and I had no option but to return to Australia early and abruptly.

CHAPTER TEN

The very last painting I did in New York was a confronting self-portrait. During our final week in the US I went into self-destruction mode. I had become distressed over having to abandon one of the biggest opportunities of my life to expand my career as I'd always dreamed. One night I drank way too much and face-planted into the footpath outside our apartment. I managed to drag myself inside where I photographed my torn and bloodied face before passing out. The resulting painting was, and always will be, a reminder to me of how powerful recognising the need for change can be.

I'd always planned to sell the thirty portraits as a collection but since I needed money to cover the cost of our American adventure I sold one of them – to Fern Mallis. Kane said he'd pack up the rest of the paintings at the Plaza with Baz's help and move them somewhere safe. He had connections with a fancy restaurant that was about to open in the Meatpacking District where he reckoned the collection would be secure until we could figure out how and where to sell it. Kane didn't know it but the guys he was dealing with were flat-out hustlers. The restaurant closed down shortly after opening and I haven't seen the paintings since. At least Fern has hers.

Back in Australia our fragile, bittersweet marriage came to an end. To cope with the sadness and the heartbreak of what divorce would mean for our beautiful little boy I decided to lose myself in work.

Baz was keen to cast Leonardo DiCaprio as Jay Gatsby but hadn't yet pitched the role to him. To help convince the actor to get onboard Baz had me do two paintings of Leo at the wheel of Gatsby's giant yellow sports car and send them to him. Baz hadn't decided on who should play Gatsby's love interest, Daisy Buchanan, so I painted Baz's wife Catherine Martin in the role, snuggled up next to Leo on the front seat in one of the paintings. I don't know how Baz did it but when I eventually saw the film two years later, one of the scenes was an exact match of the painting.

After back-to-back wins for the Archibald People's Choice Award I entered again in 2010 with a portrait of Baz. It was based on an image I'd taken of him at his house in Sydney at a time when he was under immense creative pressure.

A few days before I took the photo, Baz had sustained a cut to his forehead. The image I used to paint the Archibald entry showed the titan of Australian cinema at his most vulnerable with his face buried in his hands and a Band-Aid on his brow. I was fascinated by the image because although you couldn't see his face, it was unmistakably Baz. Should I dare enter a portrait prize where the subject's face was hidden?

We had a conversation about body language and how powerful the back of someone's head or their posture can be. It was another lesson learned on the job as opposed to university – that a portrait isn't about every wrinkle on a face; it's about telling a story and realising that sometimes less is more. Perhaps the Archibald judges didn't agree as they rejected the painting. I entered it in Australia's richest art prize instead – the Doug Moran National Portrait Prize. Not only was it accepted – it won.

Like a beaten dog I returned to the Art Gallery of New South Wales the following year with a portrait of Kimbra, the New Zealand singer who'd shot to global fame the previous year when she featured on Gotye's worldwide hit 'Somebody That I Used To Know'. When we discussed collaborating on an innovative portrait for the Archibald Prize, Kimbra played me a song called 'The Build Up' that she wrote when she was sixteen. We hit on the idea of making a film clip of the song especially for the Archibald entry.

I shot a video of Kimbra singing it in one take in a Melbourne hotel room. The clip began with my painting of her in the same room which merged with film of her performance that melted back into the portrait at the end of the song. My ever-creative friend Michael Gracey set up a barcode at the bottom of the painting that, when scanned with a smartphone, played the film clip! Pretty nifty, and definitely new ground when it came to realistic portraiture. The painting was a finalist, but it didn't win.

Although I'd been knocking on the door of the Archibald Prize since 2005, I'd always wanted to show in my home state at the National Gallery of Victoria but hadn't been offered the opportunity. That finally changed in 2012 when my friend, entrepreneur and global philanthropist Laura Anderson, proposed that the NGV host my next instalment of Thirty Portraits in Thirty Days that I planned to paint in Melbourne.

Rather than take the broadbrush demographic approach I had in Hong Kong and New York, I wanted to focus on successful, inspirational Australians this time around, and explore what made them tick. Since I was raising Luca predominantly on my own at the time, I had to juggle paintbrushes with the brightly-coloured accoutrements of single parenthood – building blocks, spinning tops, swings at the park, his tiny shoes, Dora the Explorer, plastic dinner plates, little spoons, bubble baths and ten thousand cuddles a day.

To get the ball rolling with the exhibition I tapped a few mates, including Baz and Matt, who steered me towards other subjects that fanned out into a storied line-up that included former Prime Minister Bob Hawke, world champion surfer Layne Beachley, chef George Calombaris, actress Elizabeth Debicki, Olympic swimmer Geoff Huegill, actors Joel and Nash Edgerton and AFL great Ron Barassi.

Matt suggested Asher Keddie. 'She's fantastic,' he said. 'Talented, beautiful, charismatic, hugely successful.'

'Okay. Who is she exactly?' I asked.

'She's an actor, mate!' Matt replied impatiently. 'For fuck's sake, have you never heard of *Offspring*?'

I had not, and was no doubt among the few. That night my brother Michael, whom I'd hired as an assistant for the project, googled all things Asher Keddie for me. I remember thinking, *Wow*.

Matt offered to put me in touch and before long, Asher's agent, Lee-Anne Higgins, let me know she had agreed to take part. I had no way of knowing it, but Asher's marriage had recently ended, too. She worked up to fourteen hours a day starring as obstetrician Nina Proudman on the immensely popular series *Offspring*, and when she wasn't filming she could be found among the horses at a farm she rented in rural Kyneton, an hour and a half outside Melbourne. I was delighted when she agreed to be involved in the Thirty Portraits project but I certainly wasn't planning on falling in love.

Asher's was portrait number twenty-six in the series. After nearly a month working day and night while also caring for Luca, I was pretty tired and run-down. I had trouble finding a babysitter on the day, I was disorganised, the studio looked like a bombsite and I was desperately trying to finish the painting from the night before. As the clock wound down to our appointment I became stressed and anxious that I wouldn't be ready when Asher arrived.

Minutes before she was due at the door I called her agent.

'Hi, Lee-Anne, I hate to ask but would Asher mind coming an hour later today?'

Not the greatest move. Asher had already driven for more than an hour from Kyneton (at my request!) only for me to hold up a virtual hand and tell her to drive around the block until I was ready to receive her. When Lee-Anne delivered the news, Asher was having none of it. 'I'm not waiting around for this guy! Who does he think he is? I'm turning around and going home.'

I found out later that Lee-Anne uncharacteristically tried to persuade Asher to wait and meet me. Meanwhile I continued to madly clean up the studio and at the exact moment I wheeled my garbage bins out, Asher – who was already parked outside – hung up the phone to Lee-Anne and got out of her car. We exchanged a look and I felt something I never had before in a moment like that. We walked towards one another and in those long seconds as we sized each other up, a silent connection was made.

Obviously I wasn't about to spill what was going on in my life: 'Oh, I'm sorry I'm running late, I just got separated from my wife, I'm trying to get my two-year-old son into daycare so I can do this portrait project, and this is happening, and that's happening and by the way, I don't know what the fuck I'm doing because I'm dyslexic.'

Dyslexia's close cousin, imposter syndrome, insisted that I keep all that stuff wrapped up and tucked away out of sight. I was forever worried people might see through the cracks so I kept things cool and professional with Asher as I showed her into my only slightly less shambolic workspace. As soon as I went to take some pictures I ran into another problem. After one photo the memory card was full. *Fuck!*

'Just bear with me for a sec while I get these settings right,' I said, and fiddled with the buttons on the back of the Canon. *Bam* – there it was, the first lie of the relationship. I wasn't 'getting the settings right' at all; I was deleting the last two days' worth of photos as fast as I could without letting on.

To most people it might not seem like a big deal to admit to a hiccup like that. One could reasonably say, 'Bear with me, I forgot to set up the camera.' Or, 'The memory card is full and I've got to delete some photos before we start.' Or, 'I'm running an hour late because I'm disorganised.' After all, those are normal things that normal people do, but with me it was chronic. I did stuff like that so often, day in and day out, that quickly papering over the apparent ineptitude with lies and cover stories had become instinctive.

With the memory card cleared I could finally concentrate on the subject of my next portrait. Matt was right – Asher is very beautiful, but that wasn't where the chemistry lay. I had photographed, drawn and painted attractive people my entire life

CHAPTER ELEVEN

and never before felt the way I did that day with Asher. I might not have known much about her, but suddenly I was in a big hurry to find out. I could tell she felt the same way.

I was a bit sorry for my brother Michael. He didn't know what to say or where to look as Asher and I flirted with one another. At one point I sat alongside her when the playfulness inched into the physical realm. Asher says I touched her leg but I'm quite certain it was she who touched mine. At any rate some footsy-ing took place. It was the strangest, loveliest feeling: after less than an hour together it felt like we were in a relationship.

Sometimes I describe my dyslexia as being a bit like autism or Asperger's, in the sense I'll do things that other people might not normally do – such as accidentally cross the line and hug someone for a little bit too long – but somehow it works. The shoot was meant to last one hour but Asher stayed for several more. I unintentionally crossed the line when I farewelled her with a close, lingering hug.

'This is a bit full-on,' she said, but then a funny thing happened. Instead of pulling away, Asher gently hugged me right back. At that moment my cheeky little brother snapped a photograph of us together. That picture is worth every one of the thousand words I could say about the way we both felt.

'Is it okay if I give you a call when I've finished the painting?' I asked as Asher was leaving. She nodded and smiled that famous smile. While she headed back up the freeway to her horses, I painted like a madman to finish as soon as possible so I could speak to her again. Four hours later I texted Asher a photo of the completed portrait. From then on we saw each other every day and five months later we were living together.

Asher came into my life with her eyes wide open. We both knew we weren't having a fling or a bit of fun. She understood that I was a single father and that my life was complicated. Hers was, too, not to mention exhausting and subject to the glare of media interest. As challenging as it must have been to suddenly find herself in the role of a step-parent, Asher fell head over heels in love with Luca, too. Right from the start we weren't just a couple – we were a triple. A family.

I could not quite believe that Asher loved me in spite of all the shit I had going on in my world. We came from such different places in life yet we connected deeply over the fundamentals. I took indescribable pleasure from doing the simplest things with Asher: cooking, watching movies, drinking wine and traipsing around her farm with wide-eyed Luca swinging between us. Everything fitted together. I never wanted to change anything about my life – especially because I had my treasured little boy – but I often looked at Asher and thought, *Why didn't we meet each other ten years ago?*

Still, at the back of my mind I knew Asher didn't realise just what she'd got herself into by falling in love with me – because I didn't tell her. When she entered my life I defaulted to my old ways and, if not hid it from her, I certainly downplayed the impact dyslexia had on me and would therefore have on her. It wasn't rational or fair, but I was terrified it might ruin the beautiful new thing I had found. At the beginning of the relationship I tried extra hard to ensure my text messages made sense. I'd spend ten minutes trying to proofread a simple message like 'Would you like me to pick up something for dinner?'

The messages inevitably arrived in Asher's inbox full of jumbled words and misspellings so I brushed that aside like it was no big deal. 'This won't affect our lives or anything,' I said, 'but you might notice I sometimes make spelling mistakes, or my messages don't make grammatical sense. Don't worry, I'm just a little dyslexic.'

That was the second lie of the relationship. Of course my dyslexia was going to affect our lives! Spelling and grammar wasn't the issue, though. Nobody cares about that. By omission I had lied about all the other stuff that Asher was going to have to cope with. It was very unfair and she gradually found out the hard way.

Right from the outset I wondered how long it would take before she started to notice I was not your average bear. She would have picked up on the fact that I was either absent-minded or worse, uninterested. We'd make plans to meet somewhere and I wouldn't turn up because I'd clean forget to.

Or I'd come home empty-handed when I was supposed to grab the groceries or dinner. She must have wondered, *What is this guy trying to do?*

The scale of my dyslexia wasn't the only secret I tried hard to protect. There were some deeper, darker issues at play – big ones that I hid from myself as much as anyone else. When, for instance, would Asher start asking some hard questions about why I had difficulty sleeping? Or why I jolted awake with nightmares every night? Or why I leapt out of bed and reached for a baseball bat at two in the morning? Would she ever figure out that I'd been abused?

Asher's world blew my mind. When Luca and I paid her a visit on the set of *Offspring* in Fitzroy the penny dropped on what a huge deal she was. *Oh my god, this is what she does!* I marvelled as I watched an entire television production in frantic orbit around her star. Asher had won the Logie Award for Most Popular Actress the previous year and was nominated again in 2012, not long before we became a couple (she ended up winning it six years in a row). That level of success and fame comes with a few hitches – not least the attention of the paparazzi.

A month or so after we became an item I was nominated for the GQ Artist of the Year award and Asher came with me to the event – our first public outing. As soon as we set foot on the red carpet a young TV presenter named James Tobin bounded up to us with a huge smile on his face and brimming with positive energy. 'Congratulations!' he beamed as he thrust a microphone at us. 'You guys look so happy!' We were, and it was impossible not to like James who made breaking the news a pleasant experience. He remains a good mate to this day.

The next morning we were all over the papers, with the Sydney *Daily Telegraph* reporting that, 'Keddie spoke for the first time about the blossoming relationship, revealing it was celebrity chef Matt Moran who orchestrated their first meeting and that Fantauzzo knew nothing of her TV background.' Then the floodgates opened. We couldn't go out the front door without some paparazzo hiding in a hedge to photograph us in our pyjamas. They followed us to the park, to the shops, the airport and even onto planes. Although she's the ultimate professional and is always polite, warm and charming in public, I know Asher found the constant scrutiny and lack of privacy hard to deal with. I wasn't a big fan of it, either.

Meanwhile I put my head down and painted. Thirty Portraits in Thirty Days was well received at the NGV and I sold the entire series to a major collector. In 2013 I took my annual run at the Archibald with another portrait I painted of Asher. I called it *Love Face* and it won the People's Choice Award, my third. For a guy who always thought everything was about to end, it was a nice feeling to think my work still had popular appeal, even if some in the art establishment seemed to take a perverse pleasure in tearing it down.

Writing in a major newspaper, a noted art critic described the painting of Asher as 'an elaborate oil rendition of a photograph that trivialises the art of painting and that of photography'. Ouch! He didn't stop there, though. He took a critical flamethrower to most of my work by describing the photorealistic style of painting as being to art 'what lip-syncing is to singing'. The same guy sneered that my repeated popular success at the Archibald was due to the fact I painted celebrities and, therefore, my work was superficial and meaningless.

I'm no prima donna and, coming from where I do, I can handle body shots and a bloodied nose. While I understood the role of art criticism, I didn't quite get the casual cruelty it can involve. It was as if that guy went to the Archibald every year relishing another chance to rubbish my work, not giving thought to the blood, sweat and tears I put into it. I don't know if it ever occurred to him that his flippant opinion crushed my moment, or that his serrated words might damage my career and livelihood. I'd have loved an explanation about why he was so vicious, but I knew I'd never get one.

I did, however, reflect on what he had to say about some of my celebrity subjects, bearing in mind a huge percentage of Archibald entries depict famous people. It occurred to me that the notable personalities I painted were often my friends. The reason I liked to paint them was because I found them magnetic and inspiring. They were famous in the first place because they were intriguing, and successful at what they did – something I had been fascinated by my entire life. I was lucky enough not only to get to know them but also collaborate from a perspective that most people don't get to see, be it vulnerable or dark, but almost always without the usual celebrity filter.

When I told Baz how hurt I was by the criticism he scoffed and chuckled. 'You think *you've* copped it from critics?' he said. 'All I can say is get used to it 'cos it happens for the rest of your life. Think about this, though, Vinnie: Picasso was bagged by art critics. Can you tell me the names of any of the people who criticised Picasso's work?'

I shook my head.

'Just stay focused on creating art that you believe in and you'll find your audience,' he said.

Good advice, Baz. The following year I entered a portrait that I painted purely out of a desire to. It happened to be of a non-celebrity, in the form of beautiful Luca. The portrait, which I called *All That's Good In Me*, won the People's Choice Award at the 2014 Archibald Prize.

Being with Asher made me understand the utterly unrealistic and unreasonable visions and expectations that critics, commentators and members of the public have of people whose work puts them in the public eye. For better or for worse and not by choice, we were a 'celebrity couple'. Asher, in particular, was under constant pressure to smile, be obliging, available to the media and generous with her time. And she was – for the most part. There seemed to be a weird equation in the media, though: 'You get to have a perfect life so don't you ever dare complain.'

A perfect life?

One day Asher had to go into the city for a radio interview. As she was leaving the appointment she passed by the glass panels of a studio where another FM radio duo were hosting their show live on air. The female host looked up to see Asher with her head down, lost in her own little world. 'What is wrong with Asher Keddie?' she wondered aloud to several hundred thousand listeners. 'What on earth could be wrong with that woman who has everything? She's the golden girl of Australian TV. She has a loving partner and the perfect life. Why did she just walk past here looking so sour?'

Probably because no-one's life is perfect. We all weather the same storms. When Asher found out later what had gone to air she was shocked, hurt and bemused that one woman would say that of another. The fact is we'd been trying to get pregnant from early on in our relationship. Having a child had never been an obsession for Asher, until she joined Luca and me. After that all she wanted – all we wanted – was another child to complete the circle, bring us even closer together and give Luca a sibling with whom to share the adventure of childhood. We tried but could not get pregnant.

Two weeks before the radio incident Asher and I sat in an IVF clinic having already endured half a dozen cycles, wanting to know what other treatments or medications we could try in order to throw everything at the next one. That's when our fertility specialist said, 'You're now thirty-nine and perimenopausal. The chances now of getting pregnant are low.'

Asher is a truly great actor. I knew how crushed she was as I watched her absorb the news but she held her composure and kept her emotions from spilling out in the unfamiliar drabness of the doctor's office. I'm not so good at acting and I wept for my beautiful, heartbroken girl. She'd had a marriage that didn't work out and had thrown herself into her career. It wasn't until we met that she desperately wanted to have a child, only to be told it might not happen.

When we got into the car downstairs Asher turned to face me and, with tears in her eyes, said, 'Will you still love me?'

We got married standing on the top of a hill in a thunderstorm.

Both of us had been the focus of big weddings before. Mine was like a great explosion of sparkles that quickly faded. A lot of the guests were no longer in my life and I don't think Asher spent much time looking through her first wedding album, either. We'd been there and done that, so whenever we talked about how and where to tie the knot we developed a mutual stress headache.

Should we get married in Perth, where Asher's family lived? Should we do it in Melbourne? Do we invite our pals from overseas or just do it on the down-low with our families and closest friends? If we sent out formal wedding invitations would the printer leak it to the press and would they then turn up and ruin it?

After a lot of rubbing of temples we decided not to send out any invites at all. In the autumn of 2014

CHAPTER TWELVE

we told our mums we were going to elope and not to tell a soul. We flew to Fiji with our best boy Luca and checked into Turtle Island as a wedding party of three. Aside from booking a villa and making sure there was a marriage celebrant on the island, we did next to no planning. We figured we'd check out the island and choose a nice spot on the beach or in the hills to exchange our vows. Maybe we'd hire a couple of locals to sing some songs? We didn't even realise that we needed two witnesses.

Several nights before our big day Asher and I got talking to a lovely couple during a kava evening at the resort. Brent happened to be the drummer with the American rock band the Dandy Warhols and he'd settled in Melbourne with his beautiful Australian wife, Sarah.

'Well, we've run away to get married,' Asher revealed.

A toast and congratulations all round.

Brent had a fancy camera hanging off his shoulder, so I asked him if he'd be up for taking a few snaps during the ceremony. On 9 April Asher and I held hands and faced each other at the crest of a verdant hill on Turtle Island with just Luca, Brent, a celebrant and a large group of Fijians singing their hearts out for us. As Asher and I promised ourselves to one another, towering cumulonimbus columns dragged themselves towards us across a ruffled Pacific Ocean. There was barely enough time to say 'I do'. As we put rings on each other's fingers the heavens split open and we were all instantly drenched. The Fijians assured us it was a blessing.

We piled into two open buggies and beat a hasty retreat down the hillside that had magically transformed into a waterfall. We were in fits of laughter as we slipped and slid all over the jungle track, and by the time we reached the resort to sign the papers and make it official we were covered in mud and soaked to the bone. As an added silver lining to the stormy day, Sarah and Brent became our friends for life.

When we returned home we decided to keep our nuptials under wraps until we'd had a chance to catch up with friends and family to share the news in person. The Logie Awards fell in the same week that we landed back in Melbourne and the day before the big night, news of our secret wedding broke. Our loved ones and friends were understandably upset that we'd kept them in the dark.

Over the years I'd learned just how low some people in the media stoop to get pictures. I have friends who've had their emails covertly raided while others have had their Instagram accounts hacked and their private images stolen. It's far better to just give the media some pictures and ask them to please leave it at that. I wish we'd done that because it would have saved the news breaking on the media's terms and our loved ones from feeling hurt, even though they all forgave us. The most important thing to me was that Asher and I were

CHAPTER TWELVE

relaxed and totally present (albeit filthy dirty) on our wedding day. The memories have never faded. I highly recommend eloping.

We were always happiest when far from the fray on the property at Kyneton. Not long before we tied the knot, a 110-acre property came up for sale in an achingly pretty place called the Hesket Valley at the base of Mount Macedon, right next to Hanging Rock. We bought it and moved in as soon as we returned from Fiji. The place was an old barn that had a living space above some stables where Asher kept her horse-riding gear and I stored my motorbikes and set up my trusty floor-to-ceiling ball.

Boxing remained a big part of my life, even though I'd hung up my competitive gloves following a couple of comeback fights in the twelve months before I met Asher. After Jack Rennie retired I started training at Joe Cursio's Fight Fit gym in South Melbourne. I was in it purely for the joy but Joe, a feisty warrior who was a few years older than me, encouraged me to get back in the ring and fight as a super middleweight years after I'd retired to concentrate on art. Ever since then he's been steadfastly in my corner, both as a trainer and trusted friend. He was the first one to pull me into a bear hug after my victorious final bout in front of family and supporters at the Melbourne Pavilion in 2012, and in many ways we still haven't let each other go.

I kept training with Joe after we moved to the country but whenever I felt the need on the farm

I could always pop down into the barn for a bit of floor-to-ceiling therapy. Having grown up in a series of cement boxes, I loved the idea of raising Luca in the fresh air of the great outdoors. The only downside was the fifty-minute drive into Melbourne for work each day. Luca remained enrolled in his city school, too, and spent time in Melbourne with his mum. It all added up to extra miles in the car each week, but country life was worth it for all of us. We lost ourselves among the horses, the native birds and the towering eucalypts. Luca and I went on adventures on the quad bike to see if we could spot kangaroos and possums, and the three of us planted trees and pottered in the veggie garden together for hours. It was a perfect place and a perfect time in my life.

Asher was as busy and popular as ever. She'd won Australian television's biggest prize, the Gold Logie, the previous year for her work on *Offspring*. The Logies is a huge live television event in its own right and that night Asher was front and centre. I had to do a double take when the organisers showed us to our room – the opulent Chairman's Villa at Crown Melbourne. Clearly Baz wasn't in town.

Knowing what Asher was going through behind the scenes, I watched with a mixture of pride, awe and sadness as she smiled and charmed her way through the event under the glare of lights and cameras at Crown Palladium. No-one knew that she'd just had major abdominal surgery. No-one knew that during an ad break she had to scurry up to our room and inject hormones directly into her stomach before returning to the ballroom to be everybody's golden girl. Just living that perfect life again.

Anyone who's been through it knows that the stress and invasion of IVF is off the charts: 'Try this, inject that, do this now, do that tomorrow and inject yourself with these hormones at 8 pm next Thursday.' Although we'd been told our chances of conceiving were low, Asher never gave up.

In May 2014 I was in France doing some brand ambassador promotions for the car company Audi when I received a call to say Asher had been taken to hospital after collapsing at work. Producer Imogen Banks and Asher's close friend Wizzy Molineaux never left her side for the twenty-four hours it took me to get home. Scans showed Asher's brain was severely swollen, but the neurologists couldn't figure out what was causing it.

A team of specialists carried out a barrage of tests. Finally a rheumatologist diagnosed her with systemic lupus erythematosus, an auto-immune disease that – when it flares – causes severe inflammation and the body to reject its own tissue. It sounded like the latest shattering blow until it was explained to us that lupus was possibly a contributing factor to the trouble we were having getting pregnant. Asher was put on medication to treat it and our doctors took the diagnosis into account going forward.

Mercifully, Asher fell pregnant in June 2014. Although it was considered a high-risk pregnancy due to the complication of lupus, she loved every single minute. For the first time in ten years she stopped working and blissfully spent her days on our farm, planting veggies, caring for her horses, cooking whatever she craved and nurturing all of us. It was a beautiful, simple time and Luca and I loved doting on her as much as we did driving around for hours on wacky missions to find the right pistachio gelato. It was a joy to see the wonder in Luca's eyes when he watched the baby moving in Asher's belly and to see my best friend and lover so completely contented.

On a lazy Sunday morning the following March the three of us were wandering around the farm when I noticed something about Asher wasn't quite right. She'd had a strong headache for a couple of days and told me she was just feeling heavy and very hot. I couldn't quite put my finger on it but I started to worry.

'I feel alright,' she said, although she suddenly looked concerned because I did.

We were used to closely monitoring her and the baby through the pregnancy owing to the added risk that lupus brings. We quickly checked the heartbeat and made sure the baby was moving. Everything looked normal but something just seemed a little off to me. To be on the safe side I called our obstetrician who told me to bring Asher to the hospital. We all jumped into the car with our dog and drove to

CHAPTER TWELVE

the hospital so Asher could get a bit of a once-over and make sure all was well. The obstetrician took her pulse and blood pressure, and was concerned that her lupus had started to flare. After monitoring the baby via ultrasound he said, 'I think it's best we go into surgery for an emergency caesarean right now.'

'Now?' Asher gasped.

'We're not packed or anything,' I said, as I defaulted to problem-solving on the fly. 'Our dog is in the car downstairs. Have I got time to drop him off somewhere?'

'Nope. The baby's perfectly fine, he's ready. You're going in right now,' he said.

Valentino Fantauzzo came into the world a little prematurely. Maybe he decided his mum had been through so much and waited long enough to meet him. Val was a tough guy from the start. He responded beautifully to all the measures that are put in place for premmie babies and took to feeding almost immediately. After a week in hospital it was time to take him home.

On the day we left we were nervous that the dreaded paparazzi would somehow find out. The birth of a child is an intensely private matter, and we felt strongly that it was nobody's business but ours. As soon as we entered the underground car park, however, we noticed a suspicious-looking van. A paparazzo photographed us and the images soon appeared in a magazine alongside a story that described Val's arrival in detail. They knew the sex of our baby, when he was born and even his weight. It was obvious that someone at the hospital had leaked it to the press.

Given the epic journey we'd been on to finally meet Val we had an overwhelming sense of gratitude. When Luca was born I knew I'd never be alone in the world. Now that Valentino had joined us, I breathed an even bigger sigh of relief that he and Luca would always have each other, no matter what life threw at them. Fatherhood had already made me hyper-aware of the emotional short circuits that fried much of my childhood. I was anxious that our boys wrap themselves in brotherhood, that they understood the importance of always being there for each other and that a problem shared is a problem halved.

As soon as Val could walk, Luca kicked a ball to him and they've been playing soccer together ever since. They derive such pleasure from each other, be it in sport, cooking up a storm (and a mess) in the kitchen or just making one another laugh. They're tactile, too. They share hugs and they never go to bed without saying goodnight to each other. I encourage them to talk about their days – to discuss their footy matches, their mates and what's happening at school. I try to make sure they look out for each other emotionally, too. I'm proud of the big brother Luca has become.

Sadly, fatherhood was also a reminder of my own paternal disaster zone. Dad only met Luca a couple of times. He turned up at the hospital on the day

CHAPTER TWELVE

he was born with a big, brown teddy bear and left about an hour later, never to return. He didn't bother to come and meet Val. We still have the innocent-looking teddy bear at home – the only thing he ever gave to either of our boys. In a way it means more to me than it does to them. It's one of the few things in this world I can touch that connects me to my father.

Since my family life and career had filled up with goodness, the fractures in my formative years didn't trip me up quite as much as they used to, but I never stopped chasing a relationship with Dad. He still lived in Horsham but he might as well have been on Mars. Every year I sent him a message on his birthday:

'Happy birthday, Dad! The kids would love to see you. We all would. Let me know if you want to come down and stay. Love you.'

He'd reply with two or three words: 'Sure. Thanks, son.'

Same again the next year: 'Happy birthday, Dad!'
'Thanks.'

Hmm. We'd devolved to a one-word reply.

'We'd love to have you come and see the kids. Luca's growing up. Geez, he looks a bit like you, Dad!' (Anything to try and pull him back from Mars.)

'Hey Dad, we've bought a farm! We always wanted a farm, didn't we? Why don't you come and stay with us?'

'Dad, look at the motorbike I just bought. It's like the one you used to have.'

'Hey Dad, remember you used to like Alfa Romeos? I'm a brand ambassador for them now. They gave me one to drive. We should take it for a spin.'

It was all one-way traffic, though, and it ran straight off a cliff.

One day he actually made the trip down to Melbourne to visit one of my sisters. When I got wind of it I drove around there to show him my Alfa Romeo and take him out for that drive. He didn't say a word. While his disdain and lack of interest wounded me, some of his other behaviour just pissed me off. I once bought a racing go-kart and when I moved apartments I didn't have a place to store it, so I asked Dad if I could keep it in his garage for a while.

'Yeah, sure.'

When I went to collect it six months later, he'd sold it.

The only time I got more than a handful of words out of the man was when he wanted to borrow some money: 'I was thinking I might come down and see you guys but my car rego has run out,' he'd text. 'Could you lend me $500?'

It was always a car problem, or a medical emergency. 'I've gotta go and see a specialist about this problem I'm having but I can't afford to pay for it at the moment. Can you lend me $750?'

I always loaned him the money of course, but I never got it back. And I never did get that visit.

CHAPTER TWELVE

At one point during my teenage years Dad lived with a woman who had a grandchild and, bizarrely, he was a doting grandfather figure to the baby. I visited them once and was amazed to see him babysitting. He *goo-gooed* and *gaa-gaaed*, fed the infant bottles and even changed some nappies. At the time I wondered, *Who on earth are you?* When I had children of my own – his own grandsons – I wondered, *Where on earth are you?* He had the capacity to bond with little children, I'd seen it with my own eyes, but he chose to ignore mine.

I stopped chasing after him so much after that.

We always tried to remain philosophical about the public aspect of our lives, and the media interest in Asher's in particular. It was just one of those things about her level of fame at the time. Besides, if being in her world came with some intrusion, it was nothing like the mayhem that came with her being in mine.

Most people think dyslexia describes those who find it hard to read because they see letters backwards. I don't see letters backwards and I *can* skim read, but my version of reading is different to yours. I see pictures instead of letters. Consequently the alphabet is of little use to me. In fact, I don't even know which letter comes after the last unless I sing the song. The linguistic difficulties don't end there. Even though I can get the gist of a sentence by scanning the pictures that the various letters throw up at me, if I try to read it aloud there's no way I can absorb the information.

CHAPTER THIRTEEN

Whatever tangles and knots exist in my cerebral wiring cause a lot of problems that affect me personally. Other aspects of my neurodiversity, however, can have an impact on others, particularly those nearest and dearest to me. A lot of issues flow from how my brain processes and retains information. My memory acts more like a vent than a storage facility, especially in the short term. It's a place where information goes to die or disappear like smoke in the wind. If I'm lucky it will return on a random gust hours or days later, but by then it's usually too late to be of any use.

In the early stages of our relationship, Asher would have seen this in my tendency to be late, to not arrive at all, or forget to pick up the pizza on the way home. My memory problems run so much deeper than that, but I did my best to keep them hidden from her for years.

Asher values honesty and loyalty as highly as anyone I know, whereas I spent much of my life hiding, lying and keeping secrets. Early on she knew I was holding something back from her and would often say, 'Just tell me what it is.'

Even worse, Asher sometimes felt that there was something wrong with her because of her seeming inability to understand me. Over the years – through attrition and my own growing fatigue from fibbing and concocting cover stories to mask dyslexia – Asher developed a full understanding of me. That's not to say my dyslexia can't still surprise her, or make day-to-day life any less frustrating, but she gets it and she still loves me, which was something I was afraid of losing.

Domestic foibles are one thing, but the sinkholes in my memory have deeper reaching consequences and knock-on effects. For example, I've forgotten to pay rego on the car and then been fined for unregistered driving. I've forgotten to pay at restaurants and bars all around the world. Just recently I had an expensive lunch with some mates and it wasn't until I was in the car on my way home that the information arrived in my memory on a zephyr from the void. *Fuck! Who paid?*

Well, fortunately one of my mates did after I just walked out with the meal magically covered. I thanked him later, of course. It's not so bad when it happens with close friends because they know I can't help it and they find it amusing. Not every lunch or dinner is with such understanding people, however, and I must seem like such a snake and a cheapskate in those situations when I'm the opposite. It reminds me of how I felt at school. People thought I didn't care about paying into the social contract of education. I badly wanted to learn but I just couldn't. I couldn't even remember my teachers' names. How rude that must have seemed.

It's not uncommon to be bad with names: you hear a lot of people admit to that, but not many experience it the way I do. I have a nickname for Asher's mum and I call her dad Gramps. I've known

CHAPTER THIRTEEN

my sisters' children from the day they were born and I love them, but I can't remember whose name belongs to whom. My sisters have no idea. Whenever I see them I just sing out, 'Hey! The girls!' or, 'How's the little one going today?' or, 'Hello, cheeky!' if I'm talking to the eldest. I constantly have to bluff it.

Deep down in some back alley of my mind I do know their names because they're important to me. It's just that whatever cables and synapses are plugged in back-to-front or upside down prevent the information from coming to the surface when I need it. Oddly, I somehow remember all of the lyrics to 'Ice Ice Baby'. How does that work? Some might think, *If you can remember that, why can't you remember the alphabet? Or three times six?*

I know. It's a mystery to me, too.

As a boy I was desperate to learn my times tables, if nothing more just for the achievement. I plastered them all over the house. Sometimes I'd manage to remember them for a week and then the data would simply disappear from the primary drive. It's the same with names. Whenever we have a get-together with Asher's friends or family I have to get her to brief me: 'Just remind me who we're seeing tonight.' Even though she understands why, I can tell that a small part of her cannot fathom the fact I sometimes struggle with the names of people so close to me.

There's no cure for this random amnesia. I've been encouraged to buy a beeper that would help me locate my perpetually lost sets of keys, but then I'd lose the beeper and be doubly screwed. If I got a diary I'd lose it. Technology and smartphones have been a bit of a help with alerts and reminders but I forget to set them in the first place. If I lose my phone the alarm is useless anyway. I've lost more than a dozen phones.

I became intrigued by the movie *Memento*, in which Guy Pearce stars as a man who has to tattoo clues about his life all over his body in order to unravel a mystery because he loses his memory at the end of each day. I became friends with Guy through Asher some years ago. I told him about my struggles with memory and we discussed the practicalities of the *Memento* method. I decided it wouldn't work for me because I'd forget my appointment with the tattoo artist.

Guy also features in a story that shows the different consequences dyslexia can have on something as simple as a social visit. Guy's not only a brilliant actor but a talented singer and guitarist who loves music. He'd written a whole album that he was so proud of but very self-conscious about, too. He asked me if I wanted to come over to his place and be one of the first people to hear it.

'You bet!'

I had a stuffy nose so before I set off for Guy's place I took a couple of cold and flu tablets, not realising that I downed the night-time pills by mistake. We sat in Guy's cosy home studio, had a glass of wine and when he pulled out his guitar to play the first song I went straight to sleep. I had never done that before in my life. It was beyond embarrassing: Guy had invited me into his home and was brave and vulnerable enough to play his music for me, and I responded by snoring and drooling on a cushion. He had to nudge me awake.

'Vincent. Vincent. Vinnie! Do you want me to call you an Uber?'

'Umm, yeah. Maybe,' I mumbled.

The poor fellow. I'd hate to think what was going through his mind as I lurched out the door. I didn't know that I'd taken the cold and flu medication that zonk you out so I couldn't explain myself. I only found out later when I had a closer look at the packet. Because I read in pictures, I can only get a certain amount of information onboard, which is usually enough to assess what's printed, but I can't read it word for word.

As a result my supermarket mix-ups are a dime a dozen. If I go out to buy tinned tomatoes I'll come home with red kidney beans because the shapes of the items are similar and the combination with the pictures I see in the letters on the can will confuse me. I grab coriander instead of parsley every time. It drives Asher nuts. My impromptu near-sleepover at Guy Pearce's place wasn't the only time dyslexia tripped me up with medicine. When a pill on a packet looks like the one I had last time, I just go by the size and shape of the tablet.

This backfired badly at a parent–teacher interview at Luca's school a few years ago. I had a headache so I fished around in the medicine cabinet and popped a couple of Panadol that turned out to be the dreaded oxycodone. I'd had knee surgery a few months prior and the hospital had sent me home with the heavy-duty opioid painkillers. I don't like taking the stuff. It's good for the first twenty-four hours but after that I don't want anything to do with it.

So the oxy wound up with all the other medicine in the cabinet and when I looked at the sheet of tablets and the shape of the pills, my brain told me it was Panadol. By the time I sat down with Luca's teacher I was sweating, slurring my speech and my pupils would have looked like pinholes.

Having a loving, understanding and very capable non-dyslexic life partner has been a big help. Asher assists me where she can, and she lets people know that I'm not rude, uncaring or disrespectful when I miss appointments or forget their names. However, she works some ridiculous hours and is often away from home shooting on location all over the country, but that doesn't stop me asking her to order Uber Eats for me from on set. There are plenty of times, though, when I have to battle on without her help.

Normally Asher is in charge of the Christmas shopping but one year she was away for work so the job fell to me. The list of items I needed to get for the boys required a cross-town trip to the Highpoint

CHAPTER THIRTEEN

mega-mall at Maribyrnong. Since it was the week before Christmas I had to plunge deep into the matrix of the multi-level car park with a swarm of other vehicles. When I finally found an empty spot I went inside the mall, withdrew the maximum $800 from an ATM and marched to Big W after inadvertently leaving the money in the machine.

At Big W I filled a trolley with all the presents I had to get for the boys. When I went to pay I realised I had no cash and that I must have left the money in the ATM. I tried to use my card instead but it was declined because I'd reached the transaction limit. I was forced to leave the trolley full of Christmas cheer at the check-out, run back to the ATM hoping my $800 was still there (it wasn't) and accept that the excursion had been a complete disaster. I'd dropped $800 on thin air and a wasted trip halfway across Melbourne.

Despondent, I went back out to the cavernous car park and spent nearly two hours looking for my vehicle. My stress level started to spike because I had to get back home as the boys had a babysitter who needed to be somewhere else. In desperation I climbed shakily into a shopping trolley in the middle of the car park, stood up in it and pressed my remote key in the hope the added elevation might help me see my car's lights flicker in response. When that failed I told a couple of security guards that my car might have been stolen and then I caught a taxi home.

I returned the next day and finally found the thing where I'd parked it.

Infuriating games of car park hide-and-seek are common. I'll drive to the airport, catch a plane to Sydney, fly back to Melbourne a few days later and catch an Uber home, having forgotten that I'd driven in the first place. It all adds up – the wasted time, the lost money, the forgotten names and the missed dates. Sometimes I can't help but get down on myself. The thing dyslexia robs me of the most is time, especially when my forgetfulness, my habit of losing things and being unable to read and use numbers the way most people do all combine in a perfect storm. A recent example:

I hired a van to help my sister move house. During the day I went to ring Asher but discovered that I'd lost my phone. I thought I might have left it at the van hire place whereas it had actually fallen out of my pocket into the back of the car and it was on silent. It was getting late and I knew Asher – who was also out – would be trying to call me. She tends to fret when she can't reach me.

Anxious to solve the dilemma and reconnect with my lovely, worried wife I drove home to where we now live in St Kilda. There's a keypad to gain entry to the house. I couldn't remember the code, so I had to scale the fence, clamber up to a balcony on the second floor and force my way in through a window. Once inside I figured all I had to do was find Val's iPad because I knew he used it to

CHAPTER THIRTEEN

send messages to his mum, which meant I could, too.

I sat down with Val's tablet to alert Asher that I was safe and sound at home but I couldn't remember Val's login code. I knew that his code was his birth date, I just couldn't remember when he was born. My own son. I couldn't even remember the year he arrived. I tried to count backwards but I couldn't figure it out.

Off I went in search of Val's birth certificate, passport or anything with his date of birth on it. No luck. I felt dumb all over again. *Everyone knows this stuff except me! Do I really have to get it tattooed on my wrist?* Whenever I take Val to the doctor and they ask his date of birth, and I don't know it, they must think I've stolen a child.

Finally I found my own iPad but because I'd got myself into a bit of a state I couldn't remember my login, which is a set of numbers. Since I've never known what the numbers are, I remember the login by its shape on the keypad.

One day Asher asked me, 'What's your password?'

'I don't know. I just do this,' I said, and made the shape in the air with my finger.

On this day, however, it took me time to unearth the shape from my brain. Eventually I got into my iPad but then I couldn't remember Asher's phone number so I couldn't send her a message. When she walked in the front door half an hour later she was frantic. 'Oh my god! What happened?'

she said, visibly upset. 'I thought you'd been in an accident!'

Nope. Just another day with dyslexia.

I don't know Asher's date of birth, either. Or Luca's. Or our wedding anniversary. I don't know how long we've been married. I don't know what's in our bank account. I'm lucky to remember my own birthday. The dates I have mentioned in this book are ones I've been able to check with family and friends, or they've been moments in my career that have been recorded in the media.

Dyslexia has caused me to miss out on a lot. I've missed flights, I've missed the Christmas shopping, business meetings and important appointments for portraits. Worse still, I've missed a lot of birthdays for people I love, special occasions and countless big moments on the calendar. I don't know the sequence of the months of the year. If someone tells me 'It's the fourth of the sixth' I don't know what that means. I don't know what order the seasons change in either, or where north, south, east and west are. No wonder I sometimes feel a bit lost in the world.

You would think that, being a portrait artist, I'd be great at remembering faces.

Not so. I can paint someone's likeness in fine detail, get to know them and imbue the work with all the things I discover about their personalities as I engage with them. If I see that same person out of

CHAPTER THIRTEEN

context, however, I'll walk right past them and not have a clue who they are. It doesn't happen with family and my closest friends but plenty of people whom I know quite well have passed me in the street and drawn a blank from me. Often they'll stop me and say, 'Hey, Vincent! How are you going, man?'

'Oh hey! Great to see you!' I'll reply, while madly thinking to myself, *Fuck, fuck, fuck. Where is that face from?*

Thankfully, after a bit of chitchat I can usually recall the last conversation we had and refer to that as a way of letting them know that I know who they are. I don't want people to think I can't recognise them. Bizarrely it even happens with world-famous faces, like the time I spoke with Leonardo DiCaprio at his own birthday party as if he were some random guy preventing me from getting to the bar. At *The Dark Knight* premier in New York following Heath's death I was riding an escalator in the movie complex when the guy next to me said. 'Oh! You're the artist who painted Heath! I love that painting.'

Weirdly I thought it was Heath's step-dad, Roger, but then I thought, *Why is he speaking with an American accent?*

'Thanks very much,' I replied to the gent. 'How are you going? What brings you here?'

He looked at me a bit funny.

'I was in the movie you just watched. I played the governor of Gotham City,' he said.

It was Gary Oldman.

At another film premier in New York City I wound up at the bar afterwards where I struggled to get a drink because the barman kept ignoring me. Over and over again he served others and skipped me. A woman nearby noticed it and said, 'Oh my god! I can't believe this. I'll buy you a drink.'

When the drink arrived in a flash I thanked her. 'So,' I said, 'what did you think of the movie?'

'I enjoyed making it,' she replied.

Dame Helen Mirren.

I haven't been officially diagnosed but I'm pretty sure that I suffer from face blindness, or prosopagnosia. (Fun fact: I'm also colour blind!) The sad thing about prosopagnosia is that it doesn't just affect me, it also affects the person I can't recognise. In 2024 I was in Canberra with Asher to unveil my portrait of Aboriginal elder, academic and human rights campaigner Professor Tom Calma at the University of Canberra. Suddenly a man appeared next to me and said, 'Vincent! How lovely to see you.'

It was Brian Schmidt, Vice-Chancellor of the Australian National University and a professor of astrophysics who won a Nobel Prize in 2011. I had painted his portrait years before during the Melbourne iteration of the Thirty Portraits in Thirty Days exhibition. He's a wonderful guy. I'd flown to Canberra to do his portrait and he showed me around town. We discovered we shared a love of cooking and I remember all of our conversations, and how he won the Nobel Prize for discovering the accelerating expansion of

CHAPTER THIRTEEN

the universe. I was fascinated by his description of how microscopic our existence is in the scheme of things. While he was known for big discoveries and complex thoughts Brian told me it was the simple things in life he loved the most – especially his garden and his pizza oven. I know all of that and I appreciate the man but when he walked up to me at the event and said, 'Vincent!' his face didn't map in my mind because it was out of context.

Asher could see I was very embarrassed and tried to rescue me by jumping in and introducing herself in the hope that Brian would reciprocate. I was flustered and felt the need to explain myself. 'I'm so sorry,' I told the stranger who was no stranger at all. 'I have this thing that if I don't know the context, I lose my way.'

It had nothing to do with forgetting Brian or him not being important to me. I have so much respect for the man and I was so happy to see him. I just didn't recognise him. Brian was very understanding and gracious but it had embarrassed him and it embarrasses me – every single time it happens.

When it comes to faces I'm also cognisant of a weird thing some people do when they meet celebrities. I've seen it happen a lot when people encounter Asher – they pretend not to know who she is when it's obvious that they do. 'So what do you do?' they'll usually say.

I'll stand there thinking, *You know very well what she does.*

I cringe at the thought that people might think I do this, too. I don't want to be thought of as the guy who pretends not to know who Leo DiCaprio is, or Gary Oldman or Helen Mirren. I'd give anything just to be normal when I meet people I should know.

Over the years I have gradually improved a little with written language, but not in a way that you could teach to help a dyslexic kid at school. Technology has played a part. There are a lot of different opinions about if or how dyslexic kids can find an easier path forward with their learning and I've met a lot of parents of dyslexic children who tell me things like:

'We've got our boy a tutor!'

'There's this new way of learning!'

'He's doing this new exercise for four hours a day!'

I think to myself, *Poor kid. That's not going to fix it. Give him an iPhone. Get him to start text messaging. Let him see predictive text. Get him to listen to an audiobook, or hundreds of audiobooks so he can improve his vocabulary. Let him watch a million movies. He won't even realise how much he's learning.*

Whenever I talk to parents it's important that they know there are great things that come with being dyslexic: in my case I believe I have heightened empathy and understanding of people, excellent problem-solving abilities and sharpened instincts for what might be termed 'street smarts'. Obviously one of the major gifts dyslexia has given me is an

The hug the day Asher and I met, captured by Michael.

Love Face.

Our wedding day in Fiji.
Courtesy Brent DeBoer

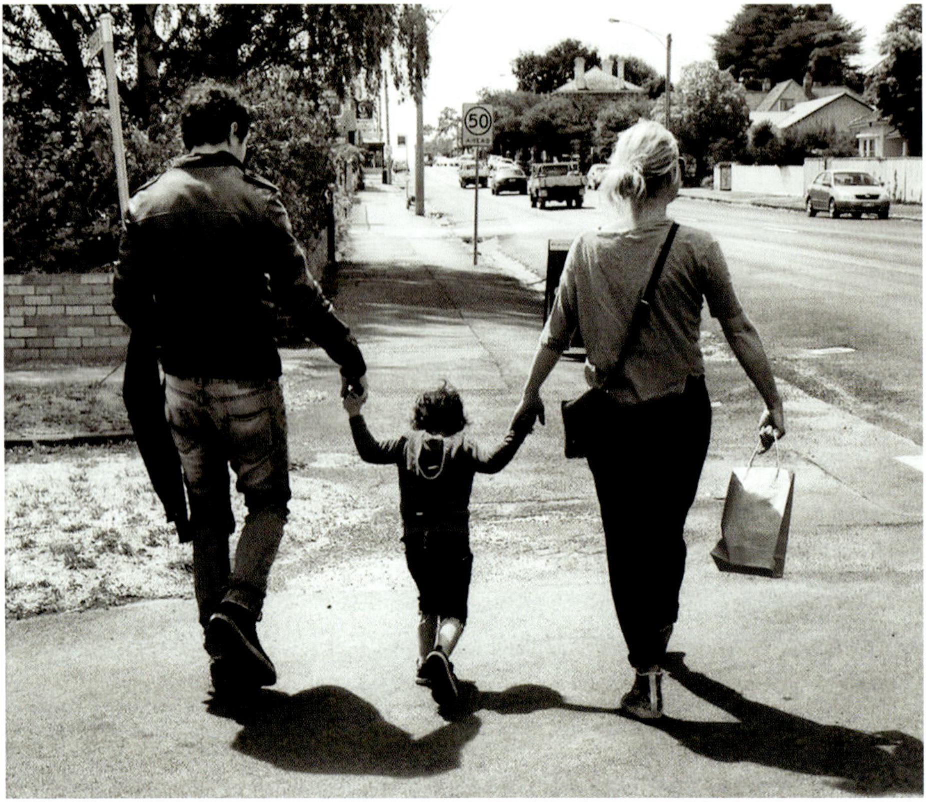

Courtesy Wizzy Mollineaux

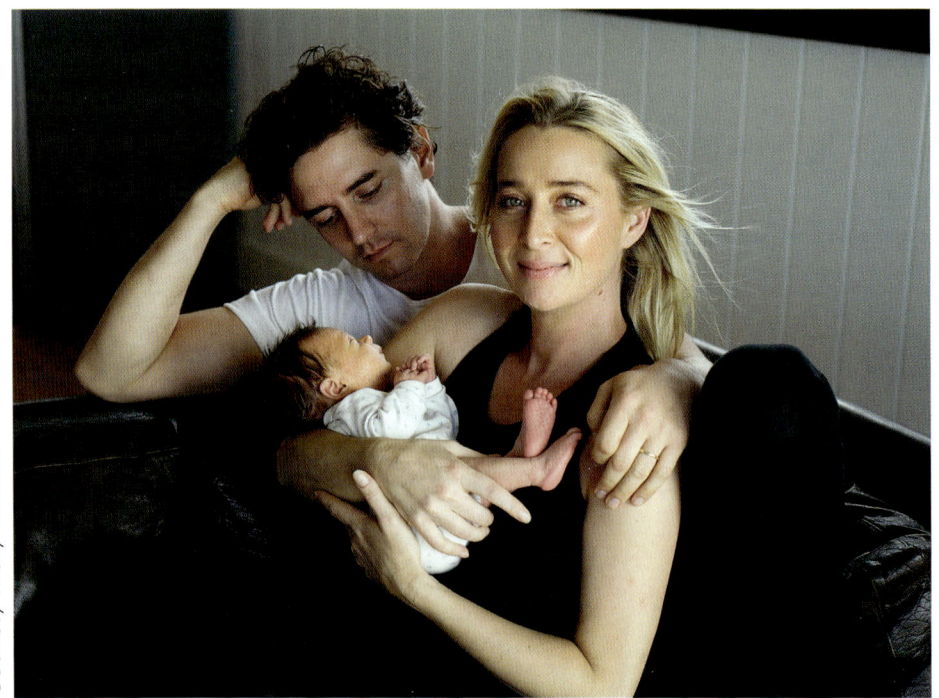

My greatest purpose in life is to be the best father, husband and friend that I can. Asher and me with Luca (*above*) and Val (*below*).

Courtesy Nicky Thomas

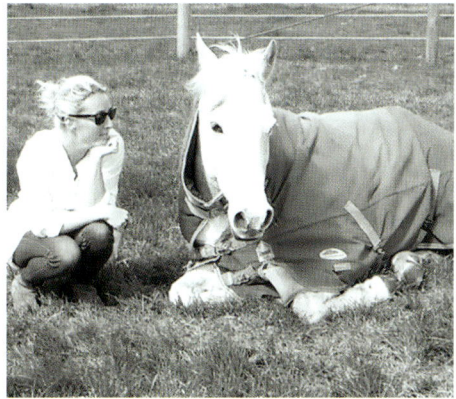

Life on the farm gives us time and space to thrive as a family.

Beach time in Thailand.

In our finery the night Asher won the Gold Logie.

Family downtime at home.

An outtake from the *Marie Claire* photo shoot.
Courtesy Michael Fantauzzo

Luca and Val derive such pleasure from each other, be it in sport, cooking up a storm (and a mess) in the kitchen or just making one another laugh – and it makes my heart so full.

Val and Luca painting at the farm.   Mum and Luca getting creative.

Marianne, Mum and Rachel.

The last time I saw Dad before he entered hospital.

Celebrating Luca's fourteenth birthday.

Another calm nighttime routine at the Fantauzzo household.

The whole family are dedicated Pies fans. Val and Luca at the 2023 AFL Grand Final at the MCG with my portrait in honour of the Australian women's cricket team winning the T20 World Cup 2020.

Michael Gudinski was the brilliant, half-mad, young-at-heart uncle I never had, and I still treasure the friendship we shared. *Inset* Asher and me with Michael and his wife, Sue.

I am fortunate that Larry Kestelman is excited by the arts and has become a big supporter of mine. Rarely do I feel further from Broadmeadows than when I'm with Larry: (*above*) Asher and me in his private plane with his wife, Anita Pahor, and (*left*) with Charlize Theron.

Nic Cester and I in front of my portrait of him. Since being introduced by Michael Gudinski, Nic and me have shared outlandish adventures, rock concerts, travel and countless hours cooking together for our families.

In my painting of Hugh that hangs in the National Portrait Gallery, I strove to capture the look in his eyes that I see when we're just chatting about the things that inspire us.

Whenever we attend a big event, our close friend and Asher's agent, Lee-Anne Higgins, is by our side. Here we are together on the 2024 Logie Awards red carpet, happily bumping into Trent Dalton.

At the launch of The Fantauzzo with (*left to right*) Imogen Banks, Asher, Matt and Richard Roxburgh.

I was totally unprepared for the impact Neale Daniher would have on me. He is an inspiration and his warmth and positivity are indescribable.

I felt an instant connection with Professor Tom Calma when we first met at an Australian Literacy and Numeracy Foundation event and hoped one day to paint him. We're at the gala dinner unveiling my portrait of him here.

I have so many good friends in my life. Celebrating Matt's fiftieth in the Tiwi Islands. Me and Asher with Richard, Matt, Sarah Hopkins and Silvia Colloca.

Hardly a month goes by without Kim Ledger phoning me to check in, and I feel blessed to still have him and Sally in my life. We're pictured at Backlot Perth with my mural of Heath as the Joker.

Recent work of two giants of sport, Scottie Pippen (*left*) and Darcy Moore (*bottom left*).

It's always a thrill to meet and conceptualise new work with people from all corners of life. Pictured here with (*left to right*) Scottie, Luc Longley, Horace Grant and Larry.

Darcy is a wonderful role model for my boys.

Every time I paint a portrait, it's a collaboration. There is a moment when something lights up – I feel it going through my body. And that's true whether the subject is a kickboxer (Alex Pereira, *left and middle*), or a Hollywood star (Guy Pearce, *bottom*).

Addressing climate change and extinction, I painted a series of creatures, displaced, with their natural environment painted over in white; to illustrate that we often do not appreciate beauty until it's gone forever.

In the spirit of making art accessible to all, I exhibited my work alongside local artists at this show in the Yarra Valley.
Inset Another pinch-me moment: giving a keynote address to graduating students of RMIT as Adjunct Professor.

I really broke through after the Archibald Prize success of *Heath*, which has always felt bittersweet. 'This painting is going to change our lives,' he told me the last time I saw him.

CHAPTER THIRTEEN

elevated ability in art. Outside of the boxing ring, the only time I can move very fluidly and in a more advanced way than other people is with a paintbrush. It provides a huge emotional counterbalance to all the other crap that makes my life hard. It delights me to know that I can do something so well that most others can't.

Some of the most brilliant people I have met are dyslexic, including former British Formula One world champion Jackie Stewart, whom I have had the pleasure of meeting and painting, and whom I admire so much. He's part of what I call the dyslexic mafia, and we're everywhere – in sports, business, the arts, science, politics and academia. It's widely thought Albert Einstein – the wild-haired man who caught my eye as a lost teenager – was dyslexic. He may have been a mathematical genius but he struggled with language and didn't speak fluently until he was six years old. Perhaps that's why he asserted that imagination is more important than knowledge.

While dyslexia tends to run in families, in my household I am a mafia of one. Luca and Val are voracious readers and good students. When it comes to the most important job in my life – being their father – dyslexia is just part of the furniture, even though it will prompt the odd eye-roll. I drive Luca to soccer three days a week, and I have to use Google Maps every single time. 'Dad! Really?' he'll ask when I program the location.

'Well, why don't *you* know the way?' I'll ask.

'Because I'm not driving the car and I'm a kid!'

Fair point. It's important to be able to laugh about it because getting down on myself isn't going to change a thing. I like that the boys don't mind teasing me a little. One night I curled up with Val as he read me *Mr Forgetful*. When he finished he paused thoughtfully.

'Dad?' he said finally.

'Yeah, Val?' I replied.

'Did that sound familiar to you?'

In contrast to the squeeze that dyslexia puts on the rest of my life, art is a magical gateway to an extraordinary meditative state where my mind opens up like a flower in the sun. The instant I begin to paint, my brain clicks onto a different setting that lets me mentally multitask in a way I usually can't. I can simultaneously think about the portrait I'm doing, the subject of it, and parts of my life that need my attention, all while absorbing information from an audiobook. I visualise the narrated story like it's cinema, and experience the characters and action in hyper-realistic detail. Concurrently, I'll be thinking about the colours I need to mix and change for the painting. I'll ruminate on the subject's life, about what they might think when it's finished and ponder what to cook the family for dinner.

Painting is where I go to sort through and solve my problems, plan my life and calm myself. Every time

I pick up a brush I feel a sense of propulsion through the universe, as though there's a gentle hand on my back steering me towards a happy and successful future. I don't even have to think about the technical side of painting – it just happens.

When I look back at my angst-ridden years at university I'm amazed at how much time I spent trying to learn things that wound up having no bearing whatsoever on how I create art. I was drilled with rule after scholarly rule about the right way and the wrong way to paint: 'You must not do this. You must not do that. You have to put these colours down first and then you have to add this layer . . .'

I was instructed in historical formulas about composition that involved balance, contrast, rhythm and movement, and on techniques like folding a piece of paper eight times. None of it made any sense to me. To my mind the composition of a painting is simple and while I spend a lot of time conceptualising, it's never in a prescriptive or formulaic way.

I'm not one to haunt art stores in search of expensive brushes, either. Some people spend hundreds of dollars – even thousands – on fancy imported paintbrushes in overpriced boutiques in the belief it will result in a better painting. I almost always paint using Mont Marte brushes that sell for $4 a pop at The Reject Shop. As a bonus to the bargain price there's no need to clean up afterwards! When I finish a painting, the spent and bent Mont Martes go straight in the bin.

CHAPTER FOURTEEN

I recall some lectures at RMIT about how to best prepare a canvas to receive paint. We were instructed to coat a canvas in a glue made from rabbit skin. We then had to sand the canvas back, add a layer of gesso, sand it again, then *repeat the process* – all before we added a single drop of paint. *Christ*, I thought as I rubbed away, *I'd better get on with this painting.*

If people want to muck about with rabbit skin glue and sandpaper, each to their own, but the idea of some poor, furry little creature giving its life for art made me feel sad. I often wondered if the vegetarian art students in my class were ever troubled because they smeared Bugs Bunny across their canvases. There's a place for such techniques of course, just as there's a place for someone to sit in front of you as you paint them live, and a place for folding pieces of paper to determine composition. My view is there's no right or wrong way to go about it.

I generally paint on whichever canvas is available when I need it. It really doesn't matter what you use so long as you feel comfortable with the surface. Admittedly a lot of my paintings have been done on linen that cost $400 a metre, some even on linen that costs $600 a metre. Sometimes, however, I spend $20 a metre and get the same result. If I want to do a painting in a hurry, I'll use a canvas that absorbs quickly so I can put down the next layer the following day.

I'm more careful when it comes to paint. I don't use the cheapest varieties because the pigments aren't as strong, but I don't necessarily go for the top-shelf names either. Average-priced oil paint is just fine. Some purists like to grind their own pigments and make their own mediums. Again, whatever makes you happy.

My approach to each work is whimsical and I never do the same thing twice. I might begin with watercolour or a can of spray paint, or I'll start with oil. One day I might commence with bold strokes and the next by diluting paint and making a watercolour-looking wash, or I'll use a brush to flick the paint to simulate the splatter of a spray can – anything that works to bring the particular painting to life. In addition to the world's cheapest brushes, I paint with my fingers all the time, or I'll use a sponge, a rag, a kitchen scourer or a toothbrush – if it's in front of me, it can be used to move paint around.

Although I said there are no rules in art, there is one – you can't put acrylic paint over oil paint because it cracks. Having said that, I did it once and got away with it by spraying an automotive coat over the top. Incidentally it was the same technique I used in order to save my Moran Portrait Prize-winning painting of Baz Luhrmann from disaster.

That particular painting was 1.6 metres high and nearly 2 metres across. The night before it was due to be sent to Sydney for judging I stayed back late to add some final touches. It was summertime so

CHAPTER FOURTEEN

I left the studio windows open in the hope it would speed up the drying process. I switched off the light, went home and when I returned the following morning I discovered the painting had fallen flat on the ground, face-down. When I lifted it up it was encrusted with dust, grit, strands of hair and assorted speckles of crap from the floor. I spent half the day trying to pick all the detritus off it, which left the painting looking pockmarked and gravelly.

Baz was on his way to Los Angeles and had flown to Melbourne first to check out the painting before I shipped it off. When he arrived at the studio and took a look at the piece, his shoulders dropped. 'Oh, no,' he lamented. 'You fucked the painting.'

'No-no,' I said. 'Hold on. I've got an idea.'

An artist mate of mine, Steve May, ran a panel-beating shop on the other side of town. Baz and I put the painting in the back of a Budget rental van, hightailed it over there and asked Steve to give it a good spray with clear coat. He ended up giving it three coats, which more than did the trick. The finished work looked like a huge sheet of glass with a painting sealed underneath. Extremely cool. What began as an accident, followed by a gamble, turned into a finishing technique that I have used quite a few times since.

I've painted on all sorts of surfaces all over the world, big and small, but one of my largest ever works was in Melbourne – home to Australia's best street art. In 2017 I decided to branch out and, with a mate, entered a partnership to open a bar in the city. We found a funky underground space in Strachan Lane just off Exhibition Street, decorated it with my artworks, called the joint Harley House Bar and Grill and threw open the doors.

We did a great trade but the entrance was in a fairly derelict-looking smoker's laneway. To brighten things up I painted some murals on the surrounding walls before I hit on the idea of decorating the road surface itself in an enormous *Alice in Wonderland*-inspired checkerboard pattern. I bought huge barrels of white non-slip pool paint and set about creating the thirty-by-five-metre piece featuring geometric dips and swirls that made it look like the ground was moving. I spent around ten days there on my hands and knees and got a bit of local press along the way. I was about halfway through transforming the laneway when a guy from Melbourne City Council turned up.

'Obviously you have permission to do this?' he asked as I stood up and wiped my hands on my jeans.

'Yeah, of course we have permission!' I said. (Of course I didn't.)

'Right, so when did you get permission?' he pressed.

'Alright, look, this is a shitty laneway and I'm just trying to clean it up and make it look nice,' I said. 'I'm not tagging it with graffiti or making it ugly. But if there's anything I need to do to get permission I'll do it, okay?'

CHAPTER FOURTEEN

After a bit of back and forth he left me alone so I kept painting. As the checkerboard took shape it received a lot of attention. Tour buses full of Japanese holidaymakers stopped by to see it and take photos, some school groups gathered to observe me at work and people snapped pictures from the top of surrounding buildings. The lively and beguiling streetscape turned up on Instagram and Facebook, too.

The day after I finished it, council workers launched a covert strike operation and arrived in Strachan Lane before dawn with sand-blasting equipment. By the time I raced to the scene on my motorbike they'd already half-removed the artwork.

'Why?' I pleaded as the noisy demolition job continued around me.

'It's unsafe,' the foreman told me above the roar of an air compressor. 'It makes the road slippery for cars.'

'It's a thirty-metre laneway with no through traffic,' I pointed out. 'There are no cars!'

'Pedestrians could slip and fall,' he pivoted.

'I used grip paint!' I said. 'Nobody's going to fall over.'

Soon news crews from Channel Seven, Channel Nine and the ABC turned up to capture the drama. I figured the press would focus on the fact that I didn't seek permission, which was true and a fair point. However, the media and public sentiment was overwhelmingly one of support. Melbourne is world renowned for its laneways and art culture and, like me, most people thought the council had got it wrong. I even appeared on Radio 3AW with Neil Mitchell and got a sympathetic hearing.

To add insult to injury, council's sand-blasting party chewed the bitumen up badly leaving the road in front of our little bar looking even uglier than it had before I started. I'd love to do it again somewhere else one day because it really did look awesome. Next time, though, I'll ask first.

While I don't have a defined technique, I definitely have a style of painting that developed as a direct result of my inability to read. Since film and television were my proxy sources of information, education and entertainment, I became fascinated with the filmic process as a boy. I freeze-framed my way through countless movies, pausing on certain shots and wondering how the cinematographers captured each moment. I obsessed over camera angles, lenses, lighting and the use of colour, and I marvelled at how they forced perspective in my mind to serve the filmmakers' storytelling intentions.

As my own art has developed I, too, think cinematically about the singular images I create. The way I see it, my paintings aren't just mugshots of people – they are moments in time that are informed by a narrative. When people look at my work I want them to feel as though something happened a split second beforehand and something else is just about to happen. Each single image has a history and a future not yet revealed.

CHAPTER FOURTEEN

By the time I reached university I realised I needed to learn to capture good images that were informed by the same methods that I loved in cinema, which is why photography became such a large component of my work. I started off with pretty cheap and nasty cameras because they were all I could afford. Later on I bought expensive SLR gear with cutting-edge lenses and all the bells and whistles because I thought they made me look more professional. (Woop-woop! Imposter alert!) I used to take two cameras to a photoshoot – the basic one that I knew I could operate easily and the flashy $15,000 camera that served the sole purpose of impressing people.

I have no chance of mastering all the operations of a modern SLR camera. The technical instructions run to thousands of words and the mathematically technical functions almost require a science degree to understand. In the art world, and Asher's adjacent world of film and television, I meet a lot of people who are technically brilliant with cameras and lighting. Publicity is part of Asher's job so it's fairly common for some of the country's best photographers to work with her.

Whenever I'm photographed for a publication myself, or I have the chance to drop into a shoot to see Asher, I watch them closely, and we inevitably end up discussing the parallels between photography and painting. I admire these artists so much, and when the respect is reciprocated, it's satisfying. Photography is one of my favourite artforms and it has given me a couple of unexpected moments to shine.

Asher was scheduled to do a photoshoot for *Marie Claire* magazine when COVID hit. As borders closed and lockdowns were enforced, the publishers looked for ways to keep the wheels turning and I was invited to photograph my wife for the cover of the venerated fashion title.

It's one thing to watch photographers at the top of their game deliver magic, but another to try to pull it off yourself. Holy fuck! There are a lot of elements that need to be achieved in a shoot of that nature, and Asher's publicist Jess Carrera facilitated everything from afar, making sure we were able to work within the magazine's parameters, but still have the creative freedom to make something original and special together.

When couture frocks were delivered we were ready to go and I had a 'Don't fuck it up' moment. With my brother Michael as my trusty assistant we shot in the backyard with no lighting, no catering and no art director. It was just me and my standard camera, the dog jumping all over us, Val throwing autumn leaves in the air to float down into the frame and a lot of arguing with Asher. It was a brilliant opportunity to collaborate with one another and we discovered we have a great creative rub that eventually gets us to where we want to be. Apparently, it was one of the bestselling issues of the year.

*

CHAPTER FOURTEEN

Pulling together a fashion shoot in the backyard is just one of the quirks of being married to Asher Keddie and it's not the only time her work has followed her home. Every time she stars in a new production she goes through a bit of a cycle that begins with a period of freaking out. 'I'm not going to be able to do this!' she'll say as she pores over a script. 'I just can't see how I'm going to play this character!'

She gets past it of course, because she's a professional and she's brilliant. Then the boys and I can look forward to phase two of the cycle in which we meet the new lady in our lives as Asher brings elements of the latest production home without realising she's doing it.

During the years that she played Nina Proudman on *Offspring*, the household was hilarious because her character was so out there. By comparison, the time Asher starred as a state premier in *Party Tricks* there was a decidedly different tone around the joint. When she played an American in *Nine Perfect Strangers*, Asher would come home and speak to us in an American accent and not realise it. The boys and I never let on because we liked it and thought it was funny. We'd nudge each other and wink. 'She's doing it again!'

Her process is lovely and funny and magical, and I wouldn't change a thing about her. One thing I wasn't properly prepared for when I fell in love with Asher, however, was that I'd have to watch her being intimate with a cast of onscreen lovers year after year. On a rational level I knew it was her job, and I knew she didn't like it, either, but I'm only human (and half Italian) so there was a bit of, *Hey! What the fuck? That's my wife!* going on inside my head. What made it weirder was that I became mates with a lot of Asher's onscreen husbands – Richard Roxburgh, Rodger Corser and Matt Le Nevez. All top blokes.

On each season of *Offspring* the writers gave Nina a brand-new handsome boyfriend and a beautifully scripted onscreen love life. In one particular season, however, she had three different love interests. It was almost too much. 'This is ridiculous!' I said one night, only half-jokingly, as Asher kissed another guy on TV. 'How many men do you have to be with on the one show?'

She threw her head back and laughed. 'How do you think *I* feel?' she said.

Imogen Banks got wind of my discomfort at Asher's occupational intimacy. 'Oh well, Nina's got a one-night stand coming up in the script,' the award-winning producer said. 'Why don't we get Vincent to do it?'

It was the perfect antidote to my insecurities because there's nothing sexy, intimate or remotely normal about filming a sex scene. I was written in as a bloke Nina meets in a bar who takes her home. I had a few lines of dialogue and then it was off to the 'bedroom' for 'sex' with my wife as twenty people fussed around with lights, boom mikes, cameras and clipboards while constantly giving me instructions. The moment I had to take my shirt off I was overwhelmed with a renewed respect for actors and how much of themselves they have to give – especially Asher.

She never complains about her life (because it's perfect, after all), but I know that feeling she's at the centre of every moment can tire her out. I see it every day. When I'm in public with her I constantly hear people say, 'It's Asher Keddie!' Or, 'Look! It's Nina!' A lot of people point at her like she's an exhibit while others feel comfortable enough to walk up and give her a hug or a kiss. Unnatural as all that attention is, I've observed some beautiful moments between Asher and complete strangers. People say the nicest things:

'I became an obstetrician because of you.'

'This is my daughter, Asher. She's named after you.'

'I was really depressed during COVID. Your face and your show saved me.'

A couple of Christmases back we took the boys on holiday to Fiji. As we walked through the airport a woman approached Asher and asked for a moment of her time. The woman explained that she was on her way interstate to be with her daughter who was in palliative care after a long battle with cancer. One of the things her daughter had always wanted to do, she said, was meet Asher Keddie. Asher went and sat with the poor grieving mum and recorded a heartfelt video for her daughter. I observed Luca watching Asher hold this woman in the middle of the airport, and I could see how proud he was. I could not stop crying.

For about five years I was woken up in the middle of the night, not only by bad dreams but also by the ringing phone. The first time it happened Asher couldn't believe it. 'Who on earth is calling you at this hour?' she groaned and pulled a pillow on top of her head.

'Sorry. It's Michael,' I whispered as his name glowed on my phone.

'Oh, alright, it's Michael,' she mumbled in a sleepy, understanding tone. Asher loved Michael Gudinski as much as I did so she forgave his late-night teleconferences.

'What are you doing?' Michael's gravelly voice growled in my ear.

'I was in bed!' I said.

'Well, fucking . . . how old are you?' he wanted to know.

'I'm forty!' I answered.

'Okay, well, I'm sixty-four years old!' he said. 'So get your young arse out of bed. I've got shit to talk about. Ideas.'

I'd be drafted into these middle-of-the-night confabs several times a week. I'd have to extract myself from under the doona and chat with Michael as he brainstormed plans for entertainment extravaganzas, mega rock'n'roll tours and one-off musical events. For some reason he sought my input on matters such as who should play the pre-match entertainment at the AFL Grand Final and whether people were still interested in Billy Joel.

'I don't even know any Billy Joel songs,' I said.

'What do you mean you don't know any Billy Joel songs?' Michael thundered incredulously. 'Please tell me you've heard of fucking *Piano Man*!'

The embarrassing truth is I hadn't, nor had I heard of the great Michael Gudinski before a friend suggested I paint his portrait in 2016. When Michael showed up to my studio we noticed straight off the bat that we made each other laugh in a way that was uncanny. It was obvious to me that Michael was a bit of a ratbag but also an extraordinary and unique human being. If Matt Moran is like a dependable older brother to me, Michael was the brilliant, half-mad, young-at-heart uncle who didn't have an off switch. I loved him from the very start.

Over a couple of hours Michael filled me in on his life story and I gained a small understanding of how he became one of the world's most legendary

CHAPTER FIFTEEN

music promoters, lauded and beloved by artists from Paul Kelly and Kylie Minogue to Bruce Springsteen and Sting. 'There's not much point in *telling* you all about what I do,' Michael said as we nattered away in my studio. 'You should come along with me and watch.'

Michael ushered me into the backrooms where the deals are made, walked me along the corridors of power and introduced me to some of the biggest names in entertainment. Hanging out backstage with the godfather of the Australian music business was a private masterclass in the politics of people and how the wheels of commerce turn. More than anything, however, Michael showed me that you don't really have to grow up or behave like an adult as you get older. He may have been closing in on seventy years old but we somehow connected with the parts of each other that were forever twenty-three.

When he brought Bruce Springsteen to Australia in 2017 Michael had a car deliver Asher and me to AAMI Park stadium where The Boss was due to play to 30,000 people that night. Michael met us at the VIP gate and led us deep into the cement intestines of the arena. He took us into a room filled with his inner fold including his amazing partner, Sue, and his best friend Nick Williams who was there with his wife, Saskia.

'Okay, Vinnie, first up we're going to do the rounds,' he said, which meant dropping into a series of rooms packed with media, corporate sponsors, artists and invited guests. Michael genuinely loved a lot of the people gathered there but I was discovering he had shorthand for specific groups of people, which usually included the word 'fucking'. God, he made me laugh.

In a room full of heavy hitters, Michael was the gravitational centre. He held court, pressed the flesh, commanded attention and conducted himself in a very poised and, dare I say it, adult manner. Back out in the corridor afterwards he reverted to Mr Twenty-Three. 'Did you hear what that fucking clown was going on about in there?' he said between fits of giggles.

Eventually he introduced me to Bruce Springsteen who, I could tell, loved the same things about Michael that I and everybody else did: the complete lack of pretence, the raw simplicity of his human connection, the loyalty and his irreverent charm. 'Bruce, this is Vinnie. Vinnie, this is Bruce,' he said, as if he was introducing a couple of blokes on a fishing trip.

Michael invited me into the inner sanctum of his business life, too. He'd call a meeting with six hugely influential entrepreneurs and tell me to come along. I'd sit there and wonder, *What am I doing here?* For whatever reason, Michael had decided to take me under his wing and teach me how the world worked. How *his* world worked. He introduced me to people in the most casual way without any explanation as to why I was suddenly involved in their day. He simply said, 'Vinnie's here,' and left it at that. After one memorable high-stakes meeting, where massive projects were discussed, I just had to ask: 'Why do you bring me along to these things, Michael?'

'Because,' he said as he put two hands on my shoulders, 'you're an important person and I value your opinion.'

Honestly, the guy made me feel like I could just about fly. I met the most amazing people through him, from billionaire titans Lloyd Williams and Lindsay Fox to global superstars like Springsteen and Ed Sheeran. He was also responsible for introducing me to one of my great mates, Nic Cester, frontman for the Melbourne rock band Jet. Michael got it in his head that Nic and I should be friends. 'I want you to meet this guy,' he said to me one day, and set Nic and me up on what was essentially a blind date. He was 100 per cent correct about us – Nic and I clicked and have stayed close ever since.

Michael wasn't only there for the good times, though. In the period I knew him I racked up numerous operations including two knee surgeries, three shoulder reconstructions and a hip replacement – the wages of martial arts and fast bikes. Every time I wound up in hospital, Michael was the first to appear at my bedside. He always brought me some fancy food and an expensive bottle of wine. Obviously, drinking vino in a post-op ward is a no-no in the eyes of medicos so he'd slyly pull it out of his jacket like a pistol from a shoulder holster and slip it under my blanket or into the bottom drawer. One time he grabbed paper cups from a water cooler and poured us a sneaky drink to toast my speedy recovery. 'What harm's it going to do?' he asked. 'Antibiotics and a bit of wine – you'll be feeling fucking great! Don't tell anyone, though, and if the nurses find it you didn't get it from me, right?'

'Right.'

'Here, drink this,' he said. 'Now have a mint.'

When I was charged with assaulting the two men outside Niddrie KFC in 1998, lawyers told me there was a strong chance I'd be going to prison. At the time the only thing I had going on in my life was the laundrette and a dribble of income from drawing sports memorabilia. Increasingly horrified at the prospect of jail, I made a panicked decision to flee Melbourne. That winter I caught a train to Sydney.

Kylie Minogue was touring Australia at the time and I'd heard on a radio station that she was due to appear at a record store in Sydney's CBD. I figured if I sketched a portrait of Kylie and got her to sign it, it would translate into dollars to finance my life as a fugitive. I found the record store, lined up for an hour with a mob of hardcore Kylie fans and eventually got the young pop princess to put her signature on the drawing. All I had to do then was sell it to the highest bidder. Since I was unwilling and quite unable to walk around the streets of an unfamiliar city and ask people if they wanted to buy a signed drawing of Kylie Minogue, I caught the next train back to Melbourne. My time on the run lasted less than forty-eight hours.

I considered telling Kylie that story as she mixed cocktails on the last night I spent with Michael. In late February 2021, Asher and I were invited to a dinner party hosted by Michael and Sue. Kylie and Asher had become friends while shooting the movie *Swinging Safari* together in 2017. They hadn't seen each other for a year and our hosts wanted them to get together while Kylie was in town. Typical Michael and Sue generosity. We had an amazing night and Michael was in better form than I'd ever seen him. His only complaint was a bad shoulder. 'It's fucking giving me hell but I've got a personal trainer,' he told me.

After dinner we adjourned to his music room. Kylie jumped behind the bar to make drinks when transport magnate Lindsay Fox arrived and dropped his pants. He was wearing tighty-whities underneath so it wasn't horrific – but he shuffled into the room with his trousers around his ankles and shook everybody's hands without saying a word.

Oh god no! Lindsay's lost his mind! I thought.

The next minute he pulled his pants back up and started talking to everyone as if nothing had happened. There were a few beats of uncomfortable silence before we all erupted with laughter. We'd had the same thoughts at the same time, but Lindsay had been winding us up – deliberately messing with the young people's heads. The man is brilliant, hilarious and, like Michael, he seems to know everyone on the planet. We got talking about motorbikes and when Lindsay needed to check a detail in the story he was telling me, he pulled out a black book of phone numbers and rang some guy in Italy. Lindsay didn't even say hello, he just asked, 'Remember the bike you rode in '78? What was it? Alright. Thanks.'

Then he turned to me and said, 'It was a Ducati.' The guy he'd called was the 1978 Grand Prix champion.

We all drank, laughed and talked into the early hours before Michael and Sue hugged us goodbye. As we left I kissed Michael on the head as I always did. Two days later I was visiting my friend Anthony who I hadn't seen in twenty years and regaling him with stories from the dinner party at Michael's when Asher phoned me. She sounded terrible. 'Are you sitting down?' she asked in a quavering voice. 'I have to tell you something.'

I knew at that moment that someone I loved had died.

'It's Michael,' she said and choked up. 'He's passed away. He's gone, Vinnie.'

I entered the same altered state I'd experienced in multiple motorcycle crashes, where everything slowed down while I was in the air as I processed every aspect of the situation and prepared for impact with the kerb. I thought about all the different things Michael and I talked about doing together that would never happen now. It registered that I would never have another conversation with him. I thought about Sue's devastation, and the torment his children Kate and Matt were going through. I winced at his grandchildren's pain at losing their granddad. I mourned the fact he wouldn't be part of *my* kids' lives, either, or how the goddamned phone would never again ring at 11.47 pm on a Wednesday. Then I hit the bitumen with a violent crack. The complete disappearance of the man left me gasping.

I had lost friends before in Heath and Aaliyah, but losing Michael was different. He was as close to me as my immediate family. When we first met he obviously said to himself, *I love this person and I am going to help him in every way that I can*. One glance around his private funeral service was to realise I was not the only lucky soul to have Michael Gudinski champion me or choose me as a friend.

His guidance and advice shaped how I approach my life, and while I was lucky to have him for five short years, I miss his counsel every day. Michael was the first person I called when ABC TV approached me to appear on *Australian Story*. I wasn't sure it was a good idea – but he was. 'I was asked to do *Australian Story* years ago and I fucking said no because I was worried about privacy,' he said. 'They never asked me again so I should have fucking done it when I had the chance. You should do it. Don't even question it.'

I could almost hear Michael's voice saying, 'Do it, Vinnie,' when I was agonising over whether or not to write this book. He was a massive supporter of my art, too, and was never afraid to speak his mind on matters financial and creative: 'Do this. Don't do that. Fucking charge them more money. You're worth more than that.'

There are a lot of things I do nowadays because of Michael that I struggled to do before he came into my life. One of the big ones is believe in myself. It was through Michael and his conviction that no-one is better than anyone else that I started to lay my imposter syndrome to rest. He had stood me in front of the biggest stars in the world and allowed me to believe that I was interesting enough to be there.

I suspect he worked that same down-to-earth magic on some of the huge international artists who loved him. Ed Sheeran was particularly close to Michael, who made a point of including me whenever Ed was in town. For a guy who can hold 100,000 people in the palm of his hand with just a guitar and a microphone to lean on, Ed is one of the humblest men I have ever had the pleasure to meet, and I imagine having Michael as a mentor only reinforced that. When Ed got married, Sue and Michael commissioned me to paint him and his bride Cherry Seaborn for their wedding present – just one of the special life experiences I gained thanks to Michael.

Other 'Michael people' are woven into my life forever, like the fabulous Nic Cester and my now confidant Nick Williams. Our friendships have become living monuments to the man who brought us together. Nic and I in particular connect in the spirit that Michael loved – outlandish adventures, rock concerts and travel. Asher and I are good friends with Michael's children, too – particularly his daughter, Kate, and her husband, Mackie. In 2024 they asked us to be godparents to their little boy. It was the first time I ever had such an honour and I felt the invisible hand of the great Gudinski at play.

Although Michael was a larger-than-life person who somehow found enough minutes in every night and every day to give himself to the world, his family meant everything to him. As naughty as he was and as much as he loved living the big life of a rock promoter, he knew what was most important and he was anxious that I knew it, too. 'You've got a good woman, Vinnie,' he'd say in solemn moments together. 'You've got a good family. Don't fuck it up.'

These days I don't cry so much when I think of Michael – only when I come across artefacts that mark his existence, like a bottle of expensive wine I snookered away after one of his post-op visits, or text messages saved on my phone. Asher and I would give anything to have his late-night phone calls once again because all I have for nocturnal company now are the nightmares.

Although I experienced poverty as a kid it was only penury when measured against the standard of life in modern metropolitan Melbourne. We struggled but we could almost always count on essentials like electricity, water on tap and refrigeration. As a boy it never occurred to me that other families in our rich and prosperous country had gone without these fundamentals for millennia. That inward-looking naïvety was shattered on my first visit to the Western Desert.

Philanthropist and Indigenous art curator, collector and advocate Ken McGregor was the one who opened my eyes to an Australia that most of us never get to see. We'd met in 2010 when Ken helped me stage some exhibitions, and I was fascinated to learn he devoted much of his life to the advancement of Indigenous people through their art. He also campaigned for improved health in remote communities. In 2015 he offered to take me into the heart of

CHAPTER SIXTEEN

the continent to meet some of the country's oldest and most treasured Indigenous artists before they were all gone.

Over several months, Ken and I made multiple trips into some of the farthest-flung and most threadbare communities smudged into the ochre sands of the vast interior. I was privileged to spend time with celebrated Indigenous artists Kudditji Kngwarreye, Linda Syddick Napaltjarri, Wentja Napaltjarri, Gloria Petyarre and Tommy Watson. These humble and ageing elders were the last of the first internationally acclaimed Indigenous artists. While I'd originally intended to paint landscapes of their Country, I quickly became far more entranced by the people and their artwork than I was of the stunning terrain they walked upon.

For weeks I sat under trees and listened to their stories, helped them mix paints and watched them bring their work to life. I camped with them beneath the desert sky as a billion constellations slowly twirled overhead, and tried not to feel so bad that I'd spent most of my life ignorant of their existence and their struggle. Iconic as they may have been, these painters were as far removed from the art world as it is possible to be. They never went to art school or an art supplies store, and they never visited galleries. Their studio was the red desert floor or a patch of shade beneath some leaves on a forty-degree day. I was in awe of them and the purity of their art.

There is no room for conceit. In Indigenous culture, everybody has the right to be an artist and tell their own stories through painting. I also loved the fact they didn't critique and judge each other the way we do in the big cities and stuffy galleries. That doesn't mean the art world doesn't exploit Indigenous painters. During nights around the campfire I heard depressing stories about art dealers paying them with KFC, alcohol and a few hundred dollars to sit in an iron shed like battery hens with brushes, just so someone could acquire an authentic painting from an Indigenous artist and then sell it for $60,000 or $100,000. It is the worst crime in art.

That's why the world needs people like Ken McGregor. He has made it his life's mission to look after the interests of Indigenous artists with respect and love. He sets up trusts for them and helps them manage their money so it's there when needed for education, vocation and healthcare for their families. That's just the beginning of the work Ken puts in. He once walked one thousand kilometres across the desert from Alice Springs to the Kiwirrkurra community in Western Australia to raise awareness and money to fight the major problems of diabetes and kidney failure in remote communities.

The project wouldn't have happened without the financial support of Larry Kestelman, either. We'd met a few years earlier through a mutual friend. Larry had built a billion-dollar business empire from scratch as the son of penniless Ukrainian migrants and, like me, he loves art as much as anything in the world. We became fast friends and have found ways of working together ever since. *Last Contact* was one of my first projects that captured Larry's imagination.

Out of the five Indigenous artists I got to know quite well, Kudditji was the closest to my heart. Like the others he was shy when we first met but we soon developed a connection. He was an old man, born in 1938 at a place called Utopia on the edge of the Tanami Desert where he spent the majority of his life working as a horseman and creating his paintings. Everything about the man was genuine and real, yet he was ethereal at the same time. Somehow he painted incredible aerial views of the landscape. Kudditji had never been in a plane or at the top of a tree but he had the ability to interpret the land from a bird's eye in his mind. His abstract composition and colour was breathtaking, too. He blew my mind.

Eventually I painted portraits of all the artists, along with a landscape from their specific part of the country. I wanted to include their own works in the series as well, so Larry kindly commissioned all five to produce a painting each. The resulting triptychs were exhibited as a collection at Nanda\ Hobbs Gallery in Sydney. Larry loved the project and what it represented so much that he bought the entire collection. When I'd finished my portrait of Kudditji I took it straight to Alice Springs where he was ill in hospital. I'd put my heart and soul into the painting because I wanted to show him how much respect I had for him and his place in the history of

Australian art. It's still up there with the best things I have ever painted.

I didn't expect to become emotional when I unveiled it for him, but to see Kudditji looking frail in a wheelchair with a crocheted blanket across his knees brought me to tears. He was so sick that he was unable to speak and when I rolled out the painting in the hospital ward he just looked at me and softly nodded his approval. Kudditji died the following year, followed a few months later by Tommy Watson. Wentja Napaltjarri and Gloria Petyarre both passed away in 2021. Only Linda Syddick Napaltjarri survives. The last nomad standing.

I learned something very honest about art making from all of them and I know younger Aboriginal artists don't want people to think the only Indigenous visual language is dot painting. They're continuing the elders' legacy and creating really interesting contemporary art. I'm so grateful to the people of the Western Desert and to Ken for the gift of understanding more about Indigenous culture. I'd have been a far poorer man had I never gone there.

After he died, I tried to enter the portrait of Kudditji in the Archibald Prize as a way of telling the nation that we'd lost a great Australian. It was rejected at the outset so it didn't even get hung. I tried again the following year with my painting of Michael Gudinski but it was also knocked back. Same story when I submitted a portrait of AFL great Neale Daniher in 2016. Indeed, I entered almost

CHAPTER SIXTEEN

every year right up until 2024 but never got a foot back in the door.

We never discussed politics at home when I was young and I don't recall my parents ever heading off on a Saturday to cast their vote. The first time politics remotely entered my thoughts was during my disastrous and short-lived return to high school. The social studies teacher spent forty long minutes trying to familiarise the class with the basics of the Westminster system. She might as well have been speaking Swahili. My head spun with talk of this party and that party, left wing versus right wing, senate this and lower house that. I definitely wasn't about to rush out and join the Young Liberals so I could figure it all out.

Even today, dyslexia makes politics bewildering to me. I struggle to sort the multitude of parties, personalities, faces, committees, elections, sitting weeks and policy platforms into an order that makes much sense. I don't know the difference between the Liberal Party and the Labor Party, and to me the Teals and the Greens are just colours I paint with. I don't even know who the current prime minister is. And yet, I consider myself somewhat political.

Art has given me a lot in life, not least a public profile and a modest media platform. Wherever I can I always look for ways to put my limited weight – and often a painting or two – behind social causes and charities I believe in. Although I shied away from politics in my younger days (because I couldn't understand it), I've since had a few things to say publicly about issues I feel strongly about. I was elated, for instance, when the same-sex marriage plebiscite passed in 2017 and I felt devastated when the Indigenous Voice to Parliament was voted down in 2023. I campaigned in favour of both.

Like everyone else, I mostly get my impressions of politicians through the distortion and noise of the mainstream media filter, so I don't put a lot of store in them and I tend not to judge. I'm well aware my general knowledge is not what most people's may be, but I do have opinions about policies and the people behind them.

A case in point came during the same-sex marriage plebiscite. I took a dislike to Tony Abbott during that time. I didn't know much about him before then, other than he liked to go to the beach in those little red swimmers. Nothing wrong with that, but I began to bristle when I heard him literally preach against marriage equality on the grounds of *his* religious beliefs. When I discovered his sister was a lesbian, and that he bitterly opposed her right to wed the person she loved, I thought he was just awful.

I still don't know what party Tony Abbott belonged to, nor did I know the political affiliations of Julia Gillard when I was asked to paint her official portrait to be hung in Parliament House in Canberra.

I was taken aback and very excited when a woman from Ms Gillard's office emailed me in late 2017. Of all the prime ministers we've had and

CHAPTER SIXTEEN

whose names I have completely forgotten, hers was one face and one name that stuck with me. The first woman to lead our nation. You don't forget someone like that.

'Julia Gillard is looking at a few people to possibly do her portrait for Parliament House,' her assistant wrote. 'She loves the series you did last year featuring Indigenous artists from the Western Desert.'

I got back to her straightaway: 'Oh wow! That's great! I'd love to paint her portrait. It's a big yes from me!'

'Well, you're not painting her portrait, yet,' came the response. 'We'd like to interview you as a candidate to *possibly* paint her portrait.'

That threw me a bit. Typically someone contacts me and asks me to paint their portrait. That's it. Simple. No-one had ever said to me, 'Would you like to apply to be a contender to do a portrait? In competition with some other artists?' Not having a clue about the culture of matters political, or if there was a special protocol that governs the painting of prime ministers, I agreed to their terms. It was to be my first job interview as an adult and only the second in my life since my failed attempt to get work in a packing factory when I was a teenager. Thankfully, the meeting was on my home turf. All I had to do to prepare was tidy up the studio and remember to keep the appointment.

Ms Gillard ('Call me Julia') was very businesslike when she arrived at the studio. Her assistant – the woman from the email – was even more intense in real life. *Bloody hell!* I thought to myself. *How am I going to convince these two that it's a good idea for me to do this portrait?*

We chatted as Julia and her assistant cast their eyes over some of the works hanging in the studio. They made some complimentary remarks and mentioned some of the other artists they were considering for the job. Even though I was nervous I just smiled and tried to be myself. We sat down and they started the interview. It was weird and a bit awkward to begin with but it ended up being pretty straightforward.

'How did you get into painting?' Julia asked.

I didn't spill all the blood and guts from my childhood but I told her in broad terms about my small beginnings, my lack of formal education or any real insight into art history or the technical aspects of painting.

'How would you go about doing the portrait?' Julia continued with a slight smile on her lips while fixing me with her probing hazel eyes.

'Well, first of all I have to get to know you,' I explained. 'Then I'd take some photos to use as reference material, I'd likely film you a little, too, and have some discussions as we go along. My portraits are really a collaborative process. We get it done together.'

Julia smiled again as I assured her there would be no formal sittings where I'd ask her to move her head slightly to the left or lift her chin up a fraction. 'I'll simply observe you,' I emphasised. 'I'll spend time with you and see if we can capture something.'

She absorbed everything in a quiet and thoughtful way. I, on the other hand, started to feel uncomfortable, since job interviews are not my happy place. By the end of it I was giving off take-it-or-leave-it vibes. Finally they stood and we shook hands.

'It's been a pleasure, Vincent,' Julia said. 'Thank you for having us.'

Six months went by, during which time I completely forgot about the whole episode until I answered my phone one day and got a surprise to hear Julia Gillard's assistant at the other end. 'I have some good news, Vincent,' she said brightly. 'If you'd still like to, Julia would love to have you paint her portrait.'

It was a massive moment for me. I'd painted some luminaries in the past including the CEOs of major banks and the heads of some of the country's most prestigious universities. I've been commissioned to do the portraits of professors, judges and even a Nobel Prize laureate. My paintings of university vice-chancellors hang in the halls of learning around the country: Monash University, Deakin University, the University of Canberra and my alma mater, the Royal Melbourne Institute of Technology.

Painting esteemed educators has provided some particularly proud moments in my career, given the horrors of my arduous academic journey. I also derived particular satisfaction from painting Marilyn Warren, the first Australian woman to become a chief justice, considering my felonious youth. Being invited to paint the official portrait of a prime minister of Australia, to be hung in Federal Parliament House alongside all the prime ministers throughout history, was on another level altogether. A huge honour.

One aspect of Julia's decision that impressed me was her apparent disregard for the political optics. I imagined she'd weighed the public relations benefits of going with a female artist, or maybe a painter from her home state of South Australia. I got a strong sense, however, that she'd looked past all of that and – knowing a bit more about me from our interview – decided, 'I'm going to give him a shot.' Julia is a bit of an outlier, too.

Prime ministers gaze back at the public from portraits long after their careers and, inevitably, their lives have ended – a final and enduring locking of eyes with a nation that once chose them to lead. Getting it right is a big responsibility for a portrait artist. I tried not to overthink it but I felt it was important to emphasise Julia's unique and historic status as Australia's first female prime minister. Her experience in the role wasn't the same as everybody else's. She faced external and internal pressures as prime minister that the twenty-six blokes who preceded her in the 109 years prior could never have conceived of.

In early 2018 Julia Gillard returned to my shabby little studio, only it was a different Julia. For one thing, she brought cakes and tea. Where our first meeting was very formal, this time she showed me who she really was.

'Vincent, I only have one request, although you could probably call it a stipulation,' Julia said, chuckling as she handed me a plate with some cake. 'I don't want this to have anything to do with fashion.'

'Right. No fashion,' I said.

'And I don't want it to look like the rest of those old men on the walls up there in Parliament House.'

I'd googled some of the other portraits and was struck by how similar many of them were: some wonderful paintings, but definitely a recurring theme of stuffy old dudes in dark suits. It occurred to me that none of those men ever had to concern themselves with what people might say about the cut and fashion appeal of said suits, or how many children they had. Those guys didn't have to worry that their choice of tie each day might end up as a hot topic in the daily news coverage.

The more we talked, the more I discovered what a sensitive human being Julia is. When people formed opinions during her prime ministership, the process was warped by the usual sneering views in newspapers and by people drawing cartoons that made fun of her fashion or her figure. Yet as far as I could see Julia remained stoic and dignified.

When we discussed these matters in my studio, I could see all of it had hurt her. I got an insight into how galling and upsetting it must have been to be literally running a country of twenty-two million people only to open the newspapers and discover some smartarse cartoonist had drawn outsize versions of your nose or your outfit or your hips. Or to tune in while a panel of wankers on TV gave their opinions about your private life, and struggled to wrap their heads around the fact you don't have kids. A lot of the acidic commentary was from other women, too. Just brutal. It certainly put my whinge about a couple of art critics into perspective.

Yet the Julia I got to know was charming, warm and wonderful company. She had no end of amazing stories and always laughed hardest at herself. I could quite ably have done the portrait using the photos and video I captured on the first day, but when that initial session wrapped she said, 'Should I come back in?'

'Yeah! You should definitely come back in!' I replied.

Julia is curious about people, which I really like about her because I am, too. On her return visit, I got a real kick out of watching the former Prime Minister of Australia sit with my brother Michael and ask him all about his life while her driver waited faithfully outside. Through it all Julia never once asked to see the painting.

As much as I was mostly in it for her company, her second sitting had a significant influence on the finished work. When I look at references such as printed photographs or digital images that I can zoom in and out of, there's a limit to how much

CHAPTER SIXTEEN

information I can extract. Colours in photographs are never the same as they are in real life, either. It's partly why it's important to me to get to know my subjects as much as possible – it helps me see beyond skin-deep.

Julia's complexion, hair colour and face were richer, but there was something else that came out of getting to know her: she's just plain funny. I decided to put the smallest hint of a smile on the edge of her lips, careful not to make it a smirk. When people are about to smile their face lifts a tiny fraction, and I noticed Julia does that a lot when she listens. The faint smile accounted for the last brushstrokes I did after her final visit.

As for her politics? We didn't get into any of that. She struck me as a truly special woman who was more than capable of handling the biggest job in the country. I could see how much she really believes in the Australian people and in the power of education.

Until the day of the unveiling I had never been to Parliament House in Canberra. Most kids go there on a special excursion during primary school but I was either deliberately excluded or we couldn't afford it. I definitely made up for it on that trip. Asher came with me and it was all very highbrow. We were picked up at Canberra Airport by a COMCAR and ushered straight into the private back rooms of Parliament House. Since I'm not great with faces I didn't recognise the powerful people swarming about. Asher did, though.

'Psst,' she whispered, nudging me with her foot. 'The Prime Minister.'

I thought she was talking about Julia but it was a bloke she nodded towards. Scott Morrison, I'm told.

At the unveiling I was more nervous than I had ever been. The national press, TV cameras and dignitaries filled the room. No-one knew what to expect. As an Australian portrait artist, moments don't get any bigger. I'd looked at all of the other prime ministerial portraits hanging on the walls and became hyper-conscious that Julia still hadn't seen our painting, and how different it was. *Oh no*, I suddenly realised. *This could go horribly wrong.*

Thankfully when we pulled back the curtain together I could tell by her smile that she loved it. I could breathe again. The applause was loud and long, too. Aside from the smile and her gender, the painting's main point of difference was, as a head-and-shoulders-style portrait, Julia's face filled the canvas leaving nothing for the fashion police to bust her for.

That afternoon I had the rare privilege of doing media interviews with Julia as she enjoyed her moment of reflection. Better still it gave me the opportunity to tell millions of Australians how brilliant – and funny – she is. The feedback from Parliament House is that Julia's portrait has eclipsed Gough Whitlam's as the most popular painting in the collection. Around one million visitors a year see it and we're told young girls are particularly drawn to it.

CHAPTER SIXTEEN

One thing I came to realise about painting a prime minister or other politicians is that people might like the artwork but cast judgement on the subject. Party politics is often taken into their personal critique. Since then, plenty of people have told me, 'I don't like Julia Gillard and I don't like politics but your portrait is very good.'

Well, I don't like politics either but I really do like Julia, and I'm very happy to know her. We've stayed in touch. If I've kicked a goal or done something worthwhile she'll text me and say, 'Saw that. Well done.' I do the same with her.

It's never lost on me that a lot of the people who have opened doors for me in life, or looked after me, have been women. Julia joins the ranks of many to whom I owe a great debt of gratitude. However I also owe her – and every other Australian, including myself – something far more important.

The reason I don't recall my parents going to vote in elections is because they never did. Mum and Dad were born overseas and neglected to take out citizenship. Australian residents? Yes. Australians citizens? No. And neither am I.

I was born in England and have spent my life travelling the world as a British citizen on a British passport. It's a discordant state of affairs considering I've represented Australia in many ways and I *am* Australian. I'm not anything else. I guess it was a clerical oversight that could have been forgiven when I was a child, but I'm closing in on my fifth decade now and I still haven't fixed the problem. Why not? Because the paperwork is like an encyclopedia. I've downloaded it plenty of times but given up as soon as I've started.

'I'll do it next year,' I'd say.

Now forty years have passed and I still haven't become a citizen. Asher downloaded the forms again not long ago and we actually made some headway, but then she got way too busy with work and the project was abandoned again. In all that time I have never voted. I feel terrible about it because I know I have a responsibility to. More than anyone, I recognise how ridiculous it seems to campaign for causes that I can't even cast a ballot for.

What do we want?

Marriage equality!

When do we want it?

When I finally get around to filling out the paperwork!

I've made a note somewhere to download the forms again. I'll get onto it this year for sure. I know it would make Julia very happy.

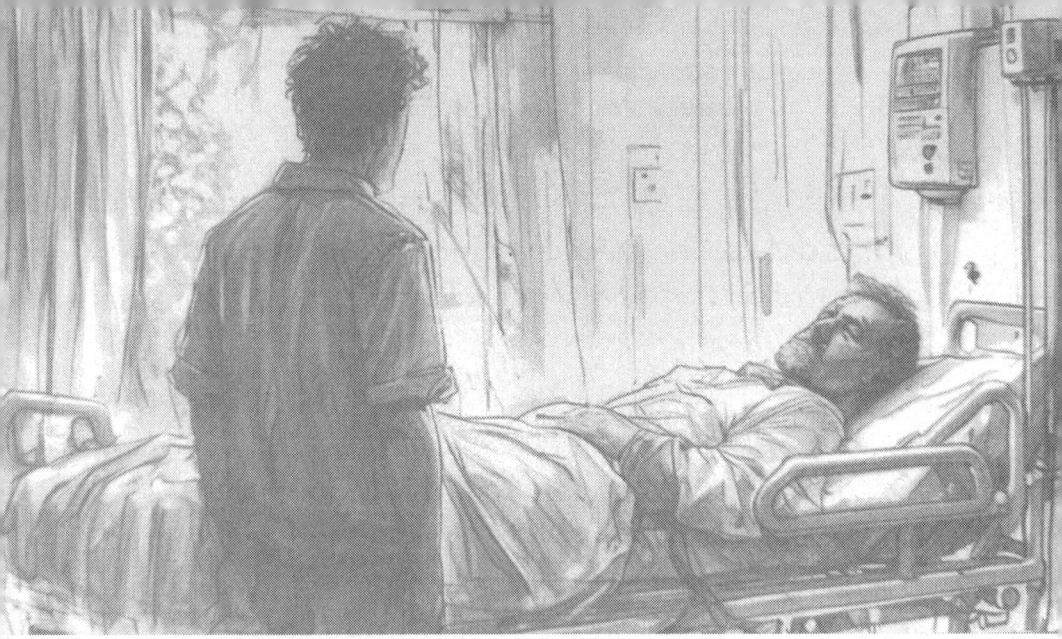

I once painted a giant mural in a boxing gym near Essendon train station of the famous image of Muhammad Ali standing over a vanquished Sonny Liston during their world heavyweight title fight in 1965. The painting reached from floor to ceiling and took up an entire wall. I was eighteen and fairly broke when I did it after striking a deal with the owners in lieu of training fees. Every time I laced up my gloves I gave Muhammad and Sonny a silent nod of thanks for taking care of my gym membership.

Twenty-five years later I received a phone call out of the blue from one of the owners. 'We're going out of business and we're selling the place,' he explained. 'That painting of Ali and Liston, what do you reckon it might be worth?'

'I couldn't tell you,' I said, 'but I can give you the name of a valuer who can come in and give you a proper appraisal.'

'That'd be great. We could definitely use an extra grand or two,' he said, trying to float a price into the conversation. I didn't want to lead him on because I honestly had no idea of its worth.

'Well, the valuer will be able to let you guys know for sure,' I said. 'Best of luck with it.'

I found out later the mural was worth $80,000. Since it was painted on gyprock, the gym owners painstakingly cut the entire wall sheet out of the building. I was thrilled for them, and touched to think Muhammad and Sonny – who'd so graciously paid for my training – had also looked after the blokes who gave me an early opportunity. I only wish I'd been there to see the looks on their faces when the valuer gave them the price.

A couple of years earlier I'd received a similar phone call from a framing shop in Collingwood. The owner was also closing the doors after many years, and had been told I was the artist responsible for one of the paintings he wanted to get rid of.

'We're trying to clear all of this junk and I came across a painting that's been sitting in the storeroom for something like twenty years,' he explained. 'Did you ever paint Johnny Famechon and Lionel Rose?'

'Yeah, I did!' I said as the hairs on my arms stood up. The moment he said those names, part of me was sitting alongside Jack Rennie as Johnny Famechon struggled to sign the prints we put in front of him. I was amazed that the painting had winged its way back to me after all those years. I could never recall

CHAPTER SEVENTEEN

what had happened to it so I figured I must have either sold it, lost it or it had been stolen.

'Well, I've got it here if you want it, but I've framed it, so you'll have to pay for that,' the shop owner said.

'That sounds fair,' I replied. 'How much do you want for the framing job?'

'It's $400. For that I'll drop it over to you if you like, or you can come and pick it up,' he offered.

'That's alright, mate. Save your petrol. I'll come and grab it off you.'

That afternoon I shook hands with the old picture framer and followed him through the dusty disarray of his dying shop. In the storeroom, Lionel and Johnny were propped up against a wall and facing off in the ring, just as I'd left them.

'There it is,' he said. 'It's a nice painting, by the way.'

'Thanks,' I replied as I peered at the boxers and recalled Johnny's displeasure at the wrong coloured shorts I'd put him in. 'It was actually one of my first.'

'Is that right?' he said. 'So, are you making a living? I might be able to give you some work. You can obviously paint.'

'That's a very kind offer,' I said.

'How much do you charge for a portrait?' he asked.

I told him the price and he nearly fell over.

'Fuck me!' he said and roared with laughter. 'You can pay me for storage! I've had this painting for twenty years!'

'How about I give you $800 for the frame instead of $400?' I proposed.

'It's a deal.'

Nowadays Johnny and Lionel live in my studio.

The mysterious boomerang arc of that painting shows that I had trouble keeping track of my work right from the start. I never catalogued paintings or knew when they were done, how much they sold for or where they ended up. I only know about some of the more famous works because they're in galleries, universities or the homes of friends, or the national media and the world wide web have courteously recorded the details for me. Countless other works were scattered to the four winds. Even entire collections have gone missing, including the New York series of Thirty Portraits in Thirty Days. (The Hong Kong version was also out of reach for many years and at the time of writing it was in storage at the gallery where it was exhibited in 2009.)

In 2015 I was given a compelling reason to finally track down all of my errant artworks. Ken McGregor introduced me to David Deague and his sons William and Jonathan who, together, run one of Australia's oldest property development companies. Back in 2009 the Deagues launched the Art Series Hotel Group – a collection of luxury hotels around Australia that are named for – and showcase the work of – famous Australian artists. The properties include The Olsen and The Cullen in Melbourne (featuring the work of John Olsen and Adam Cullen, respectively), and

CHAPTER SEVENTEEN

The Watson in Adelaide, which is hung with paintings by the late Indigenous great, Tommy Watson.

Ken, who helped the Deagues choose artists suitable for their projects, put me forward as a contender to have a new hotel in Brisbane named after me and filled with my paintings. It all sounded completely over the top to me but after a few meetings with the Deagues I was delighted to discover that we got along really well and that they were dead serious.

For such high-stakes developers they are pretty funny guys. 'Great, finally we've got someone young and cool to do a hotel with,' Will said at one point.

The patriarch, chairman David Deague, wasn't so effusive. 'Can we change your name to something people can pronounce?' he said dryly.

'Can you pronounce Caravaggio?' I replied cheekily.

After a bit of back and forth the Deagues said they were indeed going to build a $100 million hotel underneath the Storey Bridge with my name on it. Over the years I'd fielded a lot of pitches and promises from people about various projects that often came to naught. When I heard no more about it I told myself, *It's never going to happen*, and put the hotel out of my mind. I moved on with my life and, as usual, forgot all about it.

Almost two years later David Deague called me. 'We've got the site sorted and we're ready to go,' he said.

My great inner imposter – not yet interred with the help of Michael – wanted to say, 'There's been a mistake! You know it's just me, right?'

As the Deagues set about work on the six-storey five-star hotel on the banks of the Brisbane River, I was tasked with gathering together my life's work. I'd never had to think about it before and I had no idea of how to go about tracking it all down. As well as there being precious few records of sales, I didn't know what sizes they were or who owned them. In a panic, I turned to Asher.

She has been my biggest fan and champion from our first days together. In 2013 it was Asher who added fuel to my desire to break free from the galleries and go it alone. When she discovered I was paying 50–60 per cent of my earnings to other people she said, 'Are you for real?' That started a conversation about ambition and self-determination.

At the time I wanted to grow our family and provide for them, so I was determined to take control of my earning power. There was nothing to be gained by continuing to gripe about the establishment, and although there was risk involved in being a free agent – for one thing you can't show at the international art fairs unless you're aligned with a gallery – it paid off in the long run. The value of my work has increased and the middlemen are long gone.

A free agent or not, I was still hopeless at cataloguing and now that I faced the crisis of finding my lost work, it was Asher who came to the rescue. She launched into an exhaustive six-month international treasure hunt. She scoured the internet and contacted collectors, art dealers and galleries around the world and eventually compiled the first ever catalogue of my output. After countless long days and late nights, Asher located hundreds of paintings, some of which I'd completely forgotten I'd created like those of the actress Charlize Theron, gambler and art collector David Walsh, Melbourne billionaire Ron Walker and American supermodel Chanel Iman.

The Deagues invited Asher and me to participate in the interior design stage of the project, and we had final say on the placement of more than five hundred of my works throughout the 166-room hotel. Most are giclée prints but there are seven originals in there, too. The Deague family was not only generous to involve us but when it was time for the official launch party they also told us to throw the doors wide open and invite everyone we wanted to be there.

We did as we were told and dozens of friends and family flew in from interstate and overseas. On 26 March 2019 the grand opening of The Fantauzzo doubled as the big wedding reception that we'd never had. There were speeches, fireworks and live performers. I was asked to say a few words, too, and as the time drew closer I felt both overwhelmed and torn by doubt. Part of me was embarrassed that I hadn't done more with my career and felt undeserving of the honour, but I wasn't about to say that part out loud. Even so, I began my speech with another truth that spoke to my genuine mystification at all the attention. 'I wake up in the morning and I feel like I'm in a fairytale,' I said as I looked out over a room full of friends and family. 'I have to pinch myself.'

The rest of the night was a blur. Later on, Asher pulled me into a quiet corner. 'I want you to take a moment to look around and really remember this night,' she said and stroked my cheek with her finger.

'Look up there,' she continued, pointing to my name in lights above the hotel. 'This place celebrates *you* and the amazing art you have created. You deserve this.'

We woke up in the hotel the next day and life went on. From time to time I still wonder how long it will be before someone finds out that I'm bad-boy Vinnie from Shitsville and they made a big blunder, but each time I go to Brisbane the hotel and my paintings are still there. It turned out that David Deague wasn't the only one to have misgivings about my exotic surname in lights above the entrance, though. When The Fantauzzo was sold in 2020 to Syrian billionaire Ghassan Aboud, who runs the Crystalbrook Collection luxury hotel chain, the new owner renamed the place Crystalbrook Vincent.

You'd think that having a profile as an artist would be celebrated – after all, anything that brings paintings to the attention of the wider public is surely a benefit to all artists. I find it strange that the visual arts seem to be the only medium in which being outwardly and financially successful is anathema. Nobody bats an eyelid when rockstars fly in a private jet, or actors do advertisements for Chanel No. 5 or Nescafé. Similarly, no-one rolls their eyes when sportspeople have sponsorship deals. If you're a painter who wants to live the good life and enjoy the rewards of success, however, you're branded a sellout.

The good news is I long ago stopped giving a flying fig what the art world thinks of me. I'm happy to be outside of their galleries and their little clubs, and doing my own thing. I think I might even be close to dropping my obsession with winning their Archibald Prize.

I'm not ashamed that I was the first Australian artist to become a brand ambassador (initially for Audi and then Alfa Romeo) or the first artist to win a GQ Award. I'm stoked to have alignment with Ducati motorcycles and to have collaborated with several high-end brands. That's not to say sponsorships or commercial success is what drives me or my art. I don't need a Rolex or a Lamborghini, but if I work hard – like anyone else who works hard – I want to take full advantage of the opportunities that come my way and provide for my family. I want our boys to have the same outlook: that they're just as entitled to live well and aim as high as everybody else.

Aside from getting to ride their iconic motorbikes, my relationship with Ducati allowed me to fulfil a childhood dream of designing a two-wheeled machine of my own. As a half-Italian kid and the son of a major Ducati fan, I had posters of their bikes plastered over my bedroom walls. A couple of years ago I felt like I'd entered a time warp when Ducati invited me to sharpen my pencils and design my dream motorbike. Instead of sticky-taping the drawing to the back of our bedroom door, I handed it to a custom bike builder. It was one of those milestones I'd have loved my father to be around for. Maybe he would have finally said he was proud of me.

'Hey Dad! I got to design a bike for Ducati! You love Ducati! Let's go for a ride!'

I hadn't seen him in a while. The last time was at my sister Marianne's place where he flaunted his customary lack of interest in what was happening in my life. His hair was grey and thinning, and he looked a lot skinnier than he had the last time he'd bothered to come to Melbourne. I noticed he had a lump on his neck but when I asked him about it he waved away my concerns. 'It's nothing,' he grunted.

Dad generally ignored my success as a painter. He'd said a few complimentary things when I was starting out but when my career took off he saw an opportunity. *He* started painting and trying to sell works on the back of the Fantauzzo name that I had elevated. Although he had every right to – and some skill at painting – he was an average artist at best. He remained a world-class swindler, though.

CHAPTER SEVENTEEN

When I really broke through after the Archibald Prize success with *Heath* he subjected me to a deafening radio silence. From then on, after every milestone I reached in life, he had nothing to say: when I married Asher, when Val was born, when my work was hung in Parliament House and when I was made an adjunct professor at RMIT and invited to give a keynote address to graduating students. His absence always hurt but it was the family stuff that burned the most. His disdain for my boys was unforgivable.

As the years rolled along, things came up in life that reminded me of some of the sharper paternal disappointments. When Asher and I bought our dog Rocco, for example, I recalled a long-buried memory that stung as it surfaced. Before I went to England with Latifah in the late 1990s I knew I'd be gone for months so I asked Dad if he'd look after my faithful four-legged pal Cujo until I returned.

'Yeah, sure,' he said.

When I arrived back in Australia, Dad told me that Cujo had supposedly tried to bite one of his neighbours so he'd decided to get rid of him. 'I gave him to some people who have a farm,' he said.

The truth is he grew tired of looking after Cujo, took him to the vet and had him destroyed. I had truly loved that dog.

The lump on Dad's neck didn't look like 'nothing' to me. As far as I know the man never once tried to quit smoking and kept up his toxic intake of two packets a day. He'd have smoked three packs a day if he didn't have to take time out to sleep. The next time I heard anything about it was a few months later when Marianne phoned me. 'Dad's in hospital,' she said in a trembling voice. 'You'd better come and see him. He doesn't look very good.'

I drove straight to the hospital in Carlton where some of my family were gathered at his bedside. I took one look at the man and knew he was dying. By their disposition I don't think the others did, but I knew. At home that night I awoke in the grip of some kind of fit. I was soaked in sweat and shook uncontrollably. I tried to close my eyes and calm myself but I couldn't switch off the bright light that was blazing behind my eyeballs. In frightening moments of delirium I experienced awful waking nightmares and a dreadful feeling that something malevolent was inside me. It scared the hell out of Asher. 'Are you okay?' she cried. 'Are you okay?' She tried to hold me and patted me down with a cloth until I finally fell unconscious, exhausted.

I woke the next day to the sound of my phone ringing. It was someone from the hospital. 'Your father is dying,' the voice said. 'If you want to come and spend time with him, he doesn't have long. His organs are shutting down.'

Dad lasted another two weeks but he never spoke or moved again. My brothers and sisters kept a rotating bedside vigil going and – when she knew Dad's partner wouldn't be there – Mum sat beside

CHAPTER SEVENTEEN

him through the night as well. There were a lot of tears shed in that room, but not by me. The prevailing attitude towards Dad's imminent death was, 'This is a good man who is being taken from us. How will we go on without him?'

I didn't feel inclined to canonise a person who had cynically abandoned his children and deliberately made them suffer. I didn't want to hold hands and weep for a man who had declared himself bankrupt to avoid paying child support, or who gave a figurative middle finger to his own grandsons. There's nothing more painful in this world like the rejection of the people who made you and should love you the most.

I didn't take Asher or the boys to see Dad in his final weeks – they didn't need to look at a dying stranger. I didn't particularly want to, either, but I turned up when I could. I felt guilty about the rest of the family being there more than I was. They wept on his hospital blanket but I just couldn't shed a tear for Claudio Fantauzzo.

On the night that he died we were all there together. My sisters, in particular, were overcome with emotion.

'Dad, don't leave us!'

'I need my dad!'

'Please, Dad, I have nothing without you!'

Mum was a sobbing mess after he died and I was emotional, too, but mine were very mixed feelings and still I didn't cry. I wanted to feel the loss and

I couldn't understand why everyone else did except me. Didn't we share the same experiences? As much as my brain told me I should grieve, my heart refused to because the betrayal I felt was too great.

Dad's funeral was held at a small Catholic church in Macedon, which he had no connection to but happened to be quite near where Mum lived. I only took Luca with me because the lovely boy wanted to support his dad on the saddest of days. It was an hour-long drive and as we sailed along the freeway I noticed a hearse pull into our slipstream. *It couldn't be!* I thought as I peered in the rear-vision mirror. It *was* Dad, though, and his shiny black ride stayed behind my car for the rest of the journey, as if I was showing him the way to his grave.

Dad had always bagged out his parents. My nonna – as we called my grandma Vincenza – was quite a strict, robust Italian woman with lots of 'Mama mia's' and 'Donta toucha this's' that were enforced with the occasional crack across the knuckles. She laughed a lot, too, though, and seemed a pretty alright grandma to me. My nonno, Vincenzo, couldn't speak much English but he had a sense of humour and joked around with the grandkids. When he ran the cake shop in Preston he took time to sit with me and make things out of dough. He taught me how to make spinning tops, too. As far as Dad was concerned, however, Nonna and Nonno were the worst parents who'd ever lived. After he fell out with his brothers when I was just a kid, Dad shifted his antipathy to them. Even then I could see he was the one who behaved like an arsehole.

Nonna and Nonno had long departed the world but when Luca and I walked into the church in Macedon, Dad's brothers, his twin sister and my long-lost cousins were all there waiting with my siblings, Mum and his current partner. There was no-one else in attendance. Not one friend. Undertakers carried the coffin onto the little elevated stage and as everyone took their seats the room filled with the soft, funereal melodies of weeping people. I was acutely aware that I still hadn't cried since the day he died.

The Catholic priest, an Indian fellow with a strong accent, kicked off proceedings by mispronouncing my late father's name. 'Cloud was a very humble, humorous man who was devoted to his family and who also dedicated himself to the community,' he said. 'He loved God and God's people, and he was a very faithful and obedient Christian . . .'

I supposed he might have been, if you didn't count all the lying, cheating, stealing and hating. It was hard to listen to such a mindless and bloated sugar-coating of a deeply flawed man. After some more cookie-cutter eulogising from the priest, my sisters got up to say some warm and loving things about our father, describing him in saintly terms and as a rock in their lives. I squirmed in my chair feeling confused and I wondered whether we really grew up in the same household together. A reading from the Bible followed and a slideshow of photographs before the priest steered the service back towards the Catholic faith and what a huge part it had played in Cloud's life.

'Cloud was a man of deep faith who took comfort in attending his church . . .'

I'd heard enough. I stood and walked onto the little stage, then grabbed the microphone off the priest. 'I'm sorry but I can't sit here and listen to any more of this,' I said. 'I just can't.'

Turning to the priest I said, 'I'm sure you're a good man and your heart is in the right place but you're talking about a man's life and you can't even pronounce his name. It's Claudio. Not Cloud. I'm not saying my father was a bad person and I don't know who told you about his faith, but today is the very first time he's been to church since I've known him. He couldn't stand church. The thing is, I'm thankful that he's finally made it here today so for once we can all be together.'

The priest looked like a deer in the headlights. I had been asked if I wanted to speak at the funeral but originally declined because I didn't know what to say. Now that I had something to contribute, the poor priest had no choice but to listen. 'Dad might have been funny at times but he wasn't a family man,' I continued, correcting the false record. 'Not to our family anyway, and definitely not to mine. I apologise if that upsets people but I cannot sit here and listen to a version of my father that didn't exist.'

CHAPTER SEVENTEEN

I looked at his brothers who were sitting at opposite sides of the front-row pews – still estranged from each other after all those years. 'Y'know, we haven't seen any of you guys for twenty-five years, so if there's one thing that Dad *can* do it's put us all back in touch and maybe we can see each other from time to time,' I said. 'That might be nice.'

I tried to offer some kinder words about Dad, too – how he was a great cook and that I'm sure he had good intentions now and then. 'I loved him,' I said, 'and I wish that I could have sorted out the shit that we had between us. If he hadn't died maybe we would have ended up with a good relationship.' (Still chasing the man, even when he was dead and gone.)

'And maybe you guys who don't talk to each other anymore can learn from my regret,' I added. 'Maybe you can let it go.'

I handed the microphone back to the priest and resumed my seat next to Luca. No-one said a word. The only sound was people crying, but I still couldn't do it.

After some blessings and prayers from the priest it was time to carry Dad out to the hearse for his final journey. Along with my brothers, uncles and cousins, I lifted the coffin onto my shoulder. The moment I felt the earthly weight of my father press down on my body, I broke. I stumbled and struggled to stay on my feet as four decades' worth of anguish poured out of me in an uncontrolled release. I howled like an animal as a black grief rose up from deep within. My face was soaked with tears, my nose leaked like a broken tap and my chest heaved as I tried to suck in air. I was a fucking mess.

The reality that I'd refused to fully accept from the moment I laid eyes on that bulge on his neck had finally arrived. My father was gone forever and, with him, any chance of fixing the biggest thing that was broken in my life. I'd have loved to be able to say nice things about him. I wanted to love him and I wanted him to love me. I regretted all the negative stuff I'd said about him over the years because I'd heard him talk about his own parents like that and I didn't want to be that person.

Perhaps naïvely I always thought there'd be enough time for our relationship to come good. I'd seen Mum sort things out with her father before he died and I fully expected it would be the same with Dad and me: that he'd one day be a grandfather to my sons, even if it was just for five or ten years, and that I'd be able to put away my anger.

Then he went and died on me before it had a chance to happen. I couldn't believe he'd left me stranded like that. As the hearse drove him away I almost ran after it.

In late 2019 I received a phone call from Karen Quinlan, the director of the National Portrait Gallery in Canberra. In art world terms, the NPG is located somewhere in the upper atmosphere – certainly somewhere my work had never been shown. Whether you're an outsider or not, fielding a call from them is a big deal. 'We'd like to commission you to do a portrait of Hugh Jackman,' Karen said. 'Is that something you'd be interested in?'

Despite my career-long cynicism towards the establishment, I felt surprisingly electrified by the unexpected gesture of inclusion. It was like taking out a major art prize, on my birthday, after winning the lottery. 'Of course I'm interested,' I gushed. 'Thank you so much!'

I'd met Hugh a couple of times through Baz but I didn't know him well. Karen told me that when the gallery first approached him about the portrait Hugh insisted that he'd only do it with me. 'That's not the only reason for the commission,' she quickly assured me. 'We love your paintings and we'd be thrilled to have one in the collection.'

A month or so later Hugh and I met in Melbourne and got along like a house on fire. Over a couple of leisurely coffee dates we discussed ideas for what kind of painting we wanted to do, swapped war stories and generally chewed the fat. As we chatted away he told me his son, Oscar, is also dyslexic. It gave me an idea: 'Why don't you bring him along and he can help direct the photoshoot?' I proposed.

Whenever I take photos of Asher I find good light, compose the frame and focus the lens, but before I press the shutter I lift my eyes above the viewfinder. When we lock eyes she's guaranteed to give me a look that's real, be it love, annoyance or something else on the spectrum of marriage. *Click!* Asher is brilliant at telling the whole story with just one look. So is Hugh Jackman and so was Heath Ledger – that's what made them stars: they were born with a special communication wavelength, and I reckoned Oscar would help me tune directly into Hugh's.

The deadline for the portrait was a fairly loose six months away and, since there was no urgency, I took my time and caught up with Hugh more in order to hang out than to make a real start. That changed in a heartbeat after COVID hit. On the March day in 2020 that Hugh and Oscar were due to come to the studio for the shoot, the world's borders started

CHAPTER EIGHTEEN

slamming shut. Hugh – who mainly lives and works in the US – phoned me in the morning. 'We have to leave right now to get back to New York,' he said. 'I'm really sorry, mate, but I'm not going to get there.'

'Shit!' I said. 'Can't you stop by on the way to the airport?'

'I'm really, *really* sorry, Vincent,' he said. 'I literally have to get on the plane, like, right now, otherwise we'll be stranded here.'

I could have kicked myself. *The biggest commission you're going to do and you've been hanging out drinking cappuccinos with the man instead of working,* I thought ruefully. *You should have taken your camera along and shot a photo or two so you'd at least have something.*

As the COVID death toll began its alarming ascent – particularly in New York – I resisted the impulse to feel too bad about missing my opportunities with Hugh. A lot of people were having far worse days than I. Still, the deadline loomed. As the pandemic tightened its grip, society found new ways of operating, and so did I. Like millions of other people, I breathed a sigh of relief when Zoom strode confidently into my life.

A few days later I phoned Hugh in New York and got the project back on track. 'We can do this on Zoom,' I said. 'I've been thinking about it and I reckon I can direct your family to take photos of you. They'll hold the camera and I'll tell them the angles to shoot from. Or we could try using the computer as a camera. I could direct you and grab screenshots.'

I was making it up as I went but – being a true professional as well as a wonderful human being – Hugh was up for anything that would help us get a result. On a whim one night, I videoed myself walking through my house, pausing at different portraits that were hanging on the walls and describing how the process of each painting came about, and what I was after with Hugh's. I was self-conscious as I filmed myself trying to direct one of the world's great actors, but I did it with as much humour as I could in the hope it would inspire Hugh and his family to take some amazing images for me to work with.

They gave it their best shot but, for the purpose of creating an artwork to hang in the National Portrait Gallery, the photos were unusable. One that came through showed Hugh wearing a Chinese bowl on his head. It had me in fits of laughter, but I thought, *Oh no, how am I going to make this work?* I politely went back over and over, and asked them to try again but we couldn't seem to get there. It was nobody's fault but mine – the cappuccino kid.

One lovely byproduct of our communication throughout this time, however, was the bond I forged with Hugh while we hibernated with our loved ones in silent cities on opposite sides of the globe. We had some funny banter back and forth as he sent me more crap photos and I told him to try again

CHAPTER EIGHTEEN

or do something different. Finally, and unsurprisingly, the answer to our problem lay in film – the medium in which Hugh was most comfortable and the one that had informed my art since I was a little boy.

One day an email arrived with a video attached of Hugh telling a story direct to the camera. I don't know what kind of device he filmed it on but it was very high resolution, and ten times sharper and more compelling than any of the stills he'd sent. Halfway through the story Hugh started to crack up and a moment later he rested his head on his hand and smiled as wisps of laughter still clung to his face. I watched the video back a few times, then freeze-framed my way through it – just like I'd done as a cinephile kid in search of magic movie moments – until I landed on the expression that conveyed the story of Hugh I wanted to tell.

It's not how I would have approached a portrait of the man in a perfect world, but it was a bona-fide COVID-era work of art that now hangs in the National Portrait Gallery where, I'm told, it's one of the most popular on show.

I've since had two more commissions from the NPG – a painting of philanthropist Malcolm McCusker, the former barrister and Governor of Western Australia who famously worked on cases freeing wrongly convicted prisoners, and Australian community and land developer Nigel Satterley. I consider those works – particularly the hard-won portrait of Hugh – to be career victories.

Now that I'm much closer to fifty than forty I feel more comfortable in my own skin as an artist than ever before. The big prizes and marquee moments still matter to me but I'm increasingly grateful for my autonomy and to just be able to make a living doing something I love. Although I still begin each year worried that I won't get enough commissions, or that I might not have an impending exhibition, I realise I'm no different to any other sole trader or small businessperson. Everyone frets about the future to some degree. It's normal and it keeps you focused. Lately, though, I've realised I have a lot of work to do on the past as well.

The trauma of my childhood seems both a long way behind me and right up in my face. I haven't visited Broadmeadows since I don't know when, and I'm not in touch with many people from back in the day. Although I've moved on, the wider perspective has made me proud of my roots. Having spent my life getting to know people from all walks of life, listening to their stories and trying to capture the spark inside them, I have realised that everyone faces hardship. I understand that I'm not a special case and that personal struggles aren't determined by your postcode. I know people who were raised in exclusive suburbs and had the best education who are still messed up from childhood. Some took their own lives. Millions of people elevate themselves from harsh beginnings and I'm thankful that I was one of them. The real tragedy is that millions don't or, worse, they can't.

CHAPTER EIGHTEEN

While the aftershocks of my childhood trauma haven't shaped the landscape of my life anywhere near as much as my hopes and ambitions have, they've obviously left their mark. Living in constant fear of violence, molestation and even death during my formative years ingrained unhelpful reflexes deep in my psyche. It's why I wake up swinging and stash baseball bats around the house.

Nowadays my studio is in St Kilda, just down the road from a pub where I often see people teeter on the edge of violence. It's very easy to get in a fight if you're willing, but thankfully most people don't, because they're scared. I see the pub patrons yell at each other and face off as if they're going to throw punches, and I smile to myself when they walk away instead. There was a time in my life if someone did that to me – *bang*, I'd just hit them. I didn't know any other way and I was too scared to back down. I can't pinpoint exactly when I stopped doing that, but it's been a very, very long time since I was in a fight.

Still, there are times I react in ways I know I shouldn't. A couple of years ago I caught a guy trying to steal my car. I headed out to get a coffee one morning with Luca in tow when I spied someone sitting in the driver's seat with all the windows down and trying to get the thing started. I told Luca to run inside to Asher and I grabbed the nearest weapon, which happened to be a gardening shovel. I ran up to the passenger's side window of my car and cracked the thief twice in the head with the handle (not the sharp end, which I thought was considerate of me).

The guy was all tatted up, muscled like a steroid user and wearing gloves and running gear. I launched into my old 'scare them' routine. I roared as I went to rip the door open. He scrambled out the driver's side and took off down the street. I gave chase with the shovel but he was too quick. Meanwhile, inside our house, Asher turned to Luca and said, 'There's someone screaming outside! Who's screaming?'

'It's Dad,' Luca said.

When you grow up around the people I did, you know when someone's a proper bad guy. If it had just been a junkie trying to steal my car I wouldn't have reacted like that, but this guy, posing as a jogger, had 'the look'. He was the sort of person who comes into your house and hurts your family. Even so, when the dust settled, I realised my reaction might have been – as my shaken wife put it – 'disproportionate'. My brain, however, is imprinted with an animal instinct to protect the people I love immediately and at all costs. I know that if someone comes into my house to harm my wife and children, they're not coming back out.

Asher has long believed I need counselling. She lives with my nightmares, the broken sleep and my collection of baseball bats. I saw a therapist for a while but it didn't last because I couldn't see he had anything to offer me. It wasn't like I didn't know what my issues were – after all, I've lived them – and

CHAPTER EIGHTEEN

I was confident I could make sense of them by myself. During my last session I sat in his rooms thinking, *I'm telling you all this stuff and it's just going to end up as dinner-party stories for your mates.*

It was a pretty unfair take on someone whose vocation is to help people. At the time, though, I truly felt I could listen to a good book about trauma and find solutions myself. Writing my own book, however, has shifted my thinking. Reliving the events described in these pages has been a form of therapy. I've come to understand the value of talking about my problems. Do I still need counselling? I guess I'll have to wait and see. After all, these things can take time. Asher and I were together for ten years before I told her I'd been abused. What I do know is that my residual trauma can't get any worse, so maybe that means it can only get better.

Boxing training remains a huge part of my life and, like painting, it's vital to my mental health management. When I moved into my studio in St Kilda a few years ago I had the space to add a floor-to-ceiling ball and hang a punching bag from the rafters so I could train before work. I was soon joined by one of my oldest friends, Patrick Boutellier, who used to run Rolex's operations in Australasia. With such a high-pressure job we'd found it increasingly difficult to catch up for 'man time' outside of work, so he started coming by the studio at 7 am on Tuesdays and Thursdays to train with me. One day he invited a mate along, followed by another, then another . . .

Nowadays it's not unusual for a dozen men from all walks of life to file into my studio for twice-weekly morning 'Fight Club'. I've added a couple more punching bags and some of the guys have donated gym mats to cover the worn and paint-stained floorboards.

Though I train them and share my love of boxing, it's about so much more than that: camaraderie, a chance to relate to other men in an environment that isn't the pub, and an opportunity to share deeper thoughts – without judgement – about the crazy rollercoaster of life. Everyone leaves the studio feeling their best selves, mentally and physically, and some great friendships have been forged. A number of the guys have told me that Fight Club has changed their lives. I know what they mean because I feel the same way.

My memory, however, such as it is, makes me worry that I'm being stalked by another problem. I often wonder if I was born with a dementia gene and what direction my life will take as I grow older. I don't put it down to boxing because I was a defensive fighter who was never knocked out or dazed too badly. I watch teenage kids play soccer today and they get more concussions than I ever did but there are days I feel my memory might be worse than it was the year before. If I can't even find my way to Luca's soccer practice after fifty trips, how am I going to drive a car when I'm sixty-five? Thankfully I'm a very positive person because by then, I figure cars will drive themselves.

Recently I've had cause for some optimism about my brain function. Over the years a ridiculous number of people have suggested that I consider the possibility that I also suffer from attention deficit hyperactivity disorder (ADHD). Since being highly dyslexic was quite enough to deal with, I refused to even think about it. That changed in August 2024, after a number of people close to me – including the journalist and publisher Mia Freedman (who inspired the character played by Asher in the series *Strife*) – were diagnosed with ADHD.

I mentioned this to my GP, who happens to have a child with ADHD and who was a fountain of information about the condition. He organised for me to be tested and, for the first time in my life, I earned an A-plus in an exam: I scored nine from nine in two out of the three types of ADHD. After some more testing and evaluation I started taking medication to treat it. At the time of writing I noted a marked difference in the way my mind works. I have been less agitated and my myriad thoughts feel like they've converged into a steady river instead of cascading over a waterfall like they always did. Time will tell, but in a way it seems I might be onto something life-changing.

I'm not sure what to do about the anger I still feel towards Dad. My impromptu speech at his funeral sparked a few conversations among my relatives and I've been thrilled to see that Mum has since grown close to his twin sister, but there's still a lot of wreckage in the wider family.

After Dad died I yearned to have something that would connect me to him more than the lonely teddy bear that lives with us. Dad had an old Range Rover that was falling apart so I bought it off his partner and have been slowly restoring it ever since, because it was something he'd wanted to do. I'm still not finished but I know he'd have loved what I've done to it so far. While the car restoration helps me feel as though I'm in touch with him in some way it's also partly a pushback against the hard-wired psychology of my youth where shortcuts were a way of life. I have been able to fix the thing up, without cutting corners, whereas he couldn't. Nothing is simple inside my head.

I have guilt, too. I'm not proud of the fact I haven't been to my father's grave – yet. Nobody else in the family has been able to afford a headstone for him so he's out there at Macedon, practically unmarked and unremarked upon, which is something I want to fix. I will get him a proper headstone.

Memories of my father make me reflect on my purpose in life. I have a few, and one is to have children who will one day tell their kids about me in a positive light. I think about it all the time when I'm at soccer with Luca or at the skate park with Val. I never miss Luca's games. He's a very good player so he's targeted a bit on the field. One day he was shouldered and completely flattened. He wasn't embarrassed but he knew he'd been clocked and when he stood up I saw him look for me in the crowd. He didn't wave or say anything, and I didn't tell him to, 'Get up and go smash them' – we just made eye contact and I nodded my head. It was a look that told him, 'I'm here.'

I have a similar feeling about my role as a public person with dyslexia. At the moment all I can say is, 'I'm here.' It's important to share my experiences in the hope of giving confidence to others whose lives have been impacted by it, and though I want to do much more in the dyslexia space, it's hard.

A couple of my closest friends, Mac and Nicky, have an amazing boy who is also neurodivergent. He looks up to me a bit and I've been able to help him with his confidence a little. His mum and dad and I decided to start a charity for people with dyslexia. Unsurprisingly we soon discovered that the last person on earth you want to help organise a charity for dyslexics is a dyslexic. Mac and Nicky spent a lot of time and effort doing all the necessary groundwork and jumping through complex bureaucratic hoops to register the charity and now that it's complete I haven't done anything with it.

I speak to a lot of parents who have dyslexic kids – including some very wealthy people – who are more than happy to put some money into the charity and fund it, but I don't follow up. I want to, but I don't know how. I don't even know where to start. You'd think I could have someone do it for me but I find even taking a step like that too much to handle.

At the moment it's easier for me to focus on making a difference in the field I'm good in. One of my main goals in life is to make art popular. I believe everyone has the right to pursue art and to have an opinion on what's good and what has value. I like what the big name chefs like Matt Moran have done to make cooking popular and accessible. These days kids want to be top chefs and restaurateurs when they grow up, because they've been shown it's possible by people like Matt and others who have pulled back the curtain. Maybe that's the way to make art cooler, too, by somehow changing the scene from within.

I have so much more to do as an artist and I'm anxious to get on with it. One great thing about my line of work is that you don't have to retire. It excites me to think I could be more relevant at seventy-five than I am now. There aren't many jobs where you can expect to do that. Sure, you can still be working, but not at the high output level. In art you can actually peak when you're very old. Saying that, I don't want to wait or waste a minute. Every day is a blank canvas.

As I ponder these aspects of life I usually have a brush in my hand, and abstract art has become a wonderful haven for me. When I was a little boy

CHAPTER EIGHTEEN

I used to pretend I could write cursively by drawing a long, unending fluid line all over a page. To everyone else it would have looked like a giant scribble but to me it was a meditation and a way to think deeply, even back then. Nowadays my studio is filling up with similar lines writ large on canvas. I've been doing a lot of thinking lately.

My greatest purpose in life, however, is to be the best father, husband and friend that I can. My biggest fear is a broken relationship with my kids. I can't even imagine what parents go through when their children turn to drugs or crime, or leave the family. That's the scariest thing in the world to me, but then I think about my own life and some of the things I've done that my boys don't know about. They'll find out in due course and I wonder how they might look at me then. Will I still have moral authority? Hopefully they'll take after Asher. She knows everything about me and she loves me anyway. I mean the lady *really* fucking loves me, and I love her.

Luca's fifteen now and his life is just starting to fill up with other interests and people outside of the home, and he shares a close relationship with his mum, too. He's a wonderful son to us both and he's turning into a great young man who makes me extremely proud.

Lately on a Sunday – after the footy run is over and time at the skate park has wound up – I've hit on a new ritual with young Val. We raid the supermarket and load up on vegetables, meat and whatever exotic ingredients we've brainstormed together, then we scurry home and get out the pots and pans.

We can spend hours in the kitchen together. I show Val and Luca how to peel and chop up vegetables properly and how to keep things from burning. As our family DJ, my apprentice chef keeps the energy high by playing his favourite music and singing all the lyrics as we slice, stir, bake and taste our way through the afternoon. It's become one of my life's great pleasures. Sometimes, especially when we're cooking Italian, I can close my eyes and the aroma will carry me back to Sundays in the kitchen with my dad. Whenever it does, I give Val a hug and tell him how much I love him.

acknowledgements

A great many people contributed to this book, some of them in ways they'll never even know: childhood pals, old foes, ex-lovers, ex-cons, extended family, sparring partners, painters, poets, fellow travellers, long-lost friends and complete strangers. Some are no longer with us, but all of them deserve my gratitude for the roles they have played in the mad story of my life – the good, the bad, the ugly and the sublime.

Closer to home I've been blessed to have Asher Keddie by my side and in my heart during this process. I couldn't have written my story without shedding light on some of *ours*. Asher encouraged me from the outset and graciously allowed me to usher her onto these pages to share deeply personal tales of her own. Thank you for your courage, the trust you placed in me and your boundless sea of unconditional love. Your tears of empathy and long hugs of reassurance as I relived the grimmest days of my life brought me to my knees.

If it weren't for my boys, Luca and Valentino, I doubt I'd have ever attempted to write a book. I could achieve everything in this world but if I didn't get to share it with my beautiful sons none of it would mean a thing. One day you two will read this and I know it will be difficult to learn about some of the stuff your dad has done and been through in life. Just know that all I want is the very best for you both, and that I love you more than any combination of words could ever convey.

It's through raising Luca and Val that I came to truly appreciate the enormity of the task my mother faced in bringing up five children on her own. It's from you, Mum, that I learned what undying love and sacrifice mean. You always put us first and did everything you could to see us through and keep us all together. Even in the blackest of times your optimism never dimmed – a cherished trait that you have passed onto me. Thank you.

To my amazing siblings, you guys are the reassuring constant in my life. I love you to bits and I'd be lost without you. From the wider Fantauzzo family I'd like to make special mention of my cousin Enzo. An early fanner of my artistic flame, I'm so happy that you're still part of my life. I'm grateful, too, for the love and acceptance of Asher's wonderful clan who have treated me as their own from the day we first met. As for our own little family, there's no way Asher and I could function in the way we do without the care and tireless efforts of Allison Hicks. Thank you, Allly, for everything you do.

I wouldn't be the man I am today without the love and wisdom shown to me by the elders who appeared in my life precisely at the time I needed them: the late Jack Rennie, Kim Ledger, Larry Kestelman and the late Michael Gudinski. I will never stop trying to be someone they can all be proud of.

To my brothers from other mothers: Matt Moran, Rashad Haughton, Matt Pillios, Aden Clarke, Anthony Miragaya, Nick Williams, N'fa Jones, Nic Cester, Steve Smorgon, Joe Cursio (the friend who always phones just to see how I'm doing). To my beloved boxing crew, I want to mention you all individually, that's how important each of you are, but I'd be writing a whole other book. Thanks to you all for having my back in every way imaginable, especially Patrick Boutellier who was the pioneer in pulling this together, you are an unwavering support. Friends for life. A special tip of the hat to Mr Baz Luhrmann: creative genius, artistic collaborator, curry night combatant, motorcycle outlaw and dear friend.

For their valuable support and guidance I'd like to thank former RMIT vice-chancellors Margaret Gardner and Martin Bean, and Professor David Thomas for backing me when I needed it most. Thank you, also, to Julia Gillard for taking a chance on an outsider (and for making him laugh).

I'm extremely grateful to Hugh Jackman for his heartfelt words of encouragement after I gave him a sneak peek at some early chapters, and Trent Dalton for making me feel like I have as much right to be a storyteller as anyone else.

I've had a lot to say in these pages about my love-hate relationship with the art world, but it would be remiss of me if I didn't acknowledge that – even though you never really let me in – you saved my life by giving me something to strive for. All that I have and everything I've achieved stems from my years spent in pursuit of your acceptance. Who knows, maybe one day we can be really great friends?

Of course portrait artists would cease to exist without the people they have the privilege of painting. Everyone who has ever sat for me has given me an opportunity, left an impression and – in many cases – helped shape me and how I see the world. A huge thanks to every last one of you.

For a man who struggles to read and write, the idea of penning a book was terrifying on every level. Many thanks to the team at Penguin Random House, especially editor Clive Hebard for his calm approach, care and attention to detail, publisher Alison Urquhart for her support and stewardship and Sophie Ambrose for opening the door to a life-changing experience.

To all of you who I felt comfortable sharing early drafts with, and whose opinion means so much to me, you know who you are.

Penny Fowler. Thank you.

To big brain Jamie Campbell, your guidance and

ACKNOWLEDGEMENTS

straight shooting with me, always laced with a good dose of humour, is invaluable and greatly appreciated.

And finally to the inimitable Richard Roxburgh (Rox), my friend and mischievous companion, who has so generously encouraged me and narrated my story to boot. It could only have been you.

When I committed to this project at the end of 2023 I had no idea it would take me on an extraordinary emotional journey. Rummaging through a lifetime of confronting memories has fundamentally altered me – for the better. I covered more ground than I ever expected to on an arc that ranged from the depths of despair to the purest delight. I laughed, I cried *a lot*, and laughed some more. I discovered so much about who I am and who I want to be, and I learned a lot about the people who matter in my life. It's an odyssey that continues.

Being dyslexic, I obviously could not have written this book on my own. Fortunately I had a companion on the trail who has become very special to me. The term 'ghostwriter' is far too small to describe Craig Henderson. Although I'm in awe of his ability with words, he is so much more than a storyteller – he's more like my personal therapist and trusted confidant. Craig listened with compassion and patience over eight intense months as my story spilled out of me. We shed tears together, traded philosophies on life and laughed a lot, too – and he never once complained on the days when I forgot to turn up! You're my friend for life, Craig. Thank you.

resources

If you're in need of some help or you're troubled by the contents of this book please reach out and talk to someone.

Auspeld
Assists Australians with specific learning difficulties – such as dyslexia – to achieve their full learning potential through the provision of effective literacy and numeracy instruction, information, advocacy and awareness-raising among the community.
auspeld.org.au

Australian Literacy and Numeracy Foundation
A national charity assisting people in the most marginalised communities to gain vital language, literacy and communication skills. ALNF's programs address the needs of a diverse range of individuals and communities – specifically supporting First Nations, refugee and other vulnerable Australians.
alnf.org

Australian Dyslexia Association

The ADA is concerned with the wellbeing, identification and educational intervention and instruction of all who struggle with aspects of spoken and written language. It supports and provides accredited training in evidence-based instruction with the addition of a multisensory component.
dyslexiaassociation.org.au

Literacy Foundation for Children

Helps families of children with learning disabilities, particularly dyslexia, by providing them with financial support to offset some of the costs of support services.
literacyfoundation.org.au

Australian Dyslexia Foundation

Provides direct funding for individuals in need to access assistive therapies for the identification and remediation of dyslexia, dysgraphia and dyscalculia.
www.ausdys.org

Dear Dyslexic Foundation

DDF is a dyslexic-led grassroots, social enterprise that gives young people and adults a platform to share their lived experiences of dyslexia and other learning disabilities.
rethinkdyslexia.com.au/dear-dyslexic-foundation

Adult
Lifeline
Anyone across Australia experiencing a personal crisis or thinking about suicide can call Lifeline.
13 11 14
lifeline.org.au

Suicide Call Back Service
A free nationwide service providing 24/7 phone and online counselling to people affected by suicide.
1300 659 467
suicidecallbackservice.org.au

Beyond Blue
Mental health support services for anxiety, depression and suicide. You can visit the site for general information and advice, call the helpline, or chat with a counsellor online. NewAccess (currently only available in New South Wales and Queensland) is a confidential, guided, six-session mental health coaching program for anyone feeling stressed or overwhelmed about everyday life issues. It is free of charge and no GP referral is required. Visit beyondblue.org.au/get-support/newaccess-mental-healthcoaching
1300 224 636
beyondblue.org.au

Relationships Australia
Relationship support services for individuals, families and communities.
1300 364 277
relationships.org.au

MensLine Australia
Relationship advice and mental health support for men.
1300 789 978
mensline.org.au

Healthdirect
Government website with advice on where and how to get help about mental health.
healthdirect.gov.au/mental-health-where-to-get-help

Youth
Kids Helpline
Free support and talking through problems on any topic to people aged five to twenty-five. Everything discussed is private and confidential – and you can remain anonymous.
1800 551 800
kidshelpline.com.au

headspace
A site for young people looking for information about mental ill-health, and for people who want advice on supporting young people struggling with their mental health.
1800 650 890
headspace.org.au

ReachOut
A safe place to chat anonymously, get judgement-free support, and build the resilience to manage challenges now and in the future.
au.reachout.com

Other resources
1800RESPECT
Confidential information, counselling and support for people experiencing domestic, family and sexual violence.
1800 737 732
1800respect.org.au

Life in Mind
A knowledge exchange portal providing translated research, evidence, policy, data and resources in suicide prevention.
lifeinmindaustralia.org.au

Head to Health
Helps everyone access the mental health and wellbeing services that are right for them, whether they are looking for mental health support for themself, someone they care about, or just trying to improve their wellbeing.
1800 595 212
headtohealth.gov.au

National Alcohol and Other Drug Hotline
Free, confidential, 24/7 support for those struggling with addiction or worried about their drug or alcohol use.
counsellingonline.org.au

Our Watch
Preventing violence against women and their children in Australia.
ourwatch.org.au

SANE
Offers a range of free digital and telehealth support services for people over eighteen years of age with complex mental health needs, and their family, friends and carers.
sane.org

1300YARN
The first national crisis support line for Aboriginal and Torres Strait Islander folk who are feeling overwhelmed or having difficulty coping. It is a free and confidential one-on-one yarning opportunity with a Lifeline-trained Aboriginal and Torres Strait Islander Crisis Supporter – from varying demographics including age, family status, urban, rural and remote locations that have high rates of suicide and self-harm – who can provide crisis support 24 hours a day, 7 days a week.
13 92 76
13yarn.org.au

index

Note: VF denotes Vincent Fantauzzo

Abbott, Tony, 264
ABC, 239
Aboud, Ghassan, 282
Alfa Romeo brand ambassadorship, 214, 283
Ali, Muhammad, 74, 275
All That's Good in Me (2014), 201
apprenticeship in printing, 67–8
Archibald Prize
   rejected entries (2005–2007), 134
   rejected entries (2010), 188–9
   rejected entries (2016–24), 262–3
   VF moves past grip of, 149
   winner (2008), 144
   See also Packing Room Prize; People's Choice Award
Archibald Prize finalist nominations
   Heath (2008), 141–6, 142–4
   Kimbra (the build up) (2012), 190–1
   number of nominations, 148
art as meditative practice, 54–5, 233–4, 307
Art Gallery of New South Wales, 133
Art Gallery of Western Australia, 146, 147
art history, lack of confidence in, 92–3, 116–17
art schools *See* Royal Melbourne Institute of Technology (RMIT); Victorian College of the Arts (VCA)
Art Series Hotel Group, 278–82
art world, 95–7
   attempts to fit in, 124–6
   exploitation of Indigenous artists, 260
   galleries and commissions, 159, 280
   impact of harsh criticism on VF, 200–1
   predatory behaviour in, 175–8, 187
   VF's supporters, 148–9, 151
   ways to make accessible, 306–7
artist in residency programs
   10 Chancery Lane Gallery (HK), 152
   St Vincent's Hospital, 123–30

artwork
   counterfeit banknotes, 38–9
   first portrait with paints, 55
   influence of cinematography and photography, 240–2
   trouble tracking VF's, 278
   VF's approach to preparing materials, 234–7
   See also exhibitions; murals; sports memorabilia
attention deficit hyperactivity disorder (ADHD) diagnosis, 303
Audi brand ambassadorship, 209, 283
Australia (2008), 156
Australian Boxing Hall of Fame, 79, 80
Australian citizenship application, 273–4
Australian National Boxing Federation, 46
Australian Story, 255

Bachchan, Amitabh, 163–4, 167
Ball, Martin, 144, 145
Banks, Imogen, 209, 244
Barassi, Ron, 191
Barton, Del Kathryn, 144, 145
Baz Luhrmann 'Off Screen' (2011), 189
Beachley, Layne, 191
Beyoncé, 183
Blackman, Charles, portrait subject for Archibald (2007), 134
Bonegilla Migrant Reception and Training Centre, 13
Boutellier, Patrick, 301
boxing, 45
   amateur fights in England, 91
   as mental health management strategy, 301–2
   successful amateur fights, 75–8
   super middleweight division, 207
   underworld aspects, 61

INDEX

Boxing Victoria, 76
brand ambassadorships
    Alfa Romeo, 214, 283
    Audi, 209, 283
    Ducati, 283–4
Broadmeadows, 1–9
Brokeback Mountain (2005), 128, 129
Buckley Park College, 56–7

Calma, Tom, 228
Calombaris, George, 191
Campbell, Naomi, 107
Capon, Edmund, 142–3, 145–6
Carrera, Jess, 242
Cester, Nic, 251, 256–7
Channel Nine, 239
Channel Seven, 239
childhood illnesses, 4–5
childhood trauma, moving past, 298–9
The Chopping Block (2008), 179
Colombo, Giuseppe, 59, 65–6
colour blindness, 228
commissions
    Famechon and Rose fundraising painting, 79–81, 276–8
    from laundrette customers, 74–5
    from universities, 267
    Gillard's official Parliament portrait, 264–7
    Gudinski's commission, 256
    Luhrman's commission, 188
    National Portrait Gallery commissions, 293–7
Commonwealth Games, 48
Consistency Theory (album), 127–8
Corser, Rodger, 244
The Creek, 1977 installation, 169–74
    at Hong Kong Art Fair, 171, 173–4
Crown Melbourne, 208
    Chairman's Villa, 155, 208
Crystalbrook Collection luxury hotel chain, 282
Crystalbrook Vincent (hotel), 282
Cujo (pet and sidekick), 32, 47, 58, 285
Cullen, Adam, 278
The Cullen Melbourne – Art Series (hotel), 278
Cursio, Joe, 207

Daily Telegraph, 199
Daniher, Neale, 262
The Dark Knight (2008), 135, 149, 227
de Tilly, Katie, 151
Deague, David, 278, 279
Deague, Jonathan, 278

Deague, William, 278, 279
Deakin University, 267
Debicki, Elizabeth, 191
DeBoer, Brent, 205–6
DeBoer, Sarah, 205, 206
Deeds (charity), 161, 163
depression, impact on VF and peer group, 42–3, 46
DiCarlo, Trevor, 128, 140
Dianne Tanzer Gallery
    Inner Conflict (2009), 158–9
    solo exhibitions, 130
    The Nature of Fate (2007), 125–6
Diaz, Cameron, 107
DiCaprio, Leonardo, 107, 188, 227
Dippa (Moonee Ponds crew), 90
Doug Moran National Portrait Prize, 236
    Baz Luhrmann 'Off Screen' (2011), 189
dyslexia, 169
    coming to terms with, 117
    diagnosis process, 114–15
    impact on further education, 93–4, 109–16
    impact on job progression, 64, 66–7
    impact of neurodivergence in everyday life, 216–32
    impact on relationships, 197–8
    inability to remember faces, 226–7
    positive aspects, 230–1
    strategies and tactics to hide, 27–9, 69–71, 94, 194, 216
    use of technology to help, 230–1
    VF comes clean about, 111–14
    VF sets up charity for, 305–7

Edgerton, Joel, 191
Edgerton, Nash, 191
Einstein, Albert, 231
Engelman, Tony, 128
England, 23–5
    Claudio moves post-divorce, 24, 25
    Fantauzzo family moves back, 4–5
    VF follows Latifah to, 91
exhibitions
    Dianne Tanzer Gallery, 125–6, 130, 158–9
    Heath Ledger: A Life in Pictures (2017), 146
    in Hong Kong, 130, 151–2, 159, 171, 173–4
    in India, 159–63
    in New York, 185–7
    in Vietnam, 168
    Jackman Gallery, 124
    Last Contact (2016), 261–2
    The Creek, 1977 (collaboration with Luhrmann), 169–74
Ezekiel (New York portrait subject), 182, 186

face blindness (prosopagnosia), 228–9
Famechon, Johnny, 79–80, 276
The Fantauzzo Brisbane – Art Series (hotel), 281–2 See also Crystalbrook Vincent (hotel)
Fantauzzo, Claudio, 14–16
   arranges printing apprenticeship, 67–9
   attempts to bond with, 16–17, 213–15
   death, 286–7
   family business, 13
   funeral service, 289–92
   leaves family, 19
   move to Horsham, 121
   post-divorce, 23–4, 52–3
   relationship with grandsons, 212–13
   relationship with parents, 288
   relationship with VF, 37, 50, 53, 121–2, 284–5
   ways for connection, 304
Fantauzzo, Enzo (cousin), 14, 19
Fantauzzo, George (uncle), 13
Fantauzzo, Leno (uncle), 13, 14
Fantauzzo, Luca, 181, 191, 212, 231, 288, 289, 307
   birth of, 130
   portrait subject for Archibald Prize (2014), 201
   quality time with, 208, 304–5
Fantauzzo, Marianne, 5, 51, 57, 286
Fantauzzo, Michael, 5, 49, 51, 119, 122, 270
   VF's assistant, 192, 195, 242
   VF beats up bullies, 82–3
Fantauzzo, Rachel, 4, 8
   helps VF with art school applications, 88
   helps VF with job applications, 76–7
Fantauzzo, Rosaleen, 4, 11–13, 16, 20–4, 22–6, 31–4, See also Mitchell, Rosaleen
Fantauzzo, Valentino, 232
   birth of, 211
   quality time with, 304, 307–8
Fantauzzo, Vincenza (grandmother), 288
Fantauzzo, Vincenzo (grandfather), 13, 288
Fantauzzo family
   estrangement from extended family, 13–14
   life in Broadmeadows, 1–5
   life in Essendon, 22–3
   move to England, 4–5
   weekly Sunday cook-ups, 15–16
Fantauzzo family (post-divorce)
   consequences on children, 32–3
   improved conditions, 49–50
   unstable housing, 24, 31–2, 49

fatherhood ideals
   hopes for bond between sons, 212
   pre-birth jitters, 131–2
Fight Fit, 207
Fiji, VF and Keddie's elopement, 204–7
fitness as form of self-defence and protection, 44–6
Forster-Jones, N'fa, 127–8, 130, 139–40
   portrait subject for Archibald (2005), 134
Fox, Lindsay, 251, 253–4
Fox Studios, 170
Freedman, Mia, 303
friendships
   generosity of, 102–3
   with Cester, 257
   with DeBoer, 205–6
   with Forster-Jones, 127–8
   with Gudinski, 247–57
   with Haughton, 98–109
   with Ledger, 128–9, 134–9
   with Luhrmann, 153–6, 160–8, 201
   with Moran, 179–81

galleries 124, 130, 158–9
   VF breaks away from, 280
   VF breaks into scene, 125–6
gang culture, 8–9, 34–7, 48, 56–8, 100–1
Gillard, Julia, 263–73
   official Parliament portrait, 264–7
   sitting process for portrait, 269–73
Glenno (mate during teenage years), 43–4
GQ Artist of the Year award, 198, 283
Gracey, Michael, 143, 153, 190
The Great Gatsby (2013), 164, 181
Gudinski, Kate, 255, 257
Gudinski, Matt, 255
Gudinski, Michael, 247–57
   commissions Sheeran and Seaborn wedding portrait, 256
   death, 255
   dinner party, 253–4
   friendship networks, 256–7
   mentorship and belief in VF, 255–6
   portrait subject for Archibald (2016), 248–9
Gudinski, Sue, 249, 254

Harley House Bar and Grill, 238–40
Hart, Jessica, 183
Haughton, Aaliyah, 98, 99, 101–2, 140, 255
Haughton, Diane, 99
Haughton, Rashad, 98–103, 117–18, 127, 128
   VF visits New York, 104–9
Hawke, Bob, 191

Heath (2008)
  impact of painting on VF's career, 150
  popularity of painting, 146
Heath Ledger: A Life in Pictures (2017), 146
Higgins, Lee-Anne, 192, 193
Hilton, Paris, 108
Hong Kong Art Fair, 171
Hotel Le Sutra (India)
  exhibitions, 159–61
  mural project with Luhrmann, 162–3
Huegill, Geoff, 191

illiteracy *See* dyslexia
The Imaginarium of Dr Parnassus (2009), 135
Iman, Chanel, 281
imposter syndrome, 133, 135, 256, 280
India, 159–68
  exhibition at Hotel Le Sutra, 159–61
  Royal Enfield motorcycle fundraising ride, 163–8
Inner Conflict (2009), 158–9

Jackman, Hugh, 293–7
Jackman, Oscar, 294
Jackman Gallery, 124
Jagger, Mick, 183
Jay-Z, 106
Jet (band), 251
Joey's Italian Restaurant, 59–65
  underworld aspects, 60–4

Karvan, Claudia, 170
Keddie, Asher
  acting process, 243–5
  birth of Valentino, 211
  compiles and catalogues VF's artworks, 280–1
  elopes with VF to Fiji, 204–7
  falls pregnant, 209–11
  first public outing as a couple, 198–9
  generosity with fans, 245–6
  Logie Awards, 198, 206, 208
  portrait subject for Archibald (2013), 199–200
  portrait subject for Thirty Portraits in Thirty Days, 193–6
  pregnancy challenges, 203, 208–9
  pressure of being in public eye, 201–3
  VF photographs for magazine cover, 242–3
Kestelman, Larry, 148, 181, 260–1
kickboxing, 62–3, 75
Kimbra (the build up) (2012), 190–1

Kngwarreye, Kudditji, 259, 261–2
Knight, Gladys, 99

Last Contact exhibition (2016), 261
Latifah, 90–1, 99, 285
laundrette business/hustle, 72–5
Le Nevez, Matt, 244
Ledger, Heath, 128, 255
  death, 139–40
  portrait subject for Archibald (2008), 134–9, 147–8
  posthumous Academy Award, 149–50
  price of fame, 135–6
Ledger, Kim, 141, 146–7, 181
Ledger, Matilda, 135
Ledger, Sally, 137, 141, 146
Leon (Moonee Ponds crew), 90
Lewis, Lennox, 183
Liston, Sonny, 275, 276
Logie Awards, 198, 206, 208
Love Face (2013), 199–200
Luhrmann, Baz, 153–6, 191
  advice on dealing with art critics, 201
  collaborations with VF, 162–3, 169–74
  commissions VF to paint DiCaprio, 188
  helps with VF's exhibition venue in New York, 185–6
  Royal Enfield launch and fundraising ride, 160–2, 163–8
  time in New York, 181, 183–6
  portrait subject for Archibald 2010, 188–9
  portrait wins Moran Portrait Prize (2011), 189, 236–7

Mackie, Andrew, 257
Mallis, Fern, 183–5, 187
Manera, Kane, 182, 183, 185, 187
Marco Polo Gym, 45
Marie Claire, 242
marijuana hydroponic operation, 118–21
Martin, Catherine, 188
The Matrix Reloaded (2003), 99
May, Steve, 237
McCusker, Malcolm, 297
McGregor, Ken, 258–60, 278, 279
Melbourne Art Fair, 151
Melbourne City Council, removes VF's street artwork, 238–9
Melbourne Food and Wine Festival, 181
Memento, 220–1
Metro Art Awards, 174
Michelle (VF's first wife), 126–7, 129–31, 139, 145, 147, 152, 153, 178–9, 181–7
Minogue, Kylie, 252, 253

Mirren, Helen, 228
Mitchell, Rosaleen
  marriage to Claudio, 4
  partnerships post-divorce, 59, 65–6
  reconnects with Claudio's twin sister, 304
Molineaux, Wizzy, 209
Monash University, 267
Monsted, Anton, 186
Moonee Ponds Magistrates Court hearing, 83–7
Moonee Ponds Police Station, 83–5
Moonie Ponds crew, 90
Moran, Matt, 179–81, 191–2, 199, 248, 306
Morrison, Scott, 272
motorcycles and cars, 67, 71–2
  custom designs for Ducati, 283–4
  motorcycle accident, 120, 171–2
  Royal Enfield promotion and fundraising ride (India), 160–2, 166–8
murals
  Essendon boxing gym, 275–6
  Harley House Bar and Grill, 238–40
  Hotel Le Sutra (India), 162–3

Nanda\Hobbs Gallery, 261
Napaltjarri, Linda Syddick, 259, 262
Napaltjarri, Wentja, 259, 262
National Arts Club, 185–6
National Gallery of Victoria, Thirty Portraits in Thirty Days, 191–2, 199, 228–9
National Portrait Gallery (NPG) painting commissions, 293, 297
The Nature of Fate (2007), 126, 158
New York
  VF moves with Michelle and Luca, 181–7
  VF visits Haughton, 104–9
  See also Thirty Portraits in Thirty Days (New York)
New York Fashion Week, 183
Nine Perfect Strangers (2021), 243

Offspring (2010–17), 192, 198, 208, 243
  VF's cameo on, 244–5
Oldman, Gary, 227
Olsen, John, 278
The Olsen Melbourne – Art Series (hotel), 278
1200 Techniques, 127–8

Packing Room Prize
  Ball wins (2008), 144
  Matt Moran (2011), 148
Parliament House, Gillard portrait unveiling ceremony, 270–2

Party Tricks (2014), 243
Pearce, Guy, 220–1
People's Choice Award, 130, 144, 148
  All That's Good in Me (2014), 201
  Brandon (2009), 148, 158
  Heath (2008), 144, 146
  Love Face (2013), 199–200
Petyarre, Gloria, 259, 262
Pharrell Williams, 183
photography, VF shoots cover for *Marie Claire*, 241–3
Pillios, Matt, 90
Plaza Hotel, Thirty Portraits in Thirty Days exhibition, 186
predators and bullies, 17–19, 29–30, 35, 57–8, 82–3 *See also* sexual abuse
press/media
  attention after winning People's Choice Award, 145
  challenges of being in public eye, 201–2
  coverage of street art stoush with council, 239–40
  Keddie deals with paparazzi, 199
  lengths paparazzi go to get scoop, 206, 211–12
  reaction to New York Thirty Portraits in Thirty Days, 185–6
  sensationalism around *Heath* painting, 140–1
  VF's joint interviews with Gillard, 272
public housing environment, 5–9

Queen of the Damned (2002), 98, 127
Quinlan, Karen, 293

Rahman, A.R., 162
Remo (Moonee Ponds crew), 90
Rennie, Jack, 45–6, 207, 276
  coaching strategies, 75
  commissions Famechon and Rose painting, 79–81
  mentor and role model, 47–9, 147, 181
  VF gifts portrait of Rose, 78–9
Richie, Nicole, 108
Rob (Moonee Ponds crew), 90
Rock, Mick, 185
Rogers, Tim, portrait subject for Archibald (2006), 134
role models, 147, 181
Ronson, Mark, 183
Rose, Lionel, 45, 46, 276
Roxburgh, Richard, 244
Royal Enfield motorcycle promotion and fundraising launch, 160–2, 166–8

INDEX

Royal Melbourne Institute of Technology (RMIT), 267
    Bachelor of Fine Arts, 89–90, 92–4, 116–17
    impact of learning difficulties during, 109–16
    Masters of Fine Arts, 117
    memorable students, 95–7

same-sex marriage plebiscite, 264
Satterley, Nigel, 297
Schmidt, Brian, 228–9
Seaborn, Cherry, 256
self-portraits, 158–9, 187, 192
sexual abuse, 17–19, 299–300
share houses
    with Pillios, 90–1
    with Rashad, 121–2, 127
Sheeran, Ed, 256
Sing Sing Studios, 101
Sofitel Hotel, 174
SPELD Victoria, 114
sporting pursuits *See* boxing; kickboxing; taekwondo
sports memorabilia
    Famechon and Rose fundraising painting, 79–81
    underworld aspects, 74–5
Springsteen, Bruce concert (2017), 249–50
St Bernard's College, 30, 40–1, 56
St Kilda studio, as space for men to bond and box, 301–2
St Therese's School (primary years), 20–30
    VF placed in special needs class, 26–7
St Vincent's Hospital artist in residency program, 123–30
Stewart, Jackie, 231
Strife (2023–), 303
Swinging Safari (2018), 253

taekwondo, 44–5
Tanzer, Dianne, 151
teenage years, 30–81
    VF's counterfeit banknotes, 38–9, 51
    fitness as form of self-defence and protection, 44–6
    forays into boxing and kickboxing, 75–80
    introduction to drugs, 43–4, 45
    printing apprenticeship, 67–9
    behaviour around vehicles, 71–2
    work in Italian restaurants, 50–3, 59–66
    See also Buckley Park College; St Bernard's College
10 Chancery Lane Gallery (HK), 151
    artist in residency, 152
    Thirty Portraits in Thirty Days, 130
Theron, Charlize, 281
Thirty Portraits in Thirty Days (Hong Kong), 152, 278
Thirty Portraits in Thirty Days (Melbourne), 191–2, 199, 228–9
Thirty Portraits in Thirty Days (New York), 181–7
    missing paintings, 187, 278
Thirty Portraits in Thirty Days series, 129, 136
Thomas, David, 110–12, 113, 115
Tobin, James, 198–9
Trump, Donald, 105–6
Trump Tower, 106–7

University of Canberra, 267
Usher, 107

Victorian College of the Arts (VCA), 87–9, 92
violence
    Claudio's outbursts, 26
    law catches up with VF, 83–7, 252
    prevalence in Broadmeadows, 6–7
    self-defence at Moonee Ponds, 54
    VF organises Niddrie attack, 82–3
    way of hiding fear through, 9–10, 29–30
    way of life, 34–7, 40–1, 47, 56–7, 299–300

Walker, Ron, 281
Walsh, David, 281
Walters, Brandon, 156–8
Walters, Paul, 156, 157
Warne, Shane, 74
Warren, Marilyn, 267
The Watson Adelaide – Art Series (Hotel), 279
Watson, Tommy, 259, 262, 279
Western Desert trip (2015), 258–62
    exhibition inspired by, 261–2
Williams, Lloyd, 251
Williams, Michelle, 135
Williams, Nick, 249, 257
Williams, Saskia, 249
Wintour, Anna, 183

Vincent Fantauzzo, award-winning portrait artist, was born in England and grew up in Melbourne's northern suburbs. He completed a BA and a Master's in Fine Arts at RMIT, graduating in 2005. Fantauzzo truly emerged onto the portrait scene when his striking painting of his friend Heath Ledger took out the coveted People's Choice Award at the 2008 Archibald Prize. The portrait was acquired for the Art Gallery of New South Wales collection, and Fantauzzo won the People's Choice Award again in 2009, 2013 and 2014. In 2011, his Archibald-shortlisted portrait of chef Matt Moran won the Packing Room Prize; and his painting of director Baz Lurhmann was awarded the Moran National Portrait Prize the same year. In 2015, he made the first of several painting trips to Central Australia, where he collaborated with Wentja Napaltjarri, Tommy Watson, Gloria Petyarre and Kudditji Kngwarreye to create a series of triptychs. In 2018, he was commissioned by the Historic Memorials Committee to create the official portrait of Julia Gillard for the Parliament House collection. The National Portrait Gallery commissioned Fantauzzo in 2020 to create a portrait of Hugh Jackman, the first representation of the famed Australian for the collection.